WITHDRAWN

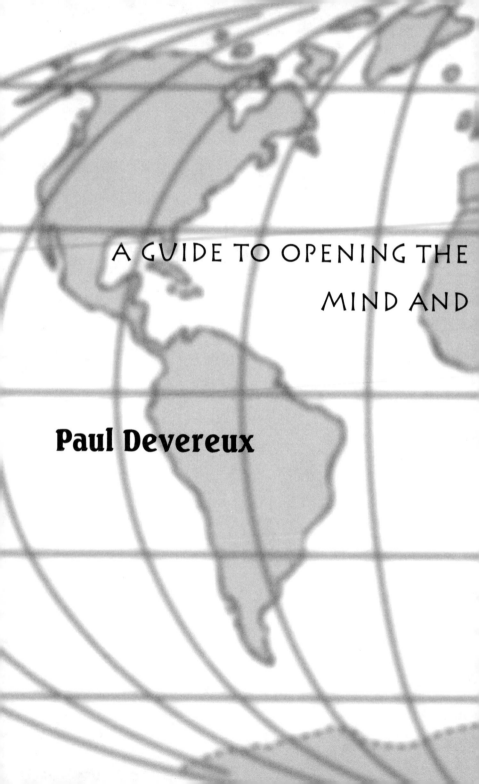

A GUIDE TO OPENING THE
MIND AND

**Paul Devereux**

# RE-VISIONING
# THE EARTH

## HEALING CHANNELS BETWEEN
## NATURE

A FIRESIDE BOOK
PUBLISHED BY SIMON & SCHUSTER

FIRESIDE
Rockefeller Center
1230 Avenue of the Americas
New York, NY 10020

FIRESIDE and colophon are registered
trademarks of Simon & Schuster Inc.

Designed by Elina D. Nudelman

Manufactured in the United States of America

10   9   8   7   6   5   4   3   2   1

Library of Congress Cataloging-in-Publication Data

Devereux, Paul.
    Re-visioning the earth : a guide to opening the healing channels
    between mind and nature / Paul Devereux
        p.      cm.
    "A Fireside book."
    Includes bibliographical references and index.
    1. Earth—Religious aspects.   2. Nature—Religious aspects.
    3. Spiritual life.   4. Sacred space.   I. Title.
    BL438.2.D48    1996
    291.2'12—dc20                          96-31403 CIP

ISBN 0-684-80063-2

For
E. Victor Walter

# CONTENTS

## 5. DREAMING
### Soul-to-Soul with *Anima Mundi*      194

# ACKNOWLEDGMENTS

A true list of acknowledgments would take many pages, so, to be purely pragmatic, I limit mention here only to those people directly involved with practical aspects of this book.

For various permissions, in addition to the general enlightenment and inspiration their work has given me, I thank Richard Bradley, Walter L. Brenneman Jr., Edmunds V. Bunke, Guy Claxton, James Cowan, Michael Dames, Anthony Donohue, Robert G. Greenway, Charles Laughlin, J. McKim Malville, John Michell, Theodore Roszak, Rana P. B. Singh, David Turnbull, E. Victor Walter.

For personally drawing my attention to useful, specific items of information used in this work, or for helping me to locate certain sources, I am grateful to Alan Bleakley, Alan Ereira, Philip Heselton, Ulrich Magin, John Palmer, William H. Rosar, Joseph Sheridan, Kim Taplin, Bob Trubshaw. Here I must particularly recall the nudges in the right direction given me by John Steele some two decades ago concerning a few of the themes that have become developed and intertwined within the subject matter of this book.

For formal permissions I acknowledge The American Museum of Natural History; Christopher Davies Publishers for Bobi Jones's poem "Small Paths"; Shirley-Ann Pager, for use of one of her late husband's tracings of San rock art; Penguin Books USA, Inc. for permission to use A. A. Milne's "Halfway Down," from *When We Were Very Young*. Copyright 1924 by E. P. Dutton, renewed 1952 by A. A. Milne. Used by permission of Dutton Children's Books, a division of Penguin Books USA, Inc. I trust all other quotes used, for which formal or informal permissions were not obtained, are within the usual bounds of fair usage, and have been correctly credited and sourced. Illustrations, other than those involved above, are either my own copyright or are out of copyright as far as is known. If other is the case with any of these matters, then copyright owners are invited to contact me.

I appreciate the role played by my agent, Sandra Martin of Paraview Inc., not to mention that by Sydny Miner at Simon & Schuster, in seeing that this book got to publication. Finally, I am, as ever, grateful to my wife, Charla, for helping in various ways to maintain the environment in which this work could be completed, and to my son, Solomon, for always being prepared to help me out when I encountered difficulties of the computerized kind.

# A CONTEXT FOR THE EARTH AS HEALER

The Planet Without, the World Within

THE ATLANTIC SEABOARD OF IRELAND IS A WILD and remarkable place. The western extremity of Europe, this sparsely populated coastline is bathed in a strange air of remoteness in both time and space. From the high cliffs of Donegal and Sligo's fairy mountain, Benbulbin, along the rocky barreness of the Burren with its gaunt prehistoric stone monuments, to the richly colored hills and lakes of Kerry and beyond, there is a refreshing (and reassuring) sense of deep nature yet undisturbed from its dreaming by that busy invasion of civilization which rolls on ceaselessly across the globe. The Irish seer George William Russell (known best by his pseudonym, "Æ") remarked earlier this century that "the whole west coast of Ireland . . . seems charged with a magical power, and I find it easiest to see while I am there," by which he meant having his mystical visions of nature. A fitting place, therefore, for one of the numerous acts of perception that have helped augment the growth of the environmental movement, and by no less a person than James Lovelock, the initiator of the Gaia Theory.

## POLLUTION IN FAIRYLAND

In 1968, Lovelock and his family bought a holiday cottage overlooking Bantry Bay. That summer, most days were clear as crystal, but there were times when a haze descended that reminded Lovelock of a Los Angeles photochemical smog. But out here, in this remote, rural place? The matter nagged at him, and the following year Lovelock brought along a gas chromatograph fitted with an electron-capture detector. The invention of this incredibly sensitive instrument by Lovelock had effectively started the environmental movement by providing the data that enabled Rachel Carson to write her seminal book, *Silent Spring* (1962), which alerted people to increasing global poisoning by chemicals like DDT. Lovelock used the device in his Irish retreat to measure CFCs (chlorofluoro-carbons), and this showed that the haze was, indeed, a photochem-ical smog, originating, as later investigation proved, in southern France and Italy. So even this fairy coast was beginning to be pol-luted by the distant clamour of civilization.

There was no escape, in fact, because it was during this work that Lovelock found a low-level presence of CFCs in even the apparently *clear* air. Where had they come from? Across the Atlantic from America? Lovelock went on to conduct global monitoring of CFCs, leading to the unwelcome discovery that these gases were building up in the atmosphere. Scientists soon realized that this would cre-ate an ever-increasing source of chlorine that would react with and help deplete stratospheric ozone. An even more important aspect to the CFCs, Lovelock saw, was that they were potent contributors to the blanketing "greenhouse effect," which causes global warming.

This grim news originating in those first observations in the Irish fairyland only went to show the exceptional interconnectedness of the global ecosystem that Lovelock had been increasingly suspect-ing ever since NASA had asked him to help devise ways of detecting life on Mars for their Viking mission. To consider this, he had to fig-ure out how he would detect life on Earth. He came to realize that our planet's atmosphere was full of "unlikely" gases, and was dy-namic—whereas the atmosphere of a dead planet would be close to a state of chemical equilibrium. The Earth's atmosphere and tem-perature range could be maintained because the planet acts like a self-regulating organism, "a tightly coupled system,"[1] comprising the totality of its life (the biosphere or biota) and its material envi-ronment—the oceans, the atmosphere, and the surface rocks. Like the French priest, paleontologist, and philosopher Teilhard de Chardin, Lovelock saw that there was only one inhabitant of Earth, and that was life itself: the biosphere created, regulated, and main-tained the environment that best suited it. This great feedback system has "emergent properties" that make it greater than the sum of its parts. The whole planet is, in a real sense, alive.

It was the novelist William Golding, a neighbor of Lovelock's, who suggested that this system be called Gaia, the ancient Greek name for the Earth Goddess. Lovelock first put forward his tentative Gaia Hypothesis in a 1969 lecture at Princeton University, to no great acclaim. But life scientist Lynn Margulis of Boston heard it, and became his principal collaborator on the development of what became in 1981 a full-fledged theory—it "is testable and has a mathematical basis."

## THE HEALING EARTH VERSUS "HEALING THE EARTH"

Not only had the Gaia Hypothesis been triggered by space research; over the years of its emergence as a theory it was accompanied by the stunning views of Earth from space that the astronauts were sending back to us. This made for a powerful cocktail. We were seeing our dazzlingly beautiful planet for the first time as a whole thing. It delighted, surprised, and perhaps shocked us. The image was widely dispersed amongst the human race (psychologist Jean Houston, for example, has reported seeing it pinned up inside remote tribal dwellings). It went into our minds—we psychically internalized our planetary home. The Gaia Theory was the intellectual parallel of this visual and emotional shock which supercharged our ecological awareness. It also raised within us a sense of spiritual awe: Lovelock was surprised to find that two-thirds of the letters he received from readers of his first book, *Gaia—A New Look at Life on Earth* (1979), were framed in religious terms. "I had no inkling that it would be taken as a religious book," he stated. But he tacitly admitted the link between the vision from space and the Gaia Theory: "When I first saw Gaia in my mind I felt as an astronaut must have done as he stood on the Moon, gazing back at our home, the Earth."[2] The emergence of this spiritual dimension should really have been expected, for the living Earth, the Mother Goddess, had been rediscovered.

But time tarnishes all things, and the image of the Earth from space has now lost much of its power. It has become sublimated into a mere icon, even a transient image used in advertising. A large strand of environmental awareness has settled into simplistic ideas of "healing the Earth" and "saving the planet," of our becoming "stewards of the planet," and of the Earth being "fragile." Lovelock has lost patience with these views. Earth, he points out, is very tough indeed. In its billions of years of existence it has withstood "at least thirty major planetesimal impacts," each capable of wiping out more than half the life present at those times. Furthermore, the heat from the sun has increased by a quarter over that vast period of time, and chemical changes have occurred within the atmosphere. Anything we can do to the planet, Lovelock reminds us, is minor by comparison. "Those who call the Earth fragile," he has written, "or who say that some human act will destroy all life on Earth, are either ignorant of what the Earth really is or are using 'Earth' metaphorically as a synonym for humans."[3] He equally dislikes phrases such as "Spaceship Earth," as if we were passengers on some vehicle, as if Earth's role were merely as a life support for us, rather than being a *whole system*, a superorganism, indivisible between all its spheres—geosphere, hydrosphere, biosphere, magnetosphere. And he thinks we are full of hubris to entertain "the dangerous illusion" that we could be stewards of the Earth.

The truth, surely, is that what we may ultimately come to do is destroy the particular type of planetary environment that sustains us and life as we know it. If that happens, then, of course, our species would die off (alas, taking many other species with it): *in the grim, final analysis, the problem would be self-correcting.* The Earth can be a stern as well as a bountiful mother, and were we to disappear she would have the ages that belong to her in which to restore herself before giving birth to other orders of life. Earth's song will go on whether or not we are part of it.

So our concern for the environment can best be seen as an awareness that we need the way the Earth is *in its present state* for our survival. It is our fate, not the fate of the planet, that is in question. We have to save ourselves. We need stewardship for our own species. Rather than thinking of healing the Earth, we should be looking to the Earth to heal us. And that is the starting point for this book: if we are the disease, then the healing of that ill is the way to save the Earth's environment as we need it to be. It is essential that we not only continue, but redouble our efforts, with practical material activities aimed at ameliorating the symptoms of ecological distress, such as by recycling, controlling our consumption of materials, encouraging ever more environmentally friendly and economical manufacturing and transportation systems, repairing environmental damage, and, above all, pressing for constantly increasing ecological awareness on the part of our corporate, financial, and governmental institutions. But none of this effort will reach the "critical mass" necessary to turn our dangerous situation around fully unless we heal the underlying sickness—our relationship with the planet, our *worldview*. This means literally changing how we perceive the world around us. And that requires the alteration of our consciousness.

## ECOPSYCHOLOGY

If our survival as part of the planet is in essence a question of state of mind, then we will need a psychology that can handle that realization, the problems that go with it, and the transformations of mind-set which it entails. It seems that such a potentially powerful tool may already be starting to emerge, under the umbrella name of "ecopsychology."

"If psychology needs ecology in order to find an adequate image of human nature," says historian Theodore Roszak, "ecology also needs psychology in order to find more sensitive ways to address the public it wishes to persuade."[4] In *The Voice of the Earth* (1992), probably the nearest thing to a primary textbook or charter for ecopsychology at the present time, Roszak suggests that to revise our relations with the environment will require the power of great conviction and strong emotional force. Reason alone can't do it. Ecological facts and figures cannot sufficiently motivate us for the psychological transformation that has to come about. For such a transformation to occur, we are going to have to *feel* the need for it. Roszak surveys the history of psychology, and finds much of it

healing than we do, one that more readily encompassed mind. Roszak wisely sees the archaic instinct of *animism* as holding out prospects to us for a reorganization of worldview. In the animistic reality, everything, whether animate or inanimate, is possessed of life or spirit in some form or another. A rock, a tree, or a mountain could be the outward form of a spiritual presence, an abode of supernatural forces, or inhabited by spirits of nature or ghosts of the ancestors. When we speak of someone as being animated, we mean he or she is full of life, lively. In our present-day mainstream worldview, the environment is no longer animated. The old animistic sensibility, Roszak argues, "may provide a better initial model than Newtonian atomism ever did." Its loss to our worldview may even be at the basis of our ecological crisis and our spiritual discontent. Traditional and archaic peoples actually *saw* the world in animistic terms; it wasn't merely metaphorical for them. Roszak calls for an "ecologically grounded form of animism."[6] He sees that childhood animism, so well documented by the experimental psychologist Jean Piaget and expressed by poets like William Wordsworth and Thomas Traherne, as an indication of "the animistic foundations of the unconscious." At some deep level, Roszak suggests, Jung's collective unconscious harbors the "ecological intelligence" of the human species. He feels we must somehow unite ... this.

...szak is by no means the only one championing the need for ...kind of an ecopsychology. Another pioneer, for instance, is ...st and psychologist Robert Greenway, who uses nature di... a sort of ecotherapy. He has taken many hundreds of peo... he wilderness in an effort to disrupt their normal habits ...nage. His Northstar Wilderness Group (see the appendix) ...e into remote nature for up to four weeks at a time. They ...days without speaking, alter their eating and sleeping ...b mountains by moonlight. Anything to help break ...bit patterns that we all fall into. "Wilderness experi... ...the way for change," Greenway avers. People return... ...rips "report an increased awakeness and power, a ...obtained from nature."[7] Even colleges and univer-

wanting in one way or another. Freud's psychotherapy he finds "separated person from planet." He notes that Freud considered the ego and the strong boundaries separating it from the outer world as being healthy, and denounced as neurosis the oceanic feeling of unity with the universe that is the hallmark of the mystical experience. Loss of boundary sense between inner and outer was the road to madness: one should feel oneself to be "inside," and nature "outside." And yet, Roszak perceptively notes, Freud admitted that originally the ego included everything and later, as one grows into an adult, "it separates off an external world from itself. Our present ego-feeling is, therefore, a shrunken residue of a much more inclusive—indeed all-embracing—feeling." That which is seen as normal ego-consciousness is, even according to Freud, a "shrunken residue" of something greater! But though Freud acknowledged nature in his work, it was from a negative angle. He viewed nature as "eternally remote."

Freud's famous pupil Carl Jung took the problem of mind and nature more readily within his scope in his earlier years. He pointed out that nature was a repressed part of the modern psyche, and he speculated about the *unus mundi*, that oceanic union with nature at the heart of mystical experience. From childhood, awareness of nature was clearly a factor in Jung's consciousness. Nevertheless, in his later years Jung developed a nonmaterial idea of the collective unconscious, a mental reservoir of the human race containing the root memories, archetypes, and psychic patterns. This powerful idea has tremendous applications, but its study has in many ways made mind even more abstract and separated from nature. Roszak notes that Jungian study and analysis of the archetypes tends to become very cerebral. Whereas Jung as a person enjoyed natural surroundings, "his formal theoretical work tends to have very little sense of *nature* to it. . . ."[5]

One development of Western twentieth-century psychological thought of which Roszak does approve is Gestalt psychology. This recognizes the importance of the wholeness of things, that phenomena are greater than the sum of their parts. So, for example, a melody can be played on many different types of instrument and still be recognizable as that particular melody. An oak tree might

have an overall quality that cannot be reduced to leaves, branches, bark, coloring, and so on. Gestalt was the first therapy to use the word "ecology" to describe the organism's relation to its environment. But overall, the image of nature as alien to consciousness broods in the background of all the major schools of psychotherapeutic thought, Roszak argues. Existentialism relegates the natural world to a kind of ugly wallpaper, a bothersome background for the individual's social and personal world. Existentialism denatures the natural environment, Roszak suggests, as one would expect from "urban therapists." The environment appears frequently in the Object Relations school of thought, but it turns out to be just the social environment. Even Humanistic psychology seeks the "transcendence of environment," to use Abraham Maslow's words (although he looked forward to a transpersonal, transhuman psychology centered on the cosmos rather than in human concerns). The outer world of Humanistic psychology tends to be limited to social relations. Behaviorism looks at observable and measurable behavior as the only guide to psychological study. It effectively removes consciousness itself from the realm of consideration, so questions of mind-nature relationships can hardly be addressed. Admittedly, the power of this school of psychology is now somewhat diminished, and few psychologists would be happy with any of its extreme forms, but only relatively recently has consciousness come into its own as a legitimate subject in mainstream research.

Most of the major strands of mainstream Western psychological thought tend to reinforce the idea of separation from nature. Psychotherapists usually work in urban environments and express urban-based ideas in which the human world is seen as the only really active factor worthy of consideration. In such an intellectual environment it is very difficult for any ideas of the natural world beyond the human mind to be entertained. A new approach is required; or, perhaps, an old approach—a relationship with nature more akin to former times yet modified to suit modern conditions.

The healing we need has to involve the earth, the mind, and tradition.

sities in America have begun to run courses on ecopsychology. One of the teachers of the Harvard ecopsychology course sees the individualism emphasized in modern psychiatry and culture as continuing to lead people to a separation from one another and from the Earth itself. Jungian psychoanalyst James Hillman has suggested "prescribing nature" as a part of therapy.[8]

These and others are signaling the need for a new psychology, one that can help us heal the rift between mind and nature that so marks our times. However, not everything is yet perfect in ecopsychology's garden. It seems that people who return from the wilderness experience, who have been "prescribed nature," report that the benefits of changed perception tend to become dulled after a time back in the city and their usual routines.[9] And some confusion about the direction ecopsychology should take is indicated by contradictions in terms used by its proponents. Roszak, for example, can in one moment recognize that, come what may in ecological terms, "the planet will, of course, endure," yet at other times use phrases such as "The Earth's cry for rescue,"[10] "if the planet is to be healed,"[11] and so on. This seems to indicate some uncertainty as to whether we or the planet needs healing, a lack of clarity in seeing that the damage to the Earth is in terms of harm to the particular, current environment that coexists with us and consequently is the one upon which we depend. Gaia can deck herself out with many different kinds of environment; it is we, surely, who should be crying out for rescue.

Also, at times it seems as if the prospectus for ecopsychology is a very anthropocentric one—humans must be the voice of the threatened biosphere, we are told. But who needs to hear other than ourselves? We are the problem—there is no other culprit within earshot. The damage to the environment that sustains us would cease if we were healed. If we are to have an ecopsychology, it must not slip into the trap of placing ourselves at the center of creation once more, of considering ourselves masters of nature again, even if this time in the guise of "healing" it. We can only heal ourselves. And the best ecopsychologist we can go to for help in that enterprise is nature, the Earth itself.

## DEEP ECOLOGY

Nevertheless, this doubtless unintentional anthropocentrism aside, the call for an ecopsychology is addressing a real need. We have to heal the inner-outer, mind-nature divide; we have to rearrange our relationship with nature; we need to change the embedded psychological structures that give us our present mainstream worldview. The ecological movement has already developed deeper dimensions behind its somewhat cerebral, statistical face. In 1972, Norwegian philosopher Arne Naess gave a seminal lecture at the Third World Future Research Conference in Bucharest. He distinguished between the "shallow" ecological movement, which he sees concerned mainly with the "health and affluence of people in the developed countries," and the "deep ecology movement." This rejected the idea of human supremacy within nature, the anthropocentric view, in favor of "biospherical egalitarianism." Naess spoke of a "relational, total-field image," rather than that of humanity inhabiting an environment, and the emergence of "an understanding from within."

This call remained unheeded for a few years, but certain individuals, particularly in the United States, picked up on it later in the 1970s, and the Deep Ecology movement commenced. A book by Bill Deval and George Sessions called *Deep Ecology—Living As If Nature Mattered* (1985) became the "bible" of the movement. Deep Ecology promotes a "state of being" in which we feel ourselves to be a more encompassing "Self," a self that includes outer nature, an ecological self—or a "transpersonal ecology," to use Warwick Fox's term. In fact, Deep Ecology has run parallel with transpersonal psychology in some respects, though the marriage has not always been a completely easy one, with some Deep Ecologists resenting what they see as a concern with nature in terms of a value system being turned into psychological theory.[12] But the psychological basis of Deep Ecology is clearly expressed in a crucial statement by Arne Naess: "I'm not so much interested in ethics or morals. I'm interested in *how we experience the world*."[13]

Before there were ecopsychologists, Deep Ecologists, or transpersonal psychologists, there were, of course, the philosophers, poets, and mystics who all expressed the deep psychological current that inheres in any full and healthy apprehension of nature. Near the close of the eighteenth century, for example, the English nature poet William Wordsworth wrote in his "Lines Composed A Few Miles Above Tintern Abbey" what could be considered the hymn of the Deep Ecologists and the ecopsychologists:

> *. . . And I have felt*
> *A presence that disturbs me with the joy*
> *Of elevated thoughts; a sense sublime*
> *Of something far more deeply interfused,*
> *Whose dwelling is the light of setting suns,*
> *And the round ocean and the living air,*
> *And the blue sky, and in the mind of man. . . .*

In the nineteenth century, to give another example, there was the great nature philosopher Ralph Waldo Emerson. "Every appearance of nature corresponds to some state of the mind," he stated in one of his most telling sentences. Like Wordsworth in "something far more deeply interfused," Emerson sensed a deeper reality within nature: "The visible creation is the terminus or the circumference of the invisible world," and "nature . . . always speaks of spirit."[14] And, like Wordsworth, he included the mind as part of nature, a fact we so easily forget.

In the twentieth century, we can take as our third example the nature mystic George William Russell, quoted earlier. He thought that his visions had various sources. Some, he felt, were fashioned from personal memory (very much in keeping with present-day neuroscientific thought) and from spiritual sources, but others came to him, he was convinced, when he participated in "the memory of nature . . . a memory greater than our own." On one occasion, while he was lying on a hill, the "Earth revealed itself to me as a living being, and rock and clay were made transparent. . . . I . . . was made partner in memory of mighty things. . . ."[15] Russell called the mystical Earth he saw in his visions "supernature." There was a "treasure-house of august memories in the innumerable being of earth."[16] Russell literally saw beyond the face of nature visible to our culture. "Walking along country roads . . . my senses were expectant of some unveiling about to take place. . . . The tinted air glowed before me with intelligible significance like a face, a voice," Russell wrote, recalling one of his earliest visions. "The visible world became like a tapestry blown and stirred by winds behind it. . . ."[17]

It is clear that ecopsychology is tapping into a current that already exists—or, rather, still survives—within the modern mind. What we hope ecopsychology can do is to make that stream more accessible to contemporary sensibility and intellectual life.

## CHANGING THE WORLD(VIEW)

We can turn Emerson's statement "Every appearance of nature corresponds to some state of the mind" on its head and consider that each state of mind provides us with a view of nature. This doesn't alter the experience of what Emerson described, but it does shift the emphasis on the dynamics involved. Mind-state and the appearance or perception of the world are highly interdependent; one feeds the other. Coleridge likewise stated: "For all we see, hear, feel and touch, the substance is and must be in ourselves," and "All things shall live in us and we shall live / In all things that surround us. . . ." Wordsworth wrote in a similar vein in *The Ruined Cottage*. In understanding these dynamics and learning how to manipulate them, we have the power to change the world we perceive, and that will result in a change in how we relate to it. What you see is what you get. Or, to put it another way, the world "is as you dream it"— as Numi, a Shuar (Jivaro) shaman told author and environmentalist John Perkins.[18] Emerson already knew it: ". . . the world is a divine dream."[19] This kind of thinking is not to be seen as somehow merely poetic or metaphorical: it is intensely real and pragmatic. How we view the world is fundamental to everything we do and is governed by two factors—our culture and our neurological processes.

Culture is the informational environment that human groups or societies weave for themselves. Types of culture vary in differing times and regions, but, whatever form it takes, culture stands between the individual and the natural world. In the simplest analysis, a culture is the concrete expression of the collective worldview of its inhabitants. But cultures have history, and develop strata like geology. Culture contains and organizes a society's collective memory. This can shape the ongoing development of the culture, which takes on a life of its own. Although culture is essentially an offspring of the human mind, that relationship soon becomes far more complex, with each person adding to the overall culture while being influenced, constrained, and modified by it in a kind of feedback loop. The culture becomes the senior partner in the relationship. It determines how a society's members interact amongst themselves and how the society as a whole views and acts on the natural world. Traditional societies develop permeable cultures that allow them considerable interaction with nature, whereas other societies' cultures effectively wall them off from it. First-world, Westernized societies of the present day share a culture of this latter kind, which is building on itself on a scale and at a depth never seen before. With the ever-increasing speed of communication and travel, and the international nature of the various forms of media, a distinct *monoculture* is forming over the globe. There may be many societies subsumed within that monoculture, with various ethnic, national, historic, linguistic, and other individual traits, but they all relate in all essential ways to the same informational system of the global monoculture. So impermeable and dense is this monoculture becoming that it has eclipsed our view of the natural world, except through carefully controlled windows that ensure that we see nature in certain limited ways. In effect, our collective mental construction of culture has become a surrogate environment or "second nature" for us in a way and on a scale not previously experienced.

It is very difficult for a people to think in terms outside those of the cultural system in which they are immersed. Because our modern culture is not bound to a defined region, and is almost global in its extent, it poses special problems in this regard and has great bearing on how we view the world. The hallmark of Westernized culture is modern science, with its trappings of technology and the philosophy of science, and is a particularly powerful and significant example of this problem. David Turnbull of Deakin University, Australia, has studied some of its aspects. He notes that "techno-science," as he calls it, actually derives from local knowledge, as does knowledge in all societies. Societies have found ways for their knowledge systems to *move*—to become portable, as it were. Various social strategies and technical devices have been used to achieve this. In the Middle Ages, the masons building the Gothic cathedrals relied on a knowledge of geometry that could be applied anywhere, needing only simple tools, like compasses, straightedge, string, and templates, which could readily guide gangs of local workers. Versions of certain formal ideas or styles could therefore be produced at any location. Other cultures have used less material, more mental, systems. This is true for the enormously complex skill of Micronesian navigation (see chapter four), or the Aboriginal dream-journey routes and Native American calendar systems (using skyline markers such as mountain peaks as mnemonics for the sun's position, for instance). In our case, our cultural knowledge system, which we call science, has been presented as a total, universal body of knowledge, neutral and objective, "floating, in some mysterious way, above culture."[20] But if we think of science as a *local* form of thinking and worldview that has simply been enormously successful in transporting itself around the world by means of books, education systems, universal notation, tables, charts, electronic transmission, and suchlike, then it can be seen on a par with other, traditional knowledge systems, rather than being the only "real" knowledge. In fact, some philosophers of science have started to re-evaluate the universality of science, which can be seen to consist of isolated elements of knowledge that have been "smoothed" into a homogenous entity by powerful means of cognitive transport so that we think of them as one body of theory and practice. Turnbull presents the argument that "scientists practising in the real world do not deduce their explanations from universal laws but rather make do with rules of thumb derived from the way the phenomena present themselves in the operation of instruments and devices."[21] There has been a recognition for some time that there is a lack of absolute standards in technical and scientific practice. The much-vaunted belief in scientific objectivity has been called the "god-trick"—the illusion that there can be "a positionless vision of everything."[22] S. L. Star has noted that scientific theory is strongly diverse in origins, with viewpoints "constantly being adduced and reconciled." Elements within a scientific community have their own viewpoints, "a partial truth consisting of local beliefs, local practices, local constants, and resources, none of which are fully verifiable across all sites."[23] This is, of course, a source of modern science's strength. We need generalizations, Turnbull acknowledges, but we also need to recognize that theory and practice are not distinct from one another, and that *theorizing is also a local practice.* The real problem with science is its *power:* it has overcome the limits of locality and now acts on the world as no other knowledge system has managed to do. Science has an awesome ability "to move and apply the knowledge it produces beyond the site of its production," Turnbull asserts. It has devised and developed social stagies and technical devices to eliminate the local to such an extent that it now supplants other knowledge systems developed outside the Westernized cultural framework. Like monoculture in agriculture, which severely limits the varieties of plant species, so, too, does our technoscientific monoculture restrict other varieties of worldview. Just as such selectivity in agriculture increases the potential risk of far-reaching effects resulting from disease in crops, so does a monocultural worldview expose us to the large-scale effects of conceptual infection.

It is important that we realize this; otherwise we can all too easily lapse into the assumption that there *is* only one real or truthful way to see the world, the way that belongs to our monoculture. In fact, it becomes increasingly difficult for us not to feel that any other way of seeing the Earth has to be inferior, superstitious, or whatever, compared with our own cultural worldview. And yet those few of us who break out from within the walls of Westernized culture report back experiences that should give us pause to reconsider such assumptions. By immersing ourselves in what survives of other cultures, we can get glimpses of other ways of seeing the environment. We can change how the world appears to us by changing our viewpoint, which effectively means by changing the state of our consciousness.

An example of just how strong this change of worldview can be—
that we are indeed not talking about some mild or metaphorical effect—is given by a couple of dramatic experiences of the German
cultural anthropologist Christian Rätsch. He had specialized in the
languages and cultures of native Mesoamerica at Hamburg University, and decided to do field study with the Lacandon Indians in the
rain forests of southern Mexico. Because these people maintain
many pre-Columbian Mayan traits, he wished to converse with
them in their own language: to use Spanish would be to erect a cultural barrier at the outset. He took Mayan linguistics at university,
then went to the Yucatán to pick up the spoken Mayan language, to
which the Lacandon language is closely related. He then set off
walking from the old Mayan city of Palenque into the rain forest,
seeking a Lacandon village a hundred kilometers away. Palenque is
the sacred center or World Navel (see chapter one), according to the
Lacandon, and Rätsch was anxious not to drop in by helicopter, for
that, too, would cause cultural dissonance. As he walked, the German anthropologist became nervous; he didn't know what to expect. "But as I walked through the jungle and saw those trees and
plants and animals somehow I got calm," he recalled. When he
made contact with the Lacandon, his long hair, along with the fact
that he just walked in to them, helped overcome their suspicions
(to them, long hair is a sign that one is a true human being; they say
that if you cut your hair you have "cut off your head"—that is, you
cannot think). When the village elder found out that Rätsch was
not a missionary, he invited the young German to stay in his house.

Rätsch was allowed to learn the Lacandon lifeway. He was taught
how to hunt and gather, and to farm in their way. The reality hit
him that "all you have to eat is what you get from your hands, what
you get from Mother Earth and from your skills. . . . It was a very
profound . . . psychological effect. When I started to hunt, my mind
changed completely." He became very sensitive to the natural environment. The Indians taught him how to see the rain forest, how to
see animals within it. "I started to walk through the jungle in a different way," he realized. "I was so amazed at the consciousness
changes . . . many very old instincts came through in my mind."

In the course of this development, he had a true reality shock.

One early morning, he was sitting on a tree trunk guarding the village's patch of nearly ripe corn against predators. A dead tree was standing about fifteen feet distant, just a trunk and a branch. A bird landed on the branch. Seeing an opportunity for getting food, Rätsch raised his gun and shot at it. "It was very easy. . . . The bird, like, exploded—I saw all the feathers flying and the bird dropped to the ground." He went over to recover the shot bird, but when he got to the tree he couldn't find it. "There was not the corpse of a bird; there was not a single feather! Then I looked up at the tree, and there was not even the branch!" He was shocked, and returned to the village to tell the village elder of the incident. The old man laughed and said such things happened quite often—it was just the jungle spirits teasing him. "Okay! That was the explanation," Rätsch accepted, "and I had to be satisfied with that."

Rätsch became increasingly fluent in the Lacandon language, and learned the Indian names for animals and plants within the rainforest environment. Eventually the Indians allowed him to take part in their ceremonies and began to tell him some of their secrets, such as the spells they used for healing. "I got inside of a magical universe I never expected to be there," Rätsch admitted. "That was the most dramatic experience, because to get involved with magical spells meant that I had to leave my German, scientific background totally." He was taught one spell that was used for healing a cut on the leg or hand—a common accident when working in the jungle with a machete. A long, complex incantation was used, full of difficult, esoteric terminology. But he learned it. The next day, he was working in the cornfield when his machete slipped and he gashed his leg seriously. There were just some village children around, and they were horrified at the sight of the great flow of blood from Rätsch's leg. He sent them back to the village for help, but he realized that he was losing blood badly and was in a dangerous predicament. There was no better alternative: he lowered himself to the ground and started the magical healing procedure he had learned just the day before. He repeated the spell twice and put some saliva on the wound—the procedure involved spitting three times and blowing on the wound. By the time he had finished performing the spell the second time, the wound had stopped bleeding. The children returned with the village elder, and they were amazed that the bleeding had stopped, but the old fellow was smiling. Rätsch was informed that whenever someone learns that spell, he invariably cuts himself a short time afterwards. It is like a test. "Now I *am* in a different reality," Rätsch thought to himself at the time. "This was nothing to do with what I learned when I grew up in Germany!"[24]

Culture affects how we see the world, and changing how we see the world actually changes the world for us. It isn't just some kind of optical illusion or parlor game with perception: the world changes, and hence one's relationship with it. And this question of worldview goes very deep indeed, beyond even culture, into the very structure of our central nervous system. Our worldview is actually *embodied* within us.

## THROUGH THE GLASS DARKLY: THE WORLD AS INFORMATION

It is very difficult to avoid the conceptual trap of thinking that we simply see the world as it is. We tend to feel that the environment is "out there" and that its reality streams in through our eyes and ears and other senses as if through open windows and doors. We think that the inside of our head is like an empty room into which all this news of outside floods in. There is our self, the real person inside us, sitting like a homunculus in the dark, empty cavity that is our brain looking out at the bright world around. But this is, of course, a fable, a story we tell ourselves. There is no space inside our brains, which is wall-to-wall tissue, blood, cells, nerve fibers. Solid. That feeling we have of a little person sitting just behind and a little above the midpoint between our eyes is a mirage, a culturally sustained phantasm, like the "ghost speaker" between two stereo loudspeakers. (I say "culturally sustained" because, if you feel your seat of consciousness is your left elbow, or your cat, or the vase on the windowsill—and are unwise enough to let on to others that this is the case—it will not be long before you are visited by "doctors" . . .) The sense of internal, mental space we have is as illusory as the three-dimensional effect produced by staring in the right way at one of those stereogram pictures. It is space that isn't there, that has never been. Princeton psychologist Julian Jaynes has argued that this "unified mind-space with its analog 'I' that we have come to call consciousness" is a relatively recent development, not existing in human beings until only a few thousand years ago.[25]

In order to gain some idea of what happens when we perceive the world, we need to turn to a relatively new area of research into consciousness, intelligent thought, and behavior that is now generally referred to as "cognitive science." This is an interdisciplinary effort, drawing together the expertise of linguists, computer scientists, philosophers, psychologists, anthropologists, and neuroscientists. Cognitive science is really still cognitive *sciences*, having not yet melded into a single discipline with a completely collective viewpoint, but nevertheless much new understanding has been achieved over recent years thanks to this collaboration of differing specialisms, together with increasingly sophisticated means of monitoring and measuring brain activity that has led to a now significant buildup of knowledge. Cognitive scientists look particularly at the structures and processes of information transmission within the central nervous system that underpin our perceptions, thinking, and behavior.

The brain is processing all the time we are perceiving, thinking, doing, sleeping. You look at a tree. How do you know you are seeing a tree? The tree in the visual signal has to be separated from its background and surroundings and compared with the information that is held in memory to do with trees (and memory itself is not some passive video library, but has to be reconstructed each time it is used, and is subject to a whole range of poorly understood dynamics). If you have seen the tree on some other occasion, there has to be an attempt to select all the memorial information relating to that tree; if there is some emotional association with that tree, then that also has to be brought out of memory and associated with the visual signal. All this information has to be linked with verbal information on trees—names, types. This in turn is transmitted to the parts of the central nervous system that control your vocal apparatus so that you can cry out, "Oh, there is the old oak tree I used to sit under with my grandfather when I was a child and listen to him telling me stories." As the visual signal is sustained, more processing brings up the memories of your grandfather, some of the stories he used to tell, how the tree's foliage has changed since you last saw it so many years ago, other instances in which you and your grandfather interacted, when he died. . . . A raging torrent of information floods the visual signal of the tree you think you are simply looking at. Filter upon filter of memory, of connections, of reconstructed emotion—nostalgia, joy, fondness—is placed on your perception of the tree—indeed, upon every perception you make. Some of these you may become conscious of; others may flash by without entering the central field of your awareness. Such processing occurs every time you do anything cognitive—listening to music or the news on the radio, speaking to your friend, solving a crossword puzzle, and so on. And in the case of your oak tree, your brain is simultaneously processing the smell of the grass, the feel of the ground, the warmth of the sun, the sound of the birds and distant voices, and these were all added, consciously or unconsciously, to your central visual perception of the old oak tree.

And you are not even seeing the tree in its "is-ness." Radiation from a narrow band of the electromagnetic spectrum we call visible light reflects from whatever it is "out there" your sensory apparatus is directed at, passes through the eyeball at around 186,000 miles a second, and impinges on the retina at the rear, where 120 million receptor nerve cells—the rods and cones—are bleached by the light energy, setting off a relay of electrochemical cellular reactions which pass along the pathway provided by the optic nerve to various locations in the brain. The raw image is processed according to wavelengths of light, light intensity, edges, contours, symmetry, and so on. The "tree," unknowable in its "thingness," its essence, has been translated via electromagnetic radiation, organic optics, and nerve reactions into a silent, invisible flux of electrochemical activity in the darkness of the brain. There and in that form it enters the exotic processing activity that gives rise to what we call our perception. You never actually "saw" the old oak tree that produced a wave of gentle nostalgia in you and may even have moved you to a tear or two. None of us ever "sees" anything, in fact, in the direct sense that we think we see: no sun, no sky, no trees, no loved one's face. We "only" receive a fabulous complex of processed information.

This initially alarming revelation has been carefully studied by a group of cognitive researchers who go under the forbidding title of "biogenetic structuralists." In their book, *Brain, Symbol and Experience*, anthropologist Charles Laughlin, cognitive scientist John McManus, and clinical psychiatrist Eugene d'Aquili state that "the principal function of our nervous system is the construction of models of the world." They call what we would think of as the external world the "operational environment," and what we would think of as our inner, mental world the "cognized environment." In their view, even the body, the organism itself, is part of the operational environment—it is part of the "outside" information that arises within in the field of cognition, the *sensorium*. Both the operational and the cognized environments are constantly changing and developing, so countless models are always being made by the brain-mind. All that we can ever be aware of are these mental models; they are the only world we are ever in contact with. Following this logic, we can therefore say that our idea of the nature of the Earth is created for us within the dark machinations of the brain. The planet we are aware of is an *informational model* which is dependent on the way our brain-minds work, and how the processing of that information is affected by the culture we are immersed in. There is always more to know about the external environment, the operational environment, than can ever be known. "The limitations upon what and how much can be known are inherent in the organization of the nervous system, as well as imposed by culture and personal history," the biogenetic structuralists tell us.[26] The brain's cognized environment can construct a landscape, horizon, distance, and perspective from a few sensory cues. Sometimes, different people can receive the same sensory cues but construct different cognitions from them—a simple example is the famous face-vase illusion. But this dissonance can work on a grander scale. The worldview of, say, Western science, which is no more than a cognized environment, differs from a tribal, shamanistic worldview—the same world, but a differing reading of it. "In fact . . . reinforcing the 'proper' views of the world is one of the principal means by which social groups enculturate their members," the bio-genetic structuralists point out.[27]

For those whose first reaction to the idea of being aware of processed information about the world rather than somehow directly apprehending its "reality" is one of depression, matters get worse: there is no "you" to receive that information. You yourself are "just" a stream of information. Your thoughts think themselves, the cognitive scientists tell us; there is no separate, interior agent doing the thinking. Your "you-ness" is sustained by constantly updated news about yourself. One of the most conspicuous forms this takes is by means of language, or, more accurately, interior narration. We are all familiar with the inner silent voice that keeps telling us stories about ourselves, a constant commentary on who we are, what we are doing or not doing, what we are planning, where we are going—an interior dialogue in which we debate about decisions or worry about consequences. When the homogeneity of mental processing breaks down, when we go "out of sync" through what is called mental illness, this interior voice can become hallucinatory and be experienced as a real, usually disembodied voice, or a voice that comes from some part of the environment. "The whole day through," one mental patient said eloquently of his voices, "they keep on telling truly my daily history of head and heart."[28]

We might think that language is a purely invented artifact, yet even schizophrenics who have been deaf from birth can hear voices, or hallucinate beings who communicate with them by sign language. This tells us that, though the particular symbolic forms of a language can be invented, the language urge itself is embedded within our brain-minds; there is a nonverbal protolanguage that is a vital process of mental life, and not only can be expressed through culturally designated symbolic systems of sounds and written marks, but can resonate internally within the brain-mind during interior dialogue, dreaming, hallucination, or divinatory and other altered mind-states. (These are matters to which we shall return in the final chapter of this book.)

The separating out of this linguistic processing into spoken words and other symbolic devices is considered by many researchers to have accompanied and cocreated the rise of conscious awareness in early humans, and it can itself begin to shape the form of consciousness we experience. Indo-European languages, for example, the languages of the founder societies of the now dominant Westernized type of culture, greatly emphasize the self, the ego, the boundary between "I" and "not-I," and generally the separateness of things. This has been a significant factor in the development of the hard-edged ego of the modern Westernized mind. Language has also allowed the brain-mind to think (as we say) in abstract ways, less tied to direct experience. "The verbal plane comes to be able to speak with its own voice," quips cognitive psychologist Guy Claxton.[29]

The whole question of the self is naturally indivisibly bound up with the riddle of the nature of consciousness, a thorny matter that is still not well understood in our culture. As a working description of how we experience consciousness, we can consider it to be the focus of our awareness at any particular moment. Guy Claxton has likened such conscious attention to the small spot of light projected by a flashlight in a dark cavern full of looming rocky shapes, deep recesses, strange noises, and so on. He points out that consciousness in this sense is a fairly recent development of cognition, and is only a part of overall mental activity. It is "the acquired tendency of the Western mind to fasten only onto what is happening in the limelight of consciousness, and to neglect the hazier activity that precedes and surrounds it," Claxton writes. "We fail to notice that consciousness is a developmental phenomenon, its contents forever arising, unfolding, and passing away, like breakers on the sea."[30] We like to think of our conscious self as encompassing the main activity of the mind, yet in reality it is like a cork bobbing on the ocean of the largely unconscious mind. *We receive more information from the environment than ever enters the limelight of our conscious awareness.* This has been shown in clinical tests with, for example, people who have a mental illness that prevents them from recognizing familiar things, such as the faces of family and friends. When they meet or are shown photographs of these people, the conductance of their skin and the size of their eye pupils change measurably, even though there is no conscious recognition. At some level, some discrimination clearly takes place. This sort of processing, bubbling away in what Henry James called "the deep well of unconscious cerebration," constantly underpins what passes into our conscious attention. (Later in this book, I will suggest that we can receive information from places and from the landscape that our conscious attention never heeds.) Cognitive philosopher Owen Flanagan refers to subjective conscious awareness as "experiential sensitivity" and to unconscious mental activity as "informational sensitivity." His parable involves telling the difference between Pepsi-Cola and Coca-Cola. A person who cannot *experientially* tell the difference between Pepsi and Coke might be *informationally* able to discriminate between the two. So someone who cannot consciously tell Pepsi from Coke and yet who repeatedly selects one in preference to the other in blind tests must be receiving information from somewhere in his or her cognitive system.

Flanagan points out that efficient and intelligent creatures could have evolved without consciousness. Intelligence does not equal consciousness, even though we might casually assume that it does. So, when computer scientists talk about "artificial intelligence," they are not, could not be, postulating about artificial consciousness. A well-programmed robot, Flanagan suggests, could be designed to mislead, but only a conscious human being can lie, for a lie requires *intent* to mislead. Many of the functions we would associate with consciousness, actually result from intelligence. "Not all our intelligent actions essentially involve consciousness," Flanagan states, "but many do."[31]

So where does all this leave the conscious self, the ego? It is an illusory "mind's 'I,' " says Flanagan; "the brain-mind contains no special-status ghost," asserts Claxton. All cognitive scientists seem to agree that the sense of self is a mirage. The sense we have of experiencing a continuous state of awareness was likened to a "stream of consciousness" by the great turn-of-the-century psychologist William James. He envisaged an individual's thoughts and perceptions as being fused together into the illusion of continuous flow, much the way the still frames in a film are presented to the eye at such a speed that they merge by means of flicker fusion to become movies. But the stream of consciousness, the cognitive people insist, is phenomenological—it is how it *feels* to be conscious—whereas objectively we know that there are many forms of discontinuities in consciousness, which are smoothed out in our experience of it. We wake up in the morning and somehow reconnect with the conscious personal identity we experienced when we went to sleep (actually, it usually takes me a while for this hookup to take place!), and even in profound cases of discontinuity, in which a person might lapse into a comatose sleep state for long periods of time, years during certain forms of mental illness, the subjective experience of a continuous self survives the time gap.

This idea of a stream, however, is a *serial* concept and still conjures the image of a person viewing the "movie" of his or her consciousness, of there being some central movie theater somewhere in the brain-mind. Contrary to that idea, neuroscientists now see the brain functioning in a *parallel* fashion, with multiple strands of processing taking place simultaneously. Someone hands you a flower. Different parts of the visual cortex process color, movement, and the distinction between the edge of the flower and the rest of the visual field. You smell the scent from the flower; this means that another part of the brain is involved in processing that sensory input. Somehow, all these multiple processes are bound together into one smoothed sensory experience. This matter of "binding" is still a profound problem for cognitive scientists to unravel, but some of them are focusing on a forty-cycles-per-second brain rhythm that has been measured and which may electrically synchronize the various neuronal firing patterns. But whatever the brain's magic trick is, it does seem that the sense of a continuous, conscious self results from a binding of parallel processing occurring in various parts of the brain. It is thought that there is no one place, no HQ in the brain, that provides the seat of the "self"—all the brain processes operate equally. They are somehow focused into a totality that gives the illusion of a separate, discrete self.

Consciousness, then, in the view of many cognitive scientists, can be seen as an *emergent* property of the brain, something like the glittering shimmer of the sun on the flowing waters of a stream. Take away the water, and this stream and the sparkling sunlight disappear. The biogenetic structuralists talk about an "entrainment" model, in which neural networks connect together like the cars of a train, and trains connect to trains:

> Consciousness and all of its aspects are functions of the on-going entrainment of neural networks. Networks of cells communicate among themselves in a particular configuration during one moment of consciousness (they become entrained), cease communicating in that configuration the next moment (they become disentrained) and link up in a whole new configuration the next moment (they re-entrain).[32]

It was the Canadian neuropsychologist Donald Hebb who, in the 1940s, developed the "neural-network" model of the brain. In this, every thought, perception, or cognitive act is underpinned by the interconnection of brain cells into ever-shifting, self-organizing networks or webs. It seems that when such neural pathways have been forged in response to a stimulus—an experience, perception, thought—the neurons are "primed" to some extent, so that the pathways can re-form more easily on subsequent occasions. The firing pattern of neurons can follow previously blazed trails. This is the way skills (such as driving a car) are learned, so that, once learned, they can slip below the threshold of conscious attention for considerable periods of time without being lost. Attitudes and opinions can also be "engraved" into neurological function like this. The biogenetic structuralists use the term "creode" to label these pathways of change, these mental canals.

The positive aspect of this is the suggestion that the neural structure of our brains can be trained and such pathways, presumably, changed if we have new experiences, or if we consciously expose ourselves to new experiences. New pathways can be forged when used more often than the old pathways. The downside is that we may react to things (mentally respond to stimuli—scenes, opinions, and so on) in habitual reflexes rather than fully conscious and exploratory ways. So we can end up just going through an automatonlike reaction to environmental stimuli we encounter regularly.

Though this can be useful, and even necessary to survival in many cases, a lack of effort to break or modify such habits or creodes in certain contexts means that we can sometimes limit the range of what we might otherwise experience to our benefit. (The practical parts of this book—the "Experiential" sections of the following chapters—are largely aimed at encouraging just such an effort.)

There are deeper forms of these primed neural pathways, according to the biogenetic structuralists: some creodes come "built into" our mental equipment—"programmed," as it were—from babyhood and even from before the time of birth (the brain in embryos develops remarkably quickly). Such inherited creodes, or "fixed action patterns," vary from species to species. In humans frowns or smiles are examples; in a dog it could be tail-wagging; in a cat it could be instinctive claw-sharpening scratching; and so on. So we need to be aware that some of our reactions to things, and some of the basic ways we cognize our environment, belong, to a greater or lesser extent, to the overall genetic heritage of our species and not to a free, independent, and individual self at all. (Again, in chapter one we will encounter an anciently manifested example of this in the cross-cultural idea of a "World Navel.")

A welcome aspect of neural-network models, Claxton points out, is that "they re-embed the 'mind' in its natural biological context, they re-connect it with the rest of the body."[33] This overcomes the "Cartesian Split," in which mind and body are held as separate entities. A healing of sorts.

Nevertheless, some cognitive scientists have a tendency to think of the brain as if it were a computer. This isn't satisfactory. The biogenetic structuralists, at least, point out that neurons are *not* inorganic microchips, but living cells. And cells are goal-seeking organisms. Brain cells, neurons, seek excitatory states as we might seek pleasure—A. Harry Knopf has termed the brain cell the "hedonistic neuron." Consequently, much of the information received by a cell is a result of its *own* activity. Our brain is a living system, just like the Earth itself. The Western, cognized environment we call science so easily overlooks the living aspect of things.

In fact, many nonscientists—and some scientists—are uncomfortable with the findings and ideas that are now pouring forth from cognitive science. There is a feeling that it is simply a new wave of materialism in thinly disguised form, and some people are inherently reluctant to consider consciousness, mind, and its close cousin spirituality in such a way. But the mystery of the matter is still present. We must remember the unique situation that prevails when people study brain-mind function: the brain is the one thing in nature of which we can study the outside and yet have the experience of the interior (hence "brain-mind"). This really comes to the fore when considering the findings of neuroscience. It is still simply unknown how electrical pulses in the brain, however complex, become our mental life. That alchemical transformation between physical processes and mental phenomena remains an enigma, as was underlined for me by Albert Hoffman, the Swiss chemist who synthesized LSD. "We can measure the light that enters the eye; we can measure the pulses that reach deep into the brain from the retina," he said, leaning across the dinner table for emphasis, "but the moment when that turns into a visual perception is lost to us. What I *see* is still a mystery."

My own view is that we can take on board the findings of cognitive science—indeed, have little option but to do so—and listen carefully to the various debates and ideas within it, but that does not necessarily mean we have to accept all the implications the cognitive scientists themselves might draw from their work. Though the architecture of the human brain must mediate consciousness in a human form, that does not necessarily explain the full nature of consciousness. To use an (imperfect) analogy, we may be becoming so involved with the TV receiver that we are overlooking clues to the TV studio that originates the material the TV screen displays, and the broadcasting system that transports to the receiver a version of what goes on in the studio. The image on the TV screen is a function of processes going on within the TV set itself, but the *origination* and *content* of the material so displayed is not. Similarly, there may be aspects of the information that enter the processing within the brain-mind that are not located in the brain. This is obviously the case with regard to the sources of sensory perception, whose full nature we can never perceive or be entirely conscious of. But it might extend to other things that come within our cognitive field.

Transpersonal experiences, for example. If you and I both see the ghost of your grandfather sitting under the old oak tree, what or where is the source of that perception? The cognized environment of mainstream Western science says ghosts do not exist. So it has to be a hallucination. But what does *that* mean? It is an explanation without meaning. In a sense, if we *really* heed the findings of cognitive science, the whole world we cognize is a form of hallucination. The procedures for *presentation* are on board in the brain, not anywhere else. We only think the consensus Western worldview is "reality" (which is—what?—a special or strong form of hallucination?) because some of the ways it arrives in the brain, though not how it arises in the mind, can be measured by the means we use and accept. But the Western worldview is highly dependent on its cultural environment, and extrasensory, transpersonal experiences are equally accepted as a part of reality in other worldviews, and can become so even to Westerners who adapt to those worldviews, as Christian Rätsch's experience with the bird and dead tree indicate.

Even within science itself there are arguments that suggest other than sensory doorways to the brain. A controversial one is biologist Rupert Sheldrake's idea of "morphic resonance," in which he hypothesizes that memory is situated outside of the brain as a field of information that extends in space and continues in time.[34] Perhaps somewhat less controversial, though nevertheless challenging, is the current research into the possible relationship of quantum-mechanical principles with consciousness. Everything arises out of the quantum field or flux, the vast sea of potentiality, and neurons are not exempt from this. Some scientists, such as Stuart Hameroff, are seeking structures within the brain where quantum effects might be located.[35]

On the other hand, the insistence by cognitive science that the self is a mirage sustained by cultural and neurophysiological factors is generally in tune with the claims of great spiritual traditions like Buddhism, and all forms of mysticism, where liberation requires ego loss, the dissolution of the image of self. The person still remains, but the mirage of self, and the illusions it generates around it, are removed. Left is the oceanic feeling of oneness. The whole brain-mind system turns on and lights up: awareness is no longer constricted to a self, a bounded ego, a streamed defining the flow of mental content. In such a state, the fully turned-on brain-mind system is *experienced* as blazing light, a paradoxically all-containing void. It is a mind-state that our language cannot describe, by its very nature. The true mystic escapes the boundaries of all cultural systems while in the full mystical state; that is why what descriptive accounts there are of the state itself, from anywhere in the world and any period of time, shorn of any cultural elements superimposed by the language used, all seem to be referring to the same basic experience. It could even be that the oceanic feeling characteristic of mystical (or "cosmic") consciousness is the interior knowledge of the quantum state.

## REMEMBERING A NEW RELATIONSHIP WITH THE EARTH

But it is not the purpose of this book to argue these matters. Rather, in seeking ways and means to use the Earth as a healer of our view of it, we want to identify certain conceptual tools cognitive science has to offer us. Perhaps the most important from our point of view here is that the world we perceive is no more, and no less, than an *informational model*. If we can accept that, then we should also be able to accept the possibility of making alterations to that model, of being able to extend the range of information it contains. Worldview is plastic; it can be molded and shaped. It is not a single, given reality. The nature of our cultural environment, and the realities of our neurological processing, can all be affected within certain limits. To effect such changes means that we sometimes have to change the state of consciousness in which we operate, even if only slightly.

In some tribal and earlier societies, the ego seems to have been "softer" and more permeable than the modern Western iron-clad sense of self. Certainly in ecstatic practices (such as shamanic trance), and perhaps to a lesser degree in the normative state in those societies, the ego could also be more mobile than in what *we* would think of as a normal state. In such mind-states, though the knowledge of "I" and "not-I" can remain present, the ego, the center or locus of consciousness, has leave to drift into a plant, a rock, even a mountain. Some tribal cultures have fostered this experience of the world, which is of course vastly different from the view of reality held by our own culture. When a Westerner enters an altered state of consciousness—however instigated, by meditative or religious practices, by trauma, by dysfunction, or by the ingesting of hallucinogens—one of the first changes of experience noticed is that the sense of the self, or ego, becomes more flexible, more mobile, and softer-edged. But since he or she belongs to our culture, the hard-nosed cognitive scientist would say that an out-of-body experience, the feeling that the locus of consciousness is floating off into some part of the environment, is a hallucination, or another version of the self being constructed in the brain. The scientist will point out that we can detect elements of memory in such visions. Of course, if the cognitive scientist takes on board her or his own findings, it has to be accepted that our apparently "real," so-called nonhallucinatory perceptions are *also* modulated by memory, and that our version of self is culturally determined. But we have already discussed the inadequacy of the explanation of hallucination, and in some ways it hardly matters if it is inadequate or not: all we have, cognitive scientists included, are models of the world, including the sense of inner and outer, of head, of brain. The important factor is that the model of the world can change in altered mind-states. *The nature and range of information is state-specific.* Western culture is *monophasic*—that is, it is locked into one particular state of consciousness. It does not follow that a perception of the world made outside of that state is somehow unreal.

The following chapters of this book identify five areas of psychological dynamics involved in mind-environment interactions that I suggest would need to be built into the foundations of an overarching ecopsychology. Each chapter is highly eclectic—it draws on a range of information from many sources in an attempt to show us ways to modify gently the automatic viewpoint of our present cultural worldview. These sources include, amongst many others, shamans, scientists, artists, archeologists, anthropologists, vagrants, as well as the Earth itself. Much of the material relates to the practices of non-Western and earlier peoples who lived in differing phases of consciousness from ours, and thus experienced different relationships with the Earth. We can think of this as the healing wisdom of the Earth working through those who were once closer to it. All the time, we must remember that *our subject is the mind, not the Earth*. It is the world*view* we are trying to heal, not the world.

The nature of this book is therefore exceptionally *cross-disciplinary*, and it will become readily apparent that all of the five areas are interrelated in various ways. This cross-disciplinary mode brings both problems and benefits. It provides headaches for librarians and bookshops ("On which shelf do we place this damn thing?"), not to mention the marketing departments of publishers, but its real downside is that much information gets lost between the boundaries of established disciplines, readerships, and "markets." The powerfully positive aspect, however, is that sums can be greater than parts, and it is at the interfaces, the margins between disciplines, where the really interesting things can happen. In this present work, the interrelating common denominator that will emerge is the one way we can redefine our model of the world by bringing extra information into it, and perhaps by doing that we can begin to modify the greater informational model of our culture. This common denominator is "mythic consciousness," or, to use an equivalent term, "imaginal consciousness." Indeed, this book is essentially an essay in mythic dynamics. But all this will be explored in greater depth as we proceed.

We must also understand what is meant by the term "healing" in this context. Not a quick cure, for sure, but, rather, a movement towards greater *wholeness*. And that of course is the root meaning of the English-language words "healing" and "health." They derive from earlier Indo-European roots through the Middle English *hole*, from the earlier *hale*, meaning "complete, healthy." The Old Norse *heill* also meant "sound, healthy," and gave us "to hail," to greet. So perhaps we need to greet the Earth again. "Therapy" likewise has a less obvious root meaning than we commonly think. It comes to us via a range of related Greek words, including *therapeuein*, to take care of; *theraps*, an attendant; *therapeia*, attendance. In his *Placeways*, Eugene Victor Walter points out that the meaning of *therapeia* varied according to context. In farming, it meant "cultivation"; regarding children, it meant "parenthood"; in religion, the worship of the gods. It meant "healing" only in association with a physician—medical attendance. Since attendance is therefore the basic meaning of "therapy," and is an act of consciousness, perhaps we need to *attend to* the Earth in order to obtain completeness, to receive its healing.

## EXPERIENTIAL: ANOTHER WAY OF KNOWING

Each chapter in the following pages contains a section labeled "Experiential," in which you will find selected aspects of the discussion presented in practical form. These practices can be seen as "exercises," but I would prefer that you think of them as simply another way of exploring the subjects we are considering—another way of knowing, if you like. The "Experiential" sections are written in a considerably less formal manner than the main body of each chapter, with more anecdote and, I hope, some fun, and they can be taken as invitations to leave behind the usual cultural and neurophysiological entrainments for a while, to experiment with some new ones, and perhaps, in the process, to open up fresh neural pathways and thus modifications of our informational model of the world. They are designed for you and me, for the denizens of Western-style culture: they would be redundant for any of the relatively few remaining tribal peoples who are still little touched by Western civilization.

You may not want actually to carry out any of the suggested experiential procedures. That is fine. The very act of reading the "Experiential" sections will extend the information in each chapter for you, and they will offer different ways of handling some of the ideas presented. Used thus, the experiential activities can be seen as the equivalents of what a physicist would call "thought experiments." But if you do decide to try out some of the suggested activities, you will find that, though you will not require much specialized equipment, a simple camera and a good portable tape recorder will prove very useful. Some of the activities are deceptively simple and quick; others are more structured and take longer to accomplish. Although the following chapters follow a generalized sort of progression, a sort of psychological journey, there is no "course" as such being laid out. You are (naturally) free to dabble with a few experiential activities if they take your fancy, and to leave the others. On the other hand, you may wish to take a more comprehensive approach and try out a wide selection of the suggested practices (this need not be as onerous as it sounds: some of them are designed to take place while you are asleep!). Whatever your choice, if you assiduously practice a selection of the experiential procedures described, you can be assured that they will begin to alter your view of the world subtly, however mild or even gamelike some of them may seem at first glance. They are experiments in ways of perception, feeling, and thinking, and will present opportunities for you to use several of your five senses, sometimes in slightly unfamiliar ways. Allow yourself the liberty of doing that, and don't let initial doubt or disbelief in the context of some of the suggested practices hold you back. It's time to kick a few creodes.

(A word of caution, however. A number of the experiential procedures outlined in this book are aimed, in one way or another, at developing a little "softening" of the edges of the self, to allow new possibilities of worldview and relationship with the environment to emerge. If you naturally experience involuntary confused ego boundaries, or if you have done so in the past, be sure to avoid procedures given in this work that would further encourage this. It is most important to be in control of all these activities. Select defined windows of time to carry out any of the experiential procedures, so that, after you "switch" one of them on, you always switch it off when completed, and return to the normal mind-state in which you go to work, the supermarket, the ball game, or whatever. Always be *state-specific*.)

It was noted earlier that, when people are exposed to nature in the raw during wilderness trips, the new vantage points they gain can be fairly quickly eroded as soon as they are reimmersed in the city and the old ruts of their lives (that is, the old ruts of their neural pathways). Information on access to properly supervised wilderness experience is given in the appendix, but we are trying to do something a little different in this book. Many of the experiential procedures outlined here—though in a few cases capable of causing significantly altered states of mind—are intended to work away gradually at some of the entrainments instilled by the prevailing cultural worldview, to which we are all victim. They are designed to be incorporated into the life-styles most of us normally lead, for it is given only to relatively few of us to share the lifeways of rainforest Indians or Australian Aborigines (and it is a good thing for those peoples that this is the case!). In this way, they will, I hope, provide you with the opportunities for creating a more sustained, abiding experience of changing worldview than the (nevertheless profoundly valuable) relatively short, sharp shock of wilderness experience.

It is important to note that all the experiential practices presented in this volume are deliberately open-ended. This has to be the case, because it is not for me to impose my experiences upon you, or to describe what you should or should not experience. You are simply offered a way of going about achieving a certain range of experience. There are no answers here, only ways of asking questions. This will, I hope, ensure that you will never again go for a walk, glance at a gnarled tree trunk or weathered rock, cross a threshold, pass through a shadow, or listen to a stream or waterfall without finding it a remarkable thing to do. As your world within changes, so will your perception of the planet without. The world begins deep inside of us.

## THE ARCHAIC WHISPER (THE WORLD AROUND US IS FALLING SILENT)

The modest suggestions outlined in the following chapters are not being put forward as the sole framework for an ecopsychology for our culture and times, but merely as one range of possibilities, an identification of source concepts and practices that could go into the creation of such a psychological tool. And we do need that tool. Our culture is the dominant one now on Earth, and is a developing monoculture; soon all earlier and different lifeways will have effectively vanished, at least from our point of worldview. This is a hard truth, but a truth nonetheless. The ancient world is almost over, but not quite. There are records of ancient traditions (though, in the main, hidden away passively in the archives and specialist publications of mainstream academic disciplines), and a limited number of fragmented tribal peoples still hold worldviews unfamiliar to us (though these are being remorselessly eroded). There are still the ancient sites and ceremonial landscapes (though many of these are increasingly coming under threat). We can learn from all these. But when this archaic whisper is finally gone or eroded to such an extent that it is no longer actively useful, when this "news of difference"—to use Gregory Bateson's term—ceases, how will we be able to compare the worldview we hold with any alternative? We must first try to hear and then listen to the archaic whisper, while it is still audible.

# CENTERING

## The Ancient Art of Being Here

Gaia, the Greek Earth Mother Goddess, once lived at Delphi, on the southern slopes of Mount Parnassus. She had a timber-built oracle house at the site, which was then called Pytho in reference to the she-dragon, Python, who dwelt there. But one day Apollo, a young god from the north, happened along and killed the dragon. The site was rededicated to him, and a temple, the first of a series at the site, was erected. A prophetess or *pythia* was set up within the Temple of Apollo, and she gave answers (usually in riddle form) to questions put to her on leaden tablets. This oracle site came to surpass all others in Greece in fame, and its authority lasted for centuries. The ruins of the temple now visible at Delphi date from the fourth century B.C. It stands within a precinct containing several other chapels and shrines, all connected by a winding Sacred Way that leads up the mountain slope. That Delphi is of the Earth strikes anyone who visits—it feels as if Gaia never really left. It has a moody, elemental beauty, surrounded by rearing cliff faces and deep chasms. The temple stands on a platform of irregular boulders, specially designed by the ancient Greeks to withstand the shock of earthquakes, to which the place is prone. Thunderstorms also frequently erupt about the site, and to witness thunder clouds roaring and flashing at eye level as they funnel through the steep valley below the precinct is to feel directly in the presence of Zeus, the king of the gods, who originally founded the site.

The memory of that foundation is lodged in a sand-colored dome of stone about three feet tall, placed in a corner of a stairway landing in the small museum at Delphi. Many visitors pass this object without knowing what it is. The legend has it that Zeus sent out two eagles from the extremities of the Earth. Where their paths crossed was the center of the world. This central point was marked with a special stone called an *omphalos*, a navel stone. Delphi was located at the World Navel. The stone in the Delphi museum, which was found at the Temple of Apollo, is certainly a mysterious object. Carved in high relief on its surface is a curious, interlaced pattern generally called an *agrenon* or "net." Some have claimed that this design represents strands of wool, whereas others have argued that it is some archaic and esoteric system of latitude and longitude,[1] and yet others have stated that it records alignments of ancient Greek temples laid out to an astrological scheme projected onto the landscape.[2]

*Omphalos* stone at Delphi.

In human beings, the navel is located about halfway down the body, and so is a center in that sense; it is also the point from which the embryo develops in the womb, and so is truly the center of life. But the navel in most people is in the form of a depression in the stomach; why did the Greeks use a dome of stone to represent the World Navel? Marie Delcourt has intriguingly pointed out that not only does the navel of a pregnant woman at the end of her term protrude, but so does the navel of a newborn baby.[3] This hints at the deep, abiding Mother Goddess association of Delphi.

Another navel stone is also to be found at Delphi, a plain cone of gray stone shot through with veins of quartz. Located at a turn on the Sacred Way, it is unlabeled and easy to miss. Other navel stones, or *omphaloi*, occur at other ancient Greek temples. A plain one was found at Claros, for instance; at Delos the *omphalos* has the carving of a serpent coiled around it. Designs of *omphaloi* on coins and relief carvings depict others in Greece, and also in Egypt and what was ancient Babylonia. In the Greek temple of Pergamum, Turkey, the *omphalos* is also depicted as being encircled by a serpent. Some pictures show navel stones with two birds, their heads turned in opposite directions. Clearly, all these motifs echo the same basic associations found at Delphi—the birds finding the center, and the "navel" being associated with the chthonic forces of the Earth symbolized by the serpent.

The monumentalizing of a notional World Center was not just an ancient Greek tradition, however. As even a cursory survey can show us, it crossed all cultures and periods of time.

## JOURNEY TO THE CENTER OF THE EARTH

The World Center took many different forms. The Etruscans of northern Italy had an *omphalos* in the form of an earthen pit which they dug at the center of their cities and from which the usually gridiron street plan was laid out.[4] This pit or shaft was thought to lead directly to the underworld, and was capped by a large stone that was lifted only on special days when the dead were allowed to mingle with the living, or when the first fruits were cast into the shaft as a harvest offering. The Romans, who took over from the Etruscans, absorbed many traditions from the older culture. The Greek writer Plutarch (who was a priest at Delphi in the latter part of his life) asserted that Romulus brought in the Etruscans at the legendary foundation of Rome. The central pit was called by the Romans *mundus*, meaning "world" or "universe," possibly deriving from whatever the Etruscan term for the central shaft was. Throughout their empire, the Romans always put a *mundus* at the center of their towns, and even their military camps. The layout of the street grid would commence from this point, where the north-south (*cardo*) and east-west (*decumanus*) roads crossed. *Cardo* gives us the *cardi*nal points of the compass, north-south, east-west. In Roman-founded British market towns, the *mundus* came to be called the "Cross" or "High Cross." The point in Oxford, though, is called the Carfax, still containing Roman echoes.

In Northern Europe, arctic Eurasia, and Siberia, the World Center was often envisaged as a World Tree or World Axis—*axis mundi*. (This vertical component of the *omphalos* theme has great significance with regard to consciousness, as we shall see later in this chapter.) The Yakuts of northeastern Siberia, for instance, believed there was a tree with eight branches standing at the "golden navel of the Earth."[5] Mongol myth told of a four-sided, pyramidical cosmic mountain with a tree in its center that the gods used as a hitching post for their horses! The most famous World Tree, however, is surely the Norse Yggdrasil, the great ash tree where the gods assembled,[6] and which linked the underworld, the world of humans, and the worlds of the gods. There are many other World Trees imaged in myths across the world, and it is likely that the European Maypole (the German *Maibaum*) and the Christmas tree are reflections of the *axis mundi*.

Ancient land division likewise reflected the concept of a sacred center, a terrestrial navel. The pagan Celtic landscape of Ireland was divided into four ancient (and surviving) provinces, Ulster, Munster, Leinster, and Connacht, which met at a fifth province in the center, Mide, of which the modern Meath is an echo. Mythographer Michael Dames has presented arguments to show that this four-plus-one scheme in Ireland long predated even the pagan Celts.[7] The hill of Usineach stood in Mide (in what is now County Westmeath). This was the ancient World Center of Celtic Ireland. More specifically, a large natural boulder called Aill na Mireann, the Stone of Divisions, on the slopes of the hill, was the *omphalos*. An ancient text tells how the god Fintan returned to this stone, complaining how long it had been since he had "taken a drink of the Deluge over the navel of Usineach." The ancient significance of the great rock, called by Joyce the "Mearing Stone" (boundary stone) in his *Finnegans Wake*, was not lost on those fighting against British rule in the early years of this century, for a hole was sunk into its top to hold a flagpole around which political meetings were held.

Returning from this western extremity of Europe, we can go on to travel east and south from the Mediterranean, where our search for the center of the Earth began. We immediately come to Jerusalem. Sacred to Judaism, Islam, and Christianity alike, this place obviously has special status as a sacred center. The most ancient, sacred core is Temple Mount, the area of the Rock, a natural outcrop beneath where is said to be the primeval waters, the *tehom*, and on which was built the legendary Temple of Solomon. Before the Jews, the Canaanites worshipped Baal there, and after King David's conquest of Jerusalam, it became a *kibleh*, or point of adoration. A series of temples were reconstructed on the spot after various sackings of Jerusalem, but the Romans destroyed the last one in 70 A.D. A temple to Jupiter was erected on the site, and this lasted until the Christianization of the Roman Empire, when a church was built there. From 325 A.D., Jerusalem experienced three hundred years of Christian and Byzantine domination. The Christians tended to see the hill of Golgotha as their *omphalos*, and the legend was that the skull of Adam was buried beneath it. In 638 A.D., the Muslims took over the city, destroying most of the Christian features that had developed in those three centuries, and a mosque, the Dome of the Rock (Qubbat al Sakrah) was built on this World Navel, enclosing a bare surface of the Rock, supposedly the precise spot from where Mohammed ascended to heaven. Nearby, a small cupola, the Dome of the Spirits, covers another area of exposed rock, where the Tablets of the Covenant were said to have rested, and which is, some researchers now claim, the true foundation stone once enclosed within the Holy of Holies of Solomon's temple.[8] To Islam, Jerusalem is the most sacred city after Mecca and Medina.

So for about four thousand years Jerusalem has been a sacred center, a World Navel to some great religions. The medieval Christians expressed this explicitly in their *mappa mundi* (maps of the world), which were schematic religious diagrams showing Jerusalem in the center. The Ebstorf map of 1235 is one of these schematic maps, with Christ's head in the north, the hands at east and west sides of the circular border, and the feet at the south. Jerusalem is specifically placed as Christ's navel. In *Talmudic Miscellany* we read the equally explicit Jewish conception: "The land of Israel is situated in the center of the world, and Jerusalem in the center of the land of Israel, and the Temple in the center of Jerusalem, and the Holy of Holies in the center of the Temple, and the foundation-stone on which the world was founded is situated in front of the ark."[9]

Before leaving this strip of geography at the eastern end of the Mediterranean known as "The Holy Land," we can note that Mount Gerizim, to the north of Jerusalem, was "doubtless invested with the prestige of the 'Center', for it is called 'navel of the earth.'"[10]

In Saudi Arabia, we have the ultimate *omphalos* of Islam—Mecca, holy even before the time of Mohammed, and focus of the *hajj*, or pilgrimage. In the court of the Great Mosque in Mecca is the Kaaba ("cube"), a pre-Islamic granite shrine. According to the Koran, the original Kaaba had been built by Abraham and Ishmael to enclose a red-brown rock known as the Black Stone which had been given to them by the archangel Gabriel as the foundation stone for a temple. This piece of basalt is encased in silver and lodged in the eastern wall of the Kaaba, where it is touched by pilgrims at the commencement of the ritual encircling of the Kaaba, the *tawaf*. It was said to have been white originally, but blackened by its contact with the sins of the pre-Islamic period. At the end of the world, it is claimed, the stone will utter speech as witness to the sins of humanity.

Indian (Hindu) cosmology had the mythic Mount Meru standing at the center of the world. Indian towns, not only temples, were built in the image of the universe, with a symbolic representation of Mount Meru in their centers. Even as late as the eighteenth century, Jaipur was built in accordance with this traditional model.[11]

This imagery of the Cosmic Mountain can be traced throughout Southeast Asia, in fact. The walls and moats of the city of Angkor in Cambodia represent the world surrounded by its chain of mountains and the cosmic ocean, and the temple in the center represents Mount Meru. Its satellite shrines represent the constellations. Thai cosmology had the world as a quadrangle with Mount Meru in the center, and the whole of Thailand was imaged as the universe, divided into four provinces with a central city, in the center of which was the royal palace—the king was placed in the center of the world. In Burma, even as late as 1857, Mandalay was built as a quadrangular image of the world with the royal palace in the center. In the cosmology of the Semang of the Malay Peninsula, the World Axis was represented by Batu Ribn, a huge rock situated at the center of the world. From its summit a massive tree trunk rose into the sky. The Dayak of Borneo have a representation of the World Tree in each of their villages. The great temple of Borobudur in Indonesia is a model of the World Mountain. The examples are virtually endless.

To the Chinese, their country was at the center of a rectangular world, with a sacred mountain on each of the four horizons. Their towns echoed this model, and the palace at the center represented the Pole Star. In the Forbidden City in Beijing, the marbled meridian, the north-south axis, passed through the Golden Throne, from where the divine emperor could govern the world.

Across the Pacific, in the Americas, the image of the world center was also decidedly present amongst Indian tribes. The best-known example is probably that recorded in the Great Vision of the Oglala Sioux holy man Black Elk in which he was taken up to the top of Harney Peak in South Dakota, the Center of the World. His vision is replete with powerful and haunting symbolism of the Center, and the Six Directions—north, south, east, west, up ("sky"), and down ("earth"). Although Harney Peak was the physical representative of the World Axis for his experience, wise old Black Elk told his biographer, John G. Neihardt, "But anywhere is the center of the world."[12] The Lakota Sioux ceremonially expressed the *axis mundi* by means of a pole. On the third day of their Sun Dance, the Lakota erect the Sun Pole at the center of the dance ground. Sweet grass, sage, and buffalo hair are placed in a fork of the pole near its top. A song accompanies this action:

*At the centre of the Earth*
*Stand looking around you.*
*Recognizing the tribe*
*Stand looking around you.*[13]

Monks Mound.

The tallest prehistoric mound in North America is the four-tiered Monks Mound, in southern Illinois. Standing over a hundred feet high and covering more than fourteen acres at its base, it was built around a thousand years ago by a people now referred to as the Mississippian Indians. It was the *omphalos* of their ceremonial city, Cahokia, where it is surrounded by the remains of a hundred smaller mounds. Some of these had a ridgelike shape, and they marked out alignments radiating in the Four Directions from Monks Mound.[14] On the summit of the great mound a king or chieftain's palace once stood, and in front of it was a mighty post which would have reached tens of feet into the air. A Sun Watching station within the Cahokia complex was so sited that the rising equinoctial sun would seem to rise out of the king's palace—a hint that he was associated with the sun, and was probably considered divine. This fits with what is known of other Indian peoples. The chief of the Natchez Indians in Louisiana, for example, was called the Great Sun. His dwelling was similarly built on a mound. He would come out of the doorway in the morning and face the rising sun, howl three times, blow tobacco smoke to the sun in the east, and then to the other three directions. The theme of the Four Directions, an essential element of the World Center cosmology, is deeply ingrained in Native American mythology.

The Pueblo peoples of the American Southwest emerged from the Earth according to their cosmology. This point of emergence is symbolized by the *sipapu*, a hole in the floor of Pueblo ceremonial kivas. The first Pueblos wandered to the four points of the compass searching for Center Place. The Tewa of the Eastern Pueblos of New Mexico consider their village center as sacred, "Earth Mother, Earth Navel, Middle Place." Another of the Pueblo peoples, the Zuñi, have a myth that gives Zuñi Pueblo—in New Mexico, near the state line with Arizona—the status of the World Center. The first Zuñi were wandering the Earth (the Zuñi word for which contains the root word for "four") but were unable to find Center Place. Eventually they asked Water Skate (K'yan asdebi) to help them in their quest. Water Skate grew to great proportions, raised himself to the zenith of the sky, and extended his six long legs to the four cardinal points and to above and below. He slowly lowered himself and said: "Where my heart and navel rest, beneath them mark the spot and build a town of the midmost, for there shall be the midmost place of the Earth Mother. . . ."[15]

The Aztec capital, Tenochtitlán, which now lies beneath modern Mexico City, was laid out to the Four Directions, with the main pyramid, Templo Mayor, at the center. Mexico City to this day has vestiges of this cosmological ground plan. The quartering of the world was deeply imprinted in Aztec lore, and we know that their holy mountains exemplified the theme—they were Cosmic Mountains. Mount Tlaloc had a temple on its summit that made use of naturally occurring rocks that happened to be spread out towards the intercardinal directions (northeast-southwest, southeast-northwest), which were especially important to prehistoric Native Americans in Mesoamerica and farther south. The ritual hill of Tetzcotzingo, however, had a row of shrines across its ridgelike summit that marked the east-west axis.[16]

In Peru, the capital of the vast Inca empire was Cuzco. In the Quechua language of the Inca, still spoken today, the name of the city means "navel." It was laid out to a slightly irregular intercardinal scheme centered on the Inca Great Plaza, Huacaypata. The Inca Empire was known as *Tahuantinsuyu*, Land of the Four Quarters, and Cuzco mirrored this in microcosm. Another, rather mysterious system of radiating alignments, called *ceques*, also laid out to a complex four-quarter system, were centered on the Coricancha, the so-called Temple of the Sun in Cuzco. If Cuzco was the navel of the empire, then the Coricancha was the *omphalos* of Cuzco itself. In Inca myth, the spot for the temple was found by Manco Capac, the first Inca, who was sent to Earth to bring civilization. He used a golden rod to seek the correct location, which he knew had been found when the rod disappeared into the ground.

Some unusual and surprising vestiges of the *axis-mundi* theme are also encountered in the Americas. As one example, voodoo temples in Haiti have a central post (*potou-mitan*) down which the spirits are said to enter during rituals. Another has been noted by Joan Halifax, who feels that a clay sculpture from Nayarit, Mexico, dated to around 100 A.D., showing a figure sitting beneath a hallucinogenic mushroom, suggests an *axis-mundi* theme.[17]

## THE TENT OF HEAVEN

The deep-rooted concept of the World Navel not only involved the center point on Earth from where the division of the four cardinal directions (and eightfold and sixteenfold subdivisions) could be made. It was also, with the axial component, where the vertical dimension cut the plane of the landscape at right angles; it was the intersection of sky and land. If the primary directions on Earth provided orientation and thus ordered space, then the division of the horizon marked the cycles of heaven, ordering time. The sky and land formed an indivisible whole for the people who lived in the ancient world, a whole which provided a matrix of profound meaning for them.

The Etruscans, whose *mundus* shaft was their World Navel, believed that the sky, like the land, was divided into quarters, each of which had esoteric significance. The Etruscan diviners or *haruspices* further divided the sky into sixteenths, each division with its own meaning. The Latin word *templum* was probably originally a term from the vocabulary of Etruscan divination for a particular area of sky, where the *haruspex* collected omens (such as scrutinizing the directions and characteristics of bird flight). During the process of interpreting the omens, the diviner faced south. "By an extension of this concept," writes Raymond Bloch, "the temple designates the place on earth devoted to the gods, the sanctuary which, in Etruria, usually faces south and represents as it were the projection on the ground of a sacred zone of sky."[18]

To many early peoples, the canopy of the heavens was viewed as a roof or tent. The stars were holes or windows in the firmament, and the Milky Way the seam. The Pole Star, Polaris, which appears fixed, held the celestial tent like a tent pole, for the sky seems to rotate or pivot around that spot. Polaris happens to mark the northern celestial pole—overhead at the North Pole, and at an angle above the horizon equivalent to the angle of latitude from which it is viewed from farther south. The Lapps and other arctic Europeans, as well as the Siberian reindeer-herder tribes, called the Pole Star the Nail Star. The Buryat of Siberia refer to it as the Pillar of the World.

The Pole Star shines above the Hindu Mount Meru, further emphasizing the World Axis nature of the mythical mountain. (In physical geography, Mount Kailas in the Himalayas represents Mount Meru. It is sacred to the Buddhists as well. The Kailas Range contains the sources of the Indian sacred rivers, the Indus and the Brahmaputra.) This symbolism is well manifested in the ancient Indian city of Vijayanagara, about two hundred miles southwest of Hyderabad. Founded in the fourteenth century, this had been one of the largest cities in the world of its day, capital of a great Hindu empire. It was laid out to a mandalic plan. The mandala is a cosmogram, appearing in its simplest, most basic structural form as a circle or square (or a circle within a square, or vice versa) with a dot at its center, used, in the form of *yantra*, for meditation and the induction of trance states—a psychological map and tool. Besides being produced as rich artwork in various Indian and Tibetan spiritual traditions, the mandala was also a basic ground-plan design in Hindu temple and royal-city architecture. Hindu temples, each a "Mount Meru," were laid out to the Vastu-purusha Mandala, which established the boundaries of the sacred enclosure, and identified the point source of emerging creation and the resulting ordering of the manifesting cosmos along the cardinal directions. "The center of the *mandala* also represents the still point of the turning universe," write researchers John McKim Malville and John M. Fritz, "the earth in a geocentric [Earth-centered] cosmos, and the surrounding square symbolizes the path of the sun, moon and planets along the ecliptic."[19] The mandala can be subdivided into a gridwork of smaller squares, each the seat of an important deity, perhaps with Brahma, the source of creation, situated in the center. Fritz has suggested that the whole royal city of Vijayanagara may be understood as a temple, for his research has shown it to contain the same mandalic spatial relationships as the classic Hindu temple.[20] Malville and Fritz studied over 150 temples and shrines within the city, and found that, though there was a cardinal pattern to many of their orientations, some temple axes showed orientations significantly skewed from the compass directions. They came to realize that these aligned to the local hills—Matanga, Anjenadri, and Malyavanta—which had seemingly been considered sacred. The sky, the temples, and the local topography had been fused together into a whole. This was probably the superposing of two imperatives: the emperors would have found most significance in the grand scheme of the cardinal directions, but the peasantry would have found the local topography to be more meaningful. Astrophysicist Malville found these elements to be powerfully synthesized when looking north at night from a ceremonial gateway on the north-south axis of Vijayanagara. From there, the eye is led to the Virabhadra temple on the summit of Matanga Hill. Malville recalls seeing the Pole Star shining above the temple:

> Standing at night inside the ceremonial gateway facing Matanga Hill with the pivot of the heavens lying immediately above it, the conjunction of celestial pole and sacred mountain could not be more clearly presented nor more dramatic. Who, watching the heavens slowly revolve around the summit of Matanga Hill, could doubt that Vi-

> jayanagara was once a magical city, sanctioned and pro-
> tected by gods and myth? . . . The symbolic *axis mundi* ex-
> tending upward from the sacred mountain actually does
> appear to intersect with the north pole of the celestial
> sphere. . . .[21]

Malville looked *along* the city axis to the Pole Star, because it naturally gets lower in the sky the farther south one goes, and is coin-
cident with the horizon at the equator. Even farther north, an
adherence to Polaris rather than a local concept of the zenith involves special design. The Omaha Indians of Nebraska, as a case in
point, had a myth recording the stabilization of their society in
which figured a great, burning cedar tree to which the forest animals had worn four trails, one from each of the cardinal directions.
In an annual ceremony, the Omaha people remembered this legendary burning cedar by setting up a sacred pole. But it was not
erected vertically, because Omaha territory covered an area around
forty-two degrees north, and to point at the Pole Star, the sacred
pole had to be angled accordingly.

Since the Pole Star does not serve as a symbol of the zenith all
that well in the Tropics, ancient people there used the phenomenon
of the zenith passage of the sun, in which the sun passes directly
overhead at noon on two days in the year, their dates depending on
where in the Tropics the location is. This is a dramatic moment, because *all shadows disappear*. It seems that prehistoric Mesoamericans
mythologically thought that the sky or sun god descended to the
Earth for a brief visit at these times. The rising and setting points of
the sun on the days of zenith passage, and on those of the nadir
passage (when the sun passes directly beneath the globe of the
Earth, as directly underfoot as the zenith is overhead), would also
have been well known at any given location and viewed with significance.

In the Southern Hemisphere, where there is no star to mark the
pole of the heavens, the zenith can be effectively marked by
the Milky Way, that glowing, diffuse band of starlight that girdles
the night sky. In the Andes, anthropologist Gary Urton made a

study of Misminay, a village community of Quechua-speaking Indians, descendants of the Incas.[22] There, the Milky Way is a striking feature of the night sky. The plane of the Milky Way is offset to that of the Earth's rotation, so its rising and set patterns seem to "tumble." When the course of the Milky Way crosses the zenith, it stretches in an intercardinal direction, say northwest-southeast; twelve hours later, when the band of the other hemisphere of the Milky Way passes through the zenith, the axis will run northeast-southwest. So, over a twenty-four-hour period, the Milky Way seems to cut two lines across the sky, crossing at the zenith and dividing the sky into four quarters. At Misminay, the point where this notional "crossing" of the two "halves" of the Milky Way occurs at the zenith is called Cruz Calvario, the Cross of Calvary. This mirrors an arrangement in the layout of the community on the ground, where two intercardinal paths cross at a point marked by a small chapel in the center of the village. This is the Crucero, Cross. The irrigation canals in Misminay also adhere to this X-shaped pattern, running alongside the courses of the paths. This water pattern has much significance for the Indians: the Milky Way is known as Mayu, River. It is thought to carry water from the Cosmic Ocean, in which the world floats, and to redistribute it as rain as it arches overhead. To the inhabitants of Misminay, the nearby Vilcanota River, which flows from southeast to northwest, is a reflection of the Milky Way. The Calvario likewise mirrors the Crucero beneath—a vertical rod could be imagined connecting the two, like an invisible axis.

## BRINGING IT ALL BACK HOME

It is nice to roam, but it's always good to come back home. . . . The primordial human instinct of the World Center that we find embodied in ancient landscapes, cities, and temples was reflected also in the old conception of the humble dwelling. Eliade put it succinctly: ". . . cosmos, land, city, temple, palace, house and hut . . . emphasize the same fundamental symbolism: each one of these images expresses the existential experience of *being in the world*, more exactly, of being situated in an organized and meaningful world. . . ."[23]

As the sky was conceived of as a vast tent supported by a central pillar by earlier tribal peoples, the herders and hunters, the central poles of their own tents were seen as being identical with the Pole Star, the World Axis. The Siberian reindeer herders such as the Soyots and Buryats saw their tent pole as the Sky Pillar. The Soyots' pole rose above the top of the yurt, its exposed end decorated with white, yellow, and blue cloths representing the colors of the celestial regions. The pole itself was sacred, and offerings were placed on a small stone altar at its base.

The central post is, or was, to be found in the structure of many tribal dwellings, including those of the Ainu of the northern Japanese islands of Hokkaido and Sakhalin, Native American peoples such as the Pomo and other northern Californian tribes and the Algonquians of the northern-woodlands–Great Lakes area, and the Khasi of northeastern India (Assam). And everywhere it was common practice to place offerings at the foot of the post.

Sometimes this is developed into more complex schemes. A dwelling of the Fali of northern Cameroon is a detailed cosmological model: the orientation of the central post, the walls and roof, and also the interior furniture is designed to accommodate the movements of the family members, who change their positions within the dwelling according to the time of day, the seasons, and changes in social status.[24] The *choom* of the Arctic Russian Nenets (Kanin Samoyed) is similarly a world model and symbolic structure.[25] Made of deerskins placed over poles, the structure is erected and dismantled only by women, in recognition of the original Mother. A special *choom* existed for childbirth, but if a baby was born in a domestic *choom* it destroyed the current "world" of the dwelling, and after various purifications the structure was dismantled and re-erected in another spot, to start a "new world." Something similar happened in the case of a death.

The Navajo hogan or hooghan ("place home") is a cosmic model and a dwelling. Like the horizon, it is circular, as most ancient and traditional dwellings were. It is traditionally built of logs chinked with mud over a shallow pit. It has upright logs at the four cardinal points and a door facing east. Hooghan songs emphasize the orientation of the dwelling, and the origin of the hooghan goes back to the Navajo world-ordering foundation myths.

The *omphalos* of any dwelling is the fire: the heart of the home is the *hearth*. In the hooghan, the fireplace is in the center, and represents Polaris. In the beginning, after the first people's emergence from the Earth, fire and poker could speak, and there was communication between the first Navajo and the fire. In Navajo custom, a "no fireplace home" means a home in which the fire has been abandoned, because of the death of a younger person.[26]

In Central Asia, herders associated not only the central post but also the smokehole of their tents and yurts with the Pole Star, because the star was a "hole in the sky" through which communication with the gods could occur. (This idea rests on the association between smoke rising up through the smokehole and the shamanic trance in which the spirit of the shaman ascends to the otherworld, as we shall shortly see.)

The Latin for the hearth is *focus*, which the English language has adapted to mean to concentrate or *center* on. In the ancient Roman household, the hearth was the center of worship and the seat of Vestia, the goddess of the hearth, the spirit of the sacred flame. Laid before the hearth would be a table containing ritual items, such as salt cake. In many ways, the hearth was the first altar. It was also the domain of the feminine, as Vestia testifies. In Celtic Ireland, to give another example of this, fire was one of the associations made with Brigit (or Brigid, Bride), a pagan goddess who was Christianized into St. Brigit. A. Carmichael described a domestic devotion that originated in Ireland called Blessing the Kindling which survived in the Hebrides until the eighteenth century, though it was of Irish origin:

> Before retiring for the night, the fire would be 'smoored' with loving care. With the hearthstone normally in the middle of the floor, the embers were evenly spread in a circle, which was then divided into three equal sections, with a small boss being left in the middle. A sod of peat was laid between each section, with each sod touching the

central boss. Then the whole circle was covered over with some ashes, and the central heap referred to as The Hearth of the Three. The woman then closed her eyes, stretched her hands, and slowly intoned 'a formula'. In Ireland this ran:

*I cover this fire*
*As noble Christ did.*
*Mary on top of the house,*
*And St Brigid in its center.*[27]

This activity was clearly the formation of a Celtic mandala. In Ireland, the central hearth was the norm, and this was true in both round and rectangular Irish buildings until as late as the seventeenth century. Inhabitants would sleep on the floor around the fire, with their feet towards it. Michael Dames traces the last known traditional central fire in Ireland to a dwelling in Galway in 1966.[28] One of the old traditions in Irish housebuilding was to light the Needfire, the first hearth-fire, by rubbing together two of the timbers going into the construction. They would be arranged in a Brigit's cross, one over the other, and the friction of their rubbing would create a spark in some kindling. A fire to warm the heart.

Lighting the "Needfire," by means of friction between timbers arranged in a Brigit's cross. [W. Wakeman, 1898.]

## BODY AND MIND

The *omphalos* as home brings the idea of the World Center down to a more intimate, human scale. Yet, even at this domestic level, it has not quite reached its deep roots, which lie in the human being—body, mind, and, ultimately, soul. The dwelling is the transition point of scales from macrocosm to microcosm, from outer to inner.

This movement inwards starts with the body, and that transition is accompanied by interchangeable concepts associated with buildings and the human body. In the Vedic tradition of the Vastu-purusha Mandala, which we have already encountered, the temple, oriented to the cardinal directions of the outside world, is also an expression of the Cosmic Man, Purusha, who is "the divine essence behind Man the builder, the altar and the fire of the altar."[29] The proportions of the temple derive from this figure; the temple is a "geometric formalization" of Purusha. Similarly with cities: the sacred city of Varanasi (Benares) is Shiva's body, and in Hindu oral tradition the city was also symbolized as Vishnu's body.[30] A Jain hatha-yoga text refers to the human body as "a house with one column and nine doors," the "column" being the spine. In Central Asia and in India there were pillars that represented the World Axis and also represented the Cosmic Man. An example of such a man-pillar is the fifty-two-foot-tall stone Yupa Sarovara, near Sarang Talab in India, which represents the Cosmic Man divided into fourteen parts, seven above the navel and seven below.[31]

The same basic association was also made in Christianity, in that the structure of a church was seen as Christ's body. This is shown literally in a drawing by the fifteenth-century architect Francesco di Giorgio, who based his ideas on the architectural philosophy of Vitruvius, a Roman engineer of the first century B.C. The idea of the ground plan of a building as an expression of the human frame was widespread in the ancient world. We can see this in more domestic terms if we return to Ireland again. In Old Irish, the word for the domestic center pole was *cliethe*, which bundled within itself the meanings "dwelling, top, the crown of the head, the heavens, firmament, and sky, culmination and perfection." The whole cosmol-

The plan of a Christian church symbolizing Christ's body, as depicted by the architect, Cataneo, in 1554, after the manner of Vitruvius.

ogy in a word! In rectangular dwellings, *cliethe* was used to describe the ridgepole, which formed the roof ridge.

So, in following the theme of the World Center, we find it is imaged in the human body, for in its simplest form this ancient and, to us moderns, rather odd and unfamiliar concept relates to the orientation of the human body. We are symmetrical beings: we have front, back, sides—the cardinal directions in body language. But there is *orientation* involved; we do not merely have four sides, we have a *front* and *back*, a *right* and *left*. It is this inherent feeling-sense that we bring to our perception of the world. The compass directions are outward projections of this feeling-sense of our body space, just as the human navel has been outwardly symbolized in the *omphalos*. Dorothy Lee (in a paper in *Explorations* 2:4, 1954/55) gives an example of this body-centering in the traditions of the Wintu Indians of northern California: "When the Wintu goes up the river, the hills are to the west, the river to the east; and a mosquito bites him on the west arm. When he returns, the hills are still to the west, but, when he scratches his mosquito bite, he scratches his east arm."[32]

Laughlin and colleagues, in *Brain, Symbol and Experience*, refer to this body image centering as a "somatocentric" worldview, and cite the (faintly patronizing) observations of the Jungian Erich Neumann: "Early man, who, without being aware of it, occupies a position in the center of the world, whence he relates everything to himself and himself to everything, fills the world around him with images of his unconscious."

But let us now take one step further—and deeper. What happens at the meeting, the intersection of the Four Directions? We have already noted that in certain traditional cosmologies, notably the Native American ones, there are not four but six directions with the inclusion of up and down, sky and earth. The human being is an *axis* at the meeting point of the four bodily directions, mirroring precisely the World Pillar, World Tree, or Cosmic Mountain at the intersection of the cardinal directions. From the depths of four millennia, the *Rig-Veda* explains what happens at the meeting of the four ways—it tells us that there is north, south, east, west . . . and *here*—zero point. It is the nothingness at the center of a wheel around which the spokes revolve. You are always here. Here is portable.

This is literally the crux of the ancient, primordial instinct of the World Center. We may have wondered how any ancient tribe, society, or religion could have fooled itself that it had the World Center, when there were clearly so many of them. But that is an abstract criticism; from our own experience, we know that "here" is always the center. Just look around you—*around* you. Are you not perceptually at the center of your world? All the billions of human beings on this planet are also at the centers of their worlds, just like you.

In the earlier half of this century, experimental psychologist Jean Piaget conducted a searching inquiry into the ways a child's perception and thinking developed. He discovered that infants have what he called the "egocentric" outlook: perceptually, they are at the center, with objects receding from them in all directions. In various experiments, Piaget and his colleagues saw that this centric view was projected into other viewpoints by children in their early years. (One set of such experiments involved the guessing of what view a doll would have from changing positions amongst three model mountains on the floor by children of various ages sitting around the sides of the layout.) The younger child is "centred exclusively on his own viewpoint, both in perception and imagination. . . . The egocentric illusion . . . prevents these children from reversing the left-right, before-behind relations and thereby rotating the perspectives along with their changing viewpoints."[33] In Piaget's opinion, it takes the more abstract model-building processes of cognition, which develop later, to be able to be conscious of perspective and assess viewpoints in space different from one's own. Geographer O. Francis G. Sitwell uses the analogy of the development of modern astronomy and cosmology, from Copernicus (who broke with the ancient Earth-centered or *geocentric* view of the universe) through Newton to Einstein, for the individual's perceptual development from being at the center to being lost in space.[34] This analogy of course reveals that by these conceptual changes our culture decentered all its people. The English word "eccentric" derives from the Greek *ekkentros*, meaning "out of center." Modern Westernized culture is truly eccentric.

Now that we are all psychologically adrift in a centerless universe which has no circumference, the *experience* of being at the center of the world has been sublimated, overlaid by our modern intellectual modeling of our place in the scheme of things. Yet, though no longer conscious within us, centricity is structured within our neurophysiology in what the experts call somatosensory and somatotopic cortical maps, touched on in the introductory chapter. Essentially, this means that a *map of the body* is projected to the brain, so that discrete patterns of neurons relate to sense receptors on the extremities of the body (though the full relationship is by no means currently known, and the edges of these areas of cortex can switch functions, so that neurons dealing with the face one week can process information from the forefinger the next!). This information from physical stimuli and body image—left, right, front, back, symmetry, bilateralism, and so on—comes into the processing arena of the brain-mind, and on these data it models a picture of the world at that moment.

The depth to which the perceptual and bodily Four Directions are unconsciously ingrained within us is indicated in C. G. Jung's identification of an archetype of quaternity, a deep psychic pattern that expresses wholeness in the Jungian view. He noted how "fourness" recurs in religious and primary concepts (such as the Four Directions), and commented on "the centering process and a radial arrangement that usually followed some quaternary system."[35]

## THE GHOST AT THE CROSSROADS

So the Four Directions, crossing at the Center, constitute a fundamental pattern that is inside us and was once experienced (that is, was conscious) and was projected out onto the physical world. It was an ordering meta-process that operated at all levels—natural, built, social, bodily, and cognitive—and was woven into religious cosmologies and folk practices alike. But now the pattern is submerged within us. The cosmic symbolism of this primary sense of sacred space is so old and so familiar, Eliade lamented, that "many are not yet able to recognize it."[36]

But who or what stands at the crossroads of the Four Directions? Cognitive science says that there is no such actual entity as a self or an ego; it is simply a useful image conjured by the machinations of the brain-mind (see the introductory chapter). So there is only a mirage, a ghost, at the crossroads. Ancient tribal wisdom says much the same thing, but in another, richer way, and with infinitely greater implications than modern science can find its way to seeing. This wisdom and knowledge take us one final stage deeper—to the center of the Center, to the core mystery around which it all revolves. To zero point.

## THROUGH THE CENTER:
## THE WAY BETWEEN THE WORLDS

At the *omphalos*, the World Navel, is the Cosmic Axis—be it imaged in the form of a cosmic mountain, a world tree, a stone pillar, the Pole Star, a celestial tent pole, or whatever. This mysterious axis is a passage between this and other worlds or states of consciousness. This is the crucial message contained in the fading archaic whisper reaching us from former and passing worldviews. ". . . the only logical direction 'perpendicular' to three dimensional space is 'within,'" psychedelic writer Jim DeKorne points out.[37]

Access to this axial element at the heart of the Center is by means of ecstatic states of consciousness. The use of such states was exemplified by shamanism, which made first and greatest use of the concept of the *axis mundi*. Shamanism developed in remote antiquity out of animism, and was the first coherent framework of magico-spiritual practice to emerge in human societies. It was not a religion starting in some particular time and place but, rather, a cross-cultural phenomenon concerning a range of techniques of ecstasy that came into independent being in many tribal societies around the world (though its "classical" expression is generally considered to be amongst the reindeer-herder tribes of Eurasia). Although it was a practical, magical form of spirituality, it nevertheless underpinned later, more intellectually sophisticated religions—including Christianity. It also underpinned later state structures such as divine kingship. And although its origins are archaic, shamanism still survives in some remaining tribal societies, especially in the rain forests of the world. (Loss of that knowledge, as well as the connected knowledge of the medical uses of plants, is one of the several ecological disasters threatened by the persistent destruction of the rain forests.)

The shaman was and is the intermediary between the human world of the tribe and the otherworlds of spirit. The basic shamanic model is of three worlds connected by a "vertical" axis: the underworld, the middle world of human existence, and the upperworld of the gods, great spirits, and celestial realms. Depending on the cultural context, this basic model can sometimes incorporate many more complex ideas, including the belief in the existence of seven or nine worlds along the axis. The shaman would "journey" to the otherworlds on behalf of the tribe, for healing, for divination, to escort the spirit of a dying tribal member, to reclaim the soul of a sick person, to gain information, and suchlike. This journeying was conducted in a trance state—the shaman's spirit went forth, leaving the body behind. It was an ecstatic or out-of-body state of consciousness (what we would nowadays technically call a "dissociated state"), effected by the use of dancing, chanting, drumming, fasting, the taking of hallucinogenic plants, sensory and sleep deprivation, or a mix of these and other techniques. This shamanic journey was often thought of as a "flight" in which the shaman's spirit flew to the World Tree, Cosmic Mountain, or whatever other form in which the *axis mundi* was culturally envisaged. The shaman went "down" or "up" this to enter the underworld or heaven world. The shaman was a voyager between the worlds.

Lapp shamans. One drums himself into trance, while the other is already "journeying" in the otherworld, as signified by the drum placed across his back. [J. Schefferus, 1673.]

The image of an axis at the World Navel as a metaphor for altered states of consciousness, for the mobility and transformation of the image of "self" at the heart of cognition, is or was powerfully reinforced in traditional shamanic lore throughout the world. The wooden frame of a Siberian shaman's drum was said to have been fashioned from a branch of the World Tree, and perhaps an image of the primordial tree would be painted on the drumskin. The Goldi shaman's ceremonial robe had a depiction of the World Tree emblazoned on it. The Siberian Chukchi saw the Pole Star as a hole in the sky through which access to the three worlds is possible, and through which the shaman travels, for the road to the sky runs through the Pole Star. The spirit of the Siberian shaman would float upwards with the smoke of the central fire through the smokehole, which was associated by many tribes with the Pole Star, as we have noted. The Chinese called the smokehole in Mongolian tents the "window of heaven," which also means "chimney" in Chinese. Sometimes the shaman would cut notches in a pole, perhaps the central tent pole, and climb it to symbolize his passage up the World Tree. This happened not only in Eurasia but around the world. The female shaman (*machi*) in Chile, for instance, would climb a nine-foot-tall notched pole called a *rewe*, at the top of which she would drum herself into trance. Shamans elsewhere might make a wing-flapping motion with their arms at the top of the pole to indicate spirit flight. In some traditions, ceremonial ladders were used, as in Vedic India, or even a rope, as in Tibet. The rungs of a ladder or the notches in a pole would usually number seven or nine, the recurring magical numbers in shamanic symbolism. Sunbeams, chains of arrows, and rainbows also functioned as axial images of the shaman's passage to the otherworlds.

At the secret center of the mind, then, is a stairway to heaven (and hell also). The World Center at the intersection of the Four Directions is the crack between the worlds, the place where communication with the spirits and gods is possible, and where access to the spiritual otherworlds can take place. It is the way we will have to take to return to paradise—a theme we will return to in our final chapter.

This fundamental experience of transformed human consciousness is at the heart of the World Center myth. Encircling that is the experience of perception and cognition related to the physical world, the "middle world" of shamanic tradition. In a wider circle around that are the projections of physical orientation, origin myths, and cosmologies. But we must not lose sight of the fact that, though the concept of the *omphalos* and *axis mundi* was an exoteric (symbolic and ceremonial) construct for most societies, for the shaman it was a metaphor for a *concrete experience*.

Only shamans and others who experience the primal ecstatic state are *conscious* at the center of the world.

## EXPERIENTIAL

But the ancient worldview has passed away, to all intents and purposes. We are now conceptually placed at random in a model of the universe whose center we cannot see and whose periphery we do not know: we are indeed lost in space. One can be homeless even within a dwelling: we increasingly live in heart(h)less rooms and, forgetting the windows, receive our sensory experience through video screens of one kind or another. Our thinking feeds more and more on itself, becomes more and more abstracted from the world of nature, so we can end up with such notorious situations as global financial institutions that find it logical to support activities such as removing rain-forest areas to make way for cattle ranches. The brave new worldview of our culture eclipses the deep physiological and perceptual building blocks of our daily experience, as we have discussed, and as denizens of our culture we are no longer centered. In that sense, we are not *here* on Earth at all. We are urban (or urbanized) astronauts who have not yet landed on Planet Earth. We float somewhere above it in the clouds of our worldview, which is less dependent on natural experience than any one before it. Even when we are in the natural landscape, we so often view it in superficial or fragmented ways, or else in terms of economic resource. We only rarely see it for its own sake. Our minds can all too often run along without reference to the world of immediate sensory experience. In his last novel, *Island*, Aldous Huxley equipped his island utopia with mynah birds that cackled at regular intervals, "Here and now, boys" and "Attention."

Though much in our culture is wonderful, is of great usefulness, and has enormous potential, and though we cannot—should not, even—pretend that we can fully and actually "go back" to other worldviews, it is healthy sometimes to make the conscious effort to explore gently other and older frames of mind, and to attempt to reintegrate our awareness of the world. It does no harm to put our automatic informational model of the world "on hold" for a little while. And it is sometimes found that these old ways of looking at things can take on a curious air of familiarity.

The following activities are suggested ways to begin this exploration, with relevance to the main theme of this chapter (methods of accessing the "shamanic state" are described later on in the book). You can take a day out to perform the following experiential activities in a sequence, or do them on separate occasions, or just pick and choose among them.

So are you ready? Prepare for a psychological landing on Planet Earth. . . .

## Being Here

Let us start simply. Find a location that is away from other people, open, and flattish—at sea, on a wide beach, in a desert, in a level landscape, on top of a hill or mountain. Stand still; breathe deeply. Consider that we are all, each of us, at the center of our world; each of us is forever in the middle of the circuit that we always see around us. Turn slowly; observe and *feel* the horizon encompassing you. Note that the skyline is also your eye-line: it always moves up or down with your head. The sky (especially at night) seems like a dome over your head, in sympathy with the dome of the cranium above the eyes. Watch for a bird flying across your field of view. Wait for it. . . . There it goes! Allow yourself the strange thought that it is flying not only in the dome of the heavens but also through the dome of your skull. If you are trying this at night, wait for a shooting star, and think the same strange thought (it's not illegal, and no one will know). Eye-line, cranium dome, front, back, sides: experience how the body models the world around you (or is it that the world models your body around you . . . ?).

Come back *here* more often. From now on, it won't matter (w)here you are, because the center of a circle whose circumference is everywhere is *now here*.

## Getting Your Bearings

Position yourself in a reasonably open and level place. Have a tall stick or bamboo pole, a measuring tape or length of string, and two or three ground markers of some kind—perhaps short pointed sticks or small pebbles. Choose a sunny early morning. Place your pole as vertically upright as possible in the ground (a beach is the simplest place to try this whole operation). Observe the shadow of your stick in the early-morning sunshine. Mark the extreme tip of the shadow and measure the length, on your tape or marked on your string, from the base of the stick to the tip of the shadow. Come back in the later afternoon, or relax, soak up the sun, and wait till then. Check the length of the pole's afternoon shadow against your tape or string. When it reaches the same length as the morning shadow, mark the tip. Find the halfway point between this marker and the one fixing the extremity of the morning's shadow. Mark the point. A line extended between this marker and the base of the stick will give you a near-as-dammit north-south axis or *meridian*. From this, you can figure out the Four Directions, so now you can *orient* yourself on this wonderful planet you have landed on. (The word "orientation," by the way, derives from the Latin verb for "to rise," particularly with reference to the sun or moon. Words like "original" and "aboriginal" have the same roots. "Orient" came to signify "east" because, of course, that is where the sun, or any heavenly body, rises.)

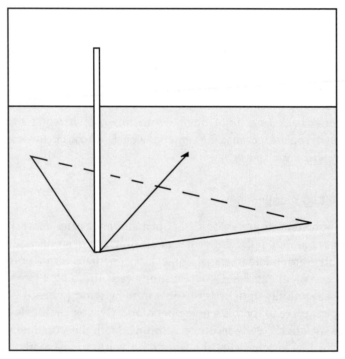

Finding a meridian using the shadows from an upright stick or pole. See text.

## DRAWING THE CIRCLE

Choose a day that has significance for you personally, such as your birthday (commemorating when your physical body arrived on Earth, though the ghost of you still had to materialize . . .). Celebrate your birthday (or whatever) not by lying in but by getting up before dawn, or at least very early. Find a fairly flat area of ground (as above), open towards the east. Take a tall stick (perhaps the same length as your height) and place it vertically in the ground. Tie one end of a roll of string or cord to the base of the stick. As the sun rises, mark off the extremity of the pole's shadow on the cord stretched tight from the pole. Use this length, or a multiple of it, as a radius for a circle. (Some tribal peoples use the shadow of a ritual pole on a specific day to give the radius of a ceremonial building.) Keeping it taut, rotate the appropriate length of cord around the central pole, marking the circumference on the ground by scratching with a pointed stick attached to the cord or by laying down small rocks or pebbles at reasonably close intervals. This circumference is a *temenos*—a boundary signifying a break between sacred and mundane space. What is within this boundary is special (to you); it is what Mircea Eliade called "a qualitively different space," and is in that sense sanctified. In drawing your circle on the ground, you have created a sanctuary—this word derives from the Latin *sanctus*, holy, and means a holy place as well as a refuge. A circle inscribed in wild nature is a potent act of consciousness that has primordial power.

(This mix of security and sanctity is an interesting one, and can be felt rather than described. One of my strongest experiences of it was at a small stone circle with the all-but-unpronounceable name of Moel ty Uchaf, in the mountains of northern Wales. It was close to sunset, and I was halfway up a mountain called Arthur's Table when I virtually stumbled across a prehistoric stone ring, subtly located just over a slight ridge in the ground. To the east rose the rest of the great bulk of Arthur's Table, while to the west, below, were rows of mountain ridges, rolling like blue waves into a gloriously golden sunset sky. The circle was only about forty feet in diameter, and nowhere were the stones more than a few feet tall, yet the moment I walked inside I felt overwhelmingly safe, with a deep sense of quiet well-being. There was a whole lot of wild nature going on all around, yet this circle of stones contained a calm center; it was the hub of the wheel.)

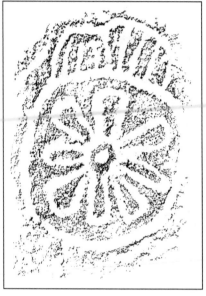

A rubbing of the eight-rayed prehistoric rock engraving on the rear chamber wall of Cairn T. Loughcrew, Ireland.

Step within your circle. Feel that qualitively different space (it is a surprisingly strong feeling). Orient yourself, either by the means indicated in the preceding activity, or by using the position of the sunrise, or, if you must "cheat," by using a compass. Mark off the cardinal directions by erecting a stick at each of the four points on your circle, or by placing a larger rock at each one. With smaller sticks or rocks, mark the midpoints. This divides the circle into eight, and eight divisions of the year produced one of the most ancient calendars, as is revealed in a five-thousand-year-old chambered cairn (stone mound) on the Loughcrew Hills in Ireland. It has an eight-petaled rock carving on the innermost stone of the chamber, facing the entrance passage. At the equinoxes (March 21 and September 21), beams from the rising sun reach right inside this stone chamber and throw a rectangle of golden light onto the carved backstone, perfectly framing the image of the sun and the eightfold year. A few thousand years later, the pagan Celts still divided the solar year into eight parts: the "quarter days" were the solstices (midwinter and midsummer) and the equinoxes, when day and night are of equal length; the "cross-quarter days" were called Imbolc (early February), Beltane (early May), Lughnasa (early August), and Samhain (early November).

As well as eight divisions to the year, there were also Eight Divisions to the day in the old Northern European tradition. These were the "tides" of the day.[38] They began at 4:30 A.M., with Morntide, and each tide lasted three hours, with its peak point in the middle. So the tide of Midnight, for example, which stretched from 10:30 P.M. to 1:30 A.M., had its midpoint at what we recognize now as midnight. The tides of the day had their feeling properties, as poet Walt Whitman similarly observed in *Specimen Days* when he wrote, "I am convinced there are hours of Nature, especially of the atmosphere, mornings and evenings, address'd to the soul. . . ." In the Northern European tradition, each tide was also associated with one of the Eight Directions. Writer Nigel Pennick has reconstructed these associations of time, sense, and space from surviving documentation, and I give a version here:

Morntide, arousing; east
Daytide (forenoon), gentleness, increase; southeast
Mid Day (noontide), sustaining; south
Undorne, receptiveness, transformation; southwest
Eventide, joy, spirituality; west
Nighttide, creativity, insights; northwest
Midnight, healing, regeneration; north
Uht (also known as "Rismal," rising time), stillness, sleep, death;
    northeast

Rotate in your circle. Stop and face each of the Eight Directions. How do you feel? Does one particular direction feel better, more welcoming or comfortable, to you? Does another direction make you feel depressed or fearful? If you can identify your "best" and "worst" directions, keep the knowledge quietly for the rest of your life. If you can manage to stay some time at your circle, spend several minutes facing the appropriate direction at the peak of the tide you are in. Again, check your feelings. It is not necessary that you make the same associations as the Northern European system; in Madagascar, to give an example from a completely different cultural context, one turns to the northeast to address the ancestors![39] In a simpler context, Henry David Thoreau maintained in his essay on "Walking" that he believed there is a "subtle magnetism in Nature," and before he set out on one of his walks he would submit himself to his instinct as to which way to go. What *is* important is that you make a conscious link between direction and feeling, or, better still, between direction, time, and feeling. This association is now unfamiliar in our culture, and that is why making it can have a useful and healing effect on your mental programming.

When it is time to leave, remove the boundary you created—scatter the rocks or rub out the scratched line in the earth or sand, pull up the sticks. Feel satisfied with yourself, for you have achieved the symbolic finding of your place, and the Greek philosopher Theophrastus, the pupil and successor of Aristotle, maintained that every living thing has its "favorable place"—its *oikeios topos*. The word *oikeios* shares a root with the modern word "ecology,"[40] so you have been truly ecological, in that you have made a conscious act of arriving on Earth. Welcome!

*Having arrived here, we must now find our place. . . .*

# PLACING

## Location and Dislocation: Knowing Our Place

WHEN SIGMUND FREUD TOILED UP THE steep steps and through the Propylaia of the Acropolis, to emerge into the blinding white-and-blue experience that the gleaming ruins and rich Athenian sky create on this sacred hilltop, he couldn't believe it. He really couldn't. Over three decades afterwards, in 1936, he wrote that what he felt there and then he had "never understood," and that it had "kept recurring to my mind." As he stood on the rocky height, surrounded by the remains of the classically beautiful Parthenon and other temples of antiquity, he felt a curious alienation. Somehow, he was not sure if he was present in a real place. "So all this really *does* exist . . ." he thought, as if to convince himself. He eventually tracked down his odd feeling of estrangement to his schooldays, when he had learned of the Acropolis. He realized that as a schoolboy he had never believed he would ever visit this famous place, yet here he was. A dissonance had been set up between his boyhood visualizations about the place and the actuality of his being there. Although, since he was Freud, his later thoughts on this experience brought in further factors, such as guilt that he was able to visit such places because he enjoyed greater success than his father, he also realized that "the original factor must have been a sense of some feeling of the unbelievable and the unreal in the situation at the moment. The situation included myself, the Acropolis and my perception of it."[1] Eugene Victor Walter, in his masterly study of the nature of place, *Placeways*, suggests that in addition, because Freud "was prepared for Athens as a place in the mind," he underwent a sense of unreality, a literal feeling of dislocation, when "he experienced the Acropolis as a place in the world."[2]

## A SENSE OF PLACE: MEANINGFUL GROUND

This brings us to the deceptively simple question of "What *is* a place?" In the growing monophasic mind-state of our culture and times, we are encouraged virtually to dismiss—certainly downgrade—ideas concerning the power of place. We are generally unconscious of place at any level other than the superficial one of its being a coordinate, an address. Something may exist or happen somewhere, but usually we concern ourselves with the event, the person, the object, rather than the location. As in a photograph, the backgound is out of focus. Modern sensibility is suffering a loss of place: as Edmunds V. Bunkśe puts it, we are beginning to experience the conditions of exile.[3] He puts this down to the change to a postindustrial society, and market forces. "Where people work, where and how they live," he writes, "is increasingly being organized according to world market criteria. . . . Global market forces, specifically consumer market forces, together with a global communications and information industry, and postmodern cultural styles and forms, are squeezing out local culture, history, society, and nature as determinants of the character and shape of places. . . . Places are either losing their identity, or entirely new 'places' are being created without a distinct identity. . . . If cultural landscapes are becoming uniform, then the distinct possibility exists that people's internal lives may be as discontinuous with their environment as it is for classic exiles."

Walter reminds us that the ancient Greeks had two senses of place, *chora* and *topos*. *Chora*, the older of the two terms, was a holistic reference to place: place as expressively potent, place as experience, place as a trigger to memory, imagination, and mythic presence. In archaic times, the Greeks used to travel and visit places in a special kind of way. They were the first theorists: what we would think of as tourism, they called *theoria*. This involved what Walter has described as "a complex but organic mode of active observation." When visiting an unfamiliar place, the Greek theorists would ask questions of locals, listen to the stories and myths of the place, observe, listen to, and obtain a "feel" for the place. "They were," writes Walter, "spectators who responded to the expressive energies of the place. . . ." Many locations had *periegetes*, guides who could explain the sites, local customs, myths, and so on. They were the living repositories of the local lore and knowledge.

*Topos*, on the other hand, signified place in much the way we think of it nowadays—simple location, and the objective, physical features of a locale. Topography. Aristotle took this sense of place and abstracted it further into the pure concept of position. Ultimately, even sacred places became *topoi*.

As Walter has commented, these differing approaches to place exemplify an important turn in the intellectual history of the West. The result is that collectively, at the mainstream intellectual level of our culture, we have lost the sense of place that *chora* implied. Individually, however, many of us still do have vestigial responses to place that relate more to *chora* than to *topos*. But such feelings about a place are admitted only quietly to intimates; culturally, it is an amusing, folk, anecdotal matter of no real consequence.

Yet can it be inconsequential to know that we actually cannot think of a place without having the elements of memory, imagination, and feeling become part of the informational model we build of it? None of us really perceives places in the neutral manner good Westerners are supposed to do. We can demonstrate this for ourselves easily with, say, any great city. Let's say that I show you a picture of the Eiffel Tower. What floods into your mind? Paris! If you haven't been there, images might include artists, dancing girls, gaiety, nightlife, wonderful food, sunlit boulevards, gendarmes, avenues of trees in blossom, and pictures of famous parts of Paris like the Champs-Élysées and the Place de la Concorde. If you actually have visited there, you may still have these impressions ready to spring to mind, but you will also have a host of other memories—dense traffic, modern buildings, and subway systems. And your own experiences can vie with the stereotypes. In my own case, whenever I see a picture of the Eiffel Tower I receive no sense of Parisian gaiety. Rather, I am reminded of my first visit to the structure as a young art student, when I sat at one end of a bench on the first stage of the tower. As I gazed out over the city, an elegant but clearly depressed middle-aged Frenchwoman at the other end of the bench spoke to me in English, asking me questions and telling me something of her life. I subsequently discovered that two hours later she had jumped to her death. So one picture can summon up a whole city of the mind. The same with, say, New York. The image of the Manhattan skyline conjures up for most Westerners ideas of exciting nightlife, an energetic city that never sleeps, the Statue of Liberty (and the separate cargo of impressions that that specific place evokes—freedom from repression, huddled masses, opportunity), Central Park, Yellow Cabs, and, in the mainstream international currency of modern mythology, TV shows—*Cagney and Lacey*, *Kojak*, *NYPD Blue*, and goodness knows what else. On the other hand, for people who live there, the same picture might create a whole range of different associations. Yet again, for some members of non-Western societies who are suspicious of, or resent, Western culture, the same picture might invoke feelings of repression by superpower imperialism, in which the skyscrapers are seen as expressions of Western arrogance, suitable as targets for a terrorist bomb.

Mind cities can be evoked by sound as well as vision. I sometimes experience Freud's sense of unreality when I find myself passing by Big Ben at Britain's Houses of Parliament. This famous clockface and tower are an icon that chimes the hours (it is the great bell that actually carries the name of Big Ben, in fact). Its computerized image opens the evening news on a main network-TV channel as the viewer hears the deep gonging notes of the bell; on BBC Worldservice Radio its secure, reassuring tones ring out, evoking in many people around the world ideas of stability, democracy, and an old-fashioned honesty—and perhaps in some the memory of World War II, when the sound echoed the only hope of freedom in occupied Europe. It can also evoke many images and associations—rainy nighttime streets, fog, Sherlock Holmes, the Queen, Buckingham Palace, the Tower of London, old pubs with dark-brown interiors. . . . As I walk or drive by this clock tower, I feel that I am passing all these true and false images and abstract ideas rather than masonry and outsized clockwork; it is like being inside a dream of a place that is real. Like Freud, I find myself caught in a limbo between *chora* and *topos*. Since I have not been culturally equipped to articulate the element that relates to *chora*, I find myself, like Freud, *dis-located*.

So just two photographs and a sound can evoke rich mythic images and memories of Paris, New York, and London, yet these mind cities all have latitude and longitude coordinates; they are specific places on the globe, represented on maps. Clearly, however, they exist on other levels than the strictly factual and rational, and exist for most people in that way. And there are starker examples of such places of the mind. Take homesickness, for example. If a person is separated from his or her homeland—perhaps a true exile, never to return—the lost country assumes a mythic quality. Bunkśe notes that the image of the homeland becomes frozen in time, as it was up to the time of departure. It becomes memory. "The homeland begins to take on mystic qualities . . ." Bunkśe points out. "It ceases to be of the contemporary world and becomes increasingly a part of the archaic past. It then joins the ziggurat landscapes of Mesopotamia, the pyramids of ancient Egypt."[4]

Our present cultural worldview is increasingly seeing the land, the place, in terms of economic and social utility. Imaginative, expressive qualities of place are remorselessly marginalized, so that even when protesters try to stop the destruction of an old woodland by road builders they have to justify their action by invoking utilitarian reasons such as leisure resources. Walter records how this worldview can be seen growing through history in the development of maps, with the mythic content in early cartographic essays gradually being shunted to the margins, until now we are left with our clinical, topographically exact maps, technical masterpieces but bereft of expressive, mythic quality (see chapter four). Geography replaced chorography. Given modern technological power, the emerging monoculture is enforcing the socioeconomic worldview with gathering speed and effectiveness. Bunkśe complains of seeing the "corporate footprint" on the ground of America, which is becoming a "landscape of economic power." Shopping malls, office and high-technology manufacturing complexes, warehousing areas, hotels, recreation centers, housing and apartment developments are "packaged" onto the landscape. Bunkśe uses Joel Garreu's term "edge cities" to define where most of this kind of development is taking place. Edge cities develop around core towns and stretch off horizontally, in some cases to cover thousands of square miles.

"Place values are increasingly sacrificed for 'jobs' and consumption," Bunkśe warns. We are becoming exiles, cut off from meaningful ground, experiencing a gnawing loss of identity. Dislocation on a grand scale. Poet and scholar Kathleen Raine puts it well, in the context of the people of the Western Isles off Scotland:

> When they look at familiar hills and islands what they see is the landscape of their imagination also, of poetry and music and songs and stories and memories familiar to them all. They inhabit both inwardly and outwardly their native place. . . .

> And what then is done to those inner worlds when whole environments are destroyed, forests felled, monocrop agriculture introduced, and the oil-rigs and petrol refineries, the nuclear waste processing and the rest that do not so much change a place but destroy place and memory altogether?[5]

When a place goes, so does a quantum of consciousness. Place and mind may be an unfamiliar association for us today, but the two are nevertheless inextricably linked. Raine insists that events in nature are not merely observed facts, but also *meanings*. Without such meaning, we could not know ourselves. We are becoming illiterate in the language of nature, which is essentially poetic, mythic.

If the full, rich, mythic sense of place is finally taken out of our cultural compass, then we will mentally inhabit a spiritual wasteland. Earth, nature, will no longer be perceived in its fullness, and our fate will be sealed. Can we avoid such a fate by starting to see place as active, as an *agent* once more, rather than as a merely passive, uniform container of things and events? Can we recognize the power of place in an open cultural way, without embarrassment, and develop a language for such a means of cognition? The rationalist will mutter darkly about the "pathetic fallacy," the delusionary projection of feelings onto external conditions. But is it not possible to see place as "a location of experience" which "evokes and organises memories, images, feelings, sentiments, meanings, and the work of the imagination," as Walter so eloquently puts it? He calls for a new paradigm to understand the environment, both natural and built, and suggests "topistics," his term for a modern *theoria*. He thinks that Freud's ontological confusion on the Acropolis was a topistic reaction that he simply did not recognize or understand.

In his *Timaeus*, Plato, on the cusp of the old mythic worldview and the new rationalist, intellectual order, struggled to define the process of becoming aware of *chora*, primeval space. He claimed that *chora* could not be apprehended by the senses alone, but required in addition a kind of "spurious reasoning"[6]—or "bastard reasoning," in Walter's translation. We perceive it "in a kind of dream,"[7]—a "dream with the power of sight," in Walter's rendering of the original Greek, which he understands as meaning "dreaming with our eyes open." This can be taken quite literally. I am one of those strange people who occasionally sleep with eyelids slightly apart, and on a number of occasions I have awoken to learn that some object in my waking dream was fashioned from something in the bedroom—an eagle can dissolve into an ornate door handle, a waving figure can transform into drapes softly disturbed by a breeze. On rousing from sleep, the mundane objects of waking consciousness become shorn of their mythic content. Visionary poet William Blake could see the mythic in the mundane in his normal waking life, for he told us that double the vision was always with him, so that a thistle across his way could also appear to him as "an old man grey."

Mythic consciousness is none other than a waking form of the dream state. This can be developed in waking consciousness, or cultivated in the dreaming sleep state, when it is called "lucid dreaming," a subject to which we shall return in the final chapter. It was the mythographer Joseph Campbell who most succinctly equated dream and myth, when he said that myths are public dreams and dreams are private myths. Weak forms of mythologizing do go on within us much of the time, it seems: an informal experiment by psychologist Jean Houston revealed that the participants spent about 75 percent of their time daydreaming while going about various activities, and philosopher Gaston Bachelard claims that the home is a place for daydreams—"the house allows one to dream in peace."[8] The dwelling collects images, so memory and imagination become fused with the physical space on a daily basis. (With time, those physical spaces become memory and imagination, too. When we move house or apartment, our former dwelling becomes a memory and not a physical space to us. First we live in a dwelling; then it becomes indwelling within us. . . .) When the Greeks—and so many other earlier and traditional peoples—apprehended gods and nature spirits in specific locales, they were merely doing the same thing on a larger scale, and with the natural environment. They were at home in nature in a way we are not.

Place is not passive. It interacts with our consciousness in a dynamic way. It contains its own memory of events and its own mythic nature, its *genius loci* or spirit of place, which may not be visible but can be apprehended by the human—and animal—interloper, especially in the appropriate mental state (the bringing of information into the focus of conscious awareness is, remember, a state-specific activity). On a less dramatic level, the forms, textures, smells, sounds, or light of a particular place can trigger associations within us that another place would not. It can bring things to the fore, into awareness, that were until then existing in the unconscious mind. Places can therefore illuminate us, and can provoke mythic imaginings within us. If we let this rich relationship with the environment decline into extinction, then we shall become lost. We shall literally cease to be fully *human* in the true sense of that word, which comes to us via the Old Latin *hemo*, meaning earthborn, out of Indo-European roots relating to earth and ground. In an inner sense, we will no longer be earthborn; and that will inevitably translate into physical implications for our species.

## ANCIENT SACRED PLACES

These considerations about place in general can be borne in mind now, as we turn to that curious, ages-old human habit of acknowledging *sacred places*. For various reasons, people have separated out certain places as being different, special, sanctified.

Sacred places take many forms. Some were recognized in the natural world and became sanctified physical locations, whereas other ones were built—these are the temples and monuments. Amongst natural sacred spots, caves were pre-eminent. All around the world, people have used the cave as the environment for initiation and contact with the spirit world. Teotihuacán, the great city of prehistoric Mexico, was founded on the site of a remarkable cave archeologists discovered beneath the Great Pyramid of the Sun. This cave is a four-lobed subterranean space, approached through a long lava-tube passage. In some remote period, the twists and turns of this passageway were deliberately exaggerated to make it even more labyrinthine: bends were narrowed and slabs used to create low ceilings, so a person was alternately standing and bending. The opening of the cave coincidentally faced the setting point of the Pleiades, of mythic significance to ancient Mesoamericans, and the later pyramid was built to the same orientation, causing the axis of the whole city to be angled accordingly. Australian Aborigines used caves for initiation, and the Chumash shaman in California would repair to a rock shelter on midwinter's eve, after ingesting the powerfully hallucinogenic Jimsonweed, and await the rays of the rising sun. And we know that in Europe people of the remote Paleolithic period would gather deep inside caves and paint images of animals and half-humans on their walls. Lascaux, in France, is the classic example, and in 1995 the discovery of a previously undisturbed cave near Avignon was announced, its interior covered with hundreds of Paleolithic paintings of animals. Untouched for twenty thousand years, these images used the natural bulges of the limestone walls to enhance the realism of the painted beasts. The skull of a bear was perched on a natural rock altar. Hills and mountains have also been natural sacred places to many peoples; to the ancient Greeks, Mount Olympus was the home of the gods. (As we shall see in chapter five, hills and mountains could express the very lineaments of the gods and goddesses themselves.) To the Wintu, Mount Shasta in northern California is where their souls go to at death, and in old Norse tradition one trusted in being able to die "into the hills." Trees and sacred groves provided natural cathedrals for the likes of the Celtic Druids. And rivers, waterfalls, and springs were everywhere venerated in ancient times—they were places where the spirits appeared, where access to the underworld could be achieved, where divination and sacred sleep could be conducted, and where healing could be effected.

Sometimes natural holy spots of antiquity and tradition are not readily recognizable by us today as "sites" in any sense we understand. What to uninitiated eyes appears to be just a boulder, to an Australian Aboriginal could be the excreta of a Dreamtime being and a place of great spritual power, or it could be the head of a Dreamtime hero projecting out of the ground.[9] In Madagascar, a hill, a tree, a rock, or even a featureless patch of ground can now be recognized as a sacred place by the modern visitor only because of the name it carries—such as Ambatosikidiana, "to the rock where one carries out divination," or Tsiandrorana, "there where one is not allowed to spit."[10]

As the nomadic wandering of hunting and gathering gave way to more settled lifeways based on agriculture and animal husbandry, the use of natural features as sacred places gradually shifted to the construction of monuments. To begin with, this human activity was minimal—the subtle enhancement of a naturally weathered boulder, the building of a wall or platform around some dramatic natural outcrop or pinnacle, or the marking of symbols on a sacred rock—but eventually completely artificial monuments and temples were constructed. Great timber posts or large standing stones (megaliths) were erected into circles, rectangles, rows, and other alignments, as well as used as solitary, free-standing markers of sanctity. Megalithic structures were raised by people in many parts of the world, but notably on the western fringes of Europe, in Scandinavia, and in the Mediterranean area. Some megalithic monuments seem to have been designed to mimic natural features; the interiors of the boxlike dolmens of France, Spain, and Britain, dating from the fourth millennium B.C., or of chambered earthen mounds and stone cairns such as Newgrange in Ireland, are reminiscent of caves. Stones in monuments might be used rough, as found, or shaped and smoothed, as at Stonehenge. In some cases, stones that had been naturally eroded into

The ruins of the Neolithic temple of Mnajdra, Malta.

the suggestive shapes of animal or human forms were used: the *seite* stones, sacrificial stones, of the Saami of northern Sweden are a case in point. Sometimes other materials would be used for the same purposes as stones—on Yttygran Island in the Senyavin Islands near the Bering Strait, for instance, a prehistoric ceremonial complex was constructed of bowhead whale skulls and mandibles!

In some cases, complexes of sacred sites spread over extensive areas, forming whole *sacred landscapes*. Archeologists call such features "core landscapes," and this principle has been accepted by the Convention Committee of UNESCO's World Heritage List of world importance. For example, Stonehenge is listed not just as a ring of stones, but as the whole Neolithic and Bronze Age ceremonial landscape for miles around, with its mounds, long barrows, and mysterious linear earthworks.

Interior of the Antequara dolmen (or passage grave), Spain.

Burial places, usually in the form of earthen mounds or kists (small stone boxes set in the ground), were everywhere considered as sacred sites, but megalithic chambers such as Ireland's New-grange or England's Stonehenge were not simply tombs, even though funerary activities may have been carried on at them. Rather, they were temples of sorts, even if most of us usually think of temples as the superb edifices of the golden eras of ancient Egypt and Greece, or the massive structures of the Maya and the Inca in the Americas.

By the time we reach the historical era, we are in the age of great religions, such as Christianity, Judaism, Hinduism, and Islam. In these, the church, temple, or mosque is seen primarily as a holy place of worship to a cosmic deity, rather than an expression of a local spirit of place. A peculiarity of Christianity, as Jane Hubert has pointed out,[11] is that it is possible to *deconsecrate* a church—that is, to cause a sacred place suddenly to not be sacred anymore, to cause the location to become mundane, if not profane, by definition. This is very different from most traditions of sanctity. Nevertheless, this

This prehistoric standing stone at Avebury, in southern England, seems to have a face emerging from it. It has been widely noted that several other stones in the Avebury complex look like human or animal shapes, and some have even been given appropriate names by locals. Did the megalithic builders deliberately choose suggestively shaped stones?

official attitude amongst great religions of minimizing the significance of place is superficial: Judaism, Islam, Christianity, and most other religions have not been above appropriating places for their buildings that were previously sacred to earlier religions. In the previous chapter, for example, we saw that the Rock in Jerusalem had hosted various temples, a church, and mosques. Even megalithic sites have been Christianized, so that the remains of dolmens can be found forming the crypts of French churches, crosses can be seen perching on the top of huge standing stones in Brittany, and English churches can be encountered within the earthworks of Neolithic ceremonial enclosures. Mosques can stand within the precincts of ancient Egyptian temples, as at the Temple of Luxor. Other great religions, too, use sites formerly sanctified by older religions, such as the Buddhist temple of Borobudur in Java, which stands on a Hindu site that in turn may well occupy the sacred place of an even earlier, local religion. In the case of holy wells in Celtic countries, the use of the waters for healing and veneration passed seamlessly from pagan to Christian usage, largely because the Celtic church was closer to paganism than the Roman church.

In the end, it seems that sanctity is nondenominational, as evidenced in India, for example, where tension between, say, Hindu and Muslim can break out into violence when both lay claim to a given place. The place in the final analysis transcends religion, because religion is not the source of spirituality but, rather, the outgrowth, the cultural (and political) development of the primary impulse of spiritual experience. Religion and spirituality should never be confused with one another.

I have been using the basic term "sacred place," but there is in fact a *range* of types of sanctity recognized at holy places. These can include spirit residences, ceremonial areas, legendary and mythological places, burial sites, resource areas for sacred materials, and locations for dream divination or for seeking visions. Some sites are seen as transformation places, where journeys to the spirit world are undertaken. Mescalero Apaches, to give just one example, identify spots specifically for this last purpose.[12] And many cultures recognize a form of nonmaterial *power* at certain spots. The Mescalero call this *diyi*, whereas other Native Americans refer to it as *Po-wa-ha* (Pueblo), *orenda* (Iroquois), *wakonda* (Sioux), *maxpe* (Crow). The Australian Aborigines have a range of words, depending on tribe, including *djang* and *kurunba*. In North Africa it is called *baraka*, and the !Kung of the Kalahari call it *n/um*. In Hindu tradition it is *prana*, and in old Chinese lore it is *ch'i* (or *ki* in Japanese spiritual tradition). Most famously, in the Pacific islands it is known as *mana*.

Places, objects, and the human body can contain or be imbued with this mystic power. It would be unwise and all too Western of us to think in terms of "energy" when considering this ancient cross-cultural concept. It may well be that these words variously relate to a feeling about a certain thing or manifestation, or the sense of being at a particular place—the sensation of *chora*, if I can put it that way.

German theologian Rudolf Otto explored this matter in his *The Idea of the Holy*. He considered feelings of eeriness or awe to be the "earliest manifestation" of the holy. This mental effect can pass away, but sometimes, he noted, it can be articulated through or by reference to a place. This is how, in Otto's opinion, the concept of the holy place developed:

> The English 'This place is haunted' shows a transition to a positive form of expression. Here we have the obscure basis of meaning and idea rising into greater clarity and beginning to make itself explicit as the notion . . . of a transcendental Something, a real operative entity of a numinous kind, which later, as the development proceeds, assumes concrete form as a 'numen loci', a daemon, an 'El', a Baal, or the like.
>
> In Genesis xxviii 17 Jacob says: 'How dreadful is this place! This is none other than the house of Elohim.' This verse is very instructive for the psychology of religion; it exemplifies the point that has just been made. The first sentence gives plainly the mental impression itself in all its immediacy, before reflection has permeated it, and before the meaning-content of the feeling itself has become clear or explicit. It connotes solely the *primal numinous awe*, which has been undoubtedly sufficient in itself in many cases to mark out 'holy' or 'sacred' places, and make them spots of aweful veneration. . . . There is no need . . . for the experient to pass on to resolve his mere impression of the eerie and aweful into the idea of a 'numen', a divine

power, dwelling in the 'aweful' place, still less need the *numen* become a *nomen*, a named power. . . . Worship is possible without this farther explicative process. But Jacob's second statement gives this process of explication and interpretation; it is no longer simply an expression of the actual experience.

The German expression *Es spukt hier* (literally, it haunts here) is also instructive. It has properly no true subject, or at least it makes no assertion as to what the *es*, the 'it', is which 'haunts'; in itself it contains no suggestion of the concrete representations of 'ghost', 'phantom', 'spectre', or 'spirit' common to our popular mythology. Rather is the statement the pure expression of the emotion of 'eerieness' or 'uncanniness' itself, when just on the point of detaching and disengaging from itself a first vaguely intimated idea of a numinous something, an entity from beyond the borders of 'natural' experience.[13]

Otto goes on to remark: "We might legitimately translate Habakkuk ii.20: 'Yaweh haunts His holy Temple.' Such a 'haunting' is frequently the meaning of the Hebrew *shaken*."

So at heart we are looking at the sacred place as a focus of *numinosity* (Jung's noun, coined from Otto's adjective "numinous"[14]), a place provoking a feeling of awe, eeriness, or, in mythical terms, possessing a haunting quality of localized spirit, a *numen loci*.

Mircea Eliade considered a sacred place to be that symbolic or mythic "center" we discussed in the previous chapter, and, like Otto, a place where a breakthrough between the material and spiritual worlds could occur, a manifestation of the supernatural he called a "hierophany."

## PREHISTORY AS THE UNCONSCIOUS

What, then, in the context of the discussion earlier in this chapter, are we to make of sacred places? I have spent more than half my life exploring, studying, being at ancient sacred sites around the world, and I have a working conceptual framework that I use. I think of prehistory as analogous to the unconscious mind, and the sacred sites as being like fragments of dreams we struggle to remember. It is therefore apt that the word "monument" derives from the Latin *monere*, to remind, via *monumentum*, which has the meaning "anything that recalls the mind."[15,16]

This is more than simply an analogy. The nature of "prehistory" is qualitively different from the condition we call "history." History is recorded, documented time; it presupposes writing along with any other form of documentation. We all too readily think of prehistory as a kind of illiterate history, but the difference is more fundamental than this. To chronicle, document, write, record requires a particular type of mentation, a certain kind of consciousness, as compared with the consciousness of a people who do not write, who do not chronicle and record in that way. "Prehistory" and "history" are really labels for different overall states of mind. They are not connected with chronological absolutes, for prehistory ends at different times in different parts of the world (in most cases it dates from whenever the European mind arrived there). History floats on the ocean of prehistory in the way the waking, conscious self or ego floats on the vasty deeps of the unconscious mind. The two are mirror images of one another. Protohistory we could liken to the waking dream, those transitionary moments in which the mythic dissolves away, leaving the bleached bones and gaunt stones of the mundane—the stuff of archeology.

In attempting to understand the long, silent change of worldview that has occurred from the unchronicled, archaic past to the present, documented, linear time, we have to recognize that the ego, the sense of the self, has changed, causing the advent of the type of consciousness that inhabits history. In prehistory, the mind experienced time as slow, cyclical, and seasonal, and the ego was soft-edged and merged with the physical world in a dreamy way. Now we watch the clock and count the seconds; our ego sense is hardened; its boundaries are clear-cut; self and other are clearly demarcated. This has its expression on the land. Land becomes property. We have physical boundaries defining and containing our property, and they are recorded in legal documents. There are fences (sometimes electrified), walls, hedges, barbed wire, and antipersonnel wire. The idea of enclosed land, within the boundaries of which was the private land, the farmstead, emerged naturally from the settling of human beings and the beginning of agriculture. This simply became more defined, more exact, more entrenched "as time went on" (a phrase that is itself an expression of the historical mind-set). Prior to such settlement, people moved across the land, hunting and gathering. Land was not seen in blocks, in defined areas, any more than it is today by the tribal Aborigine. It wasn't documented on maps; it wasn't settled in static farms. The ego, the sense of self, was likewise soft-edged, diffused. *State of consciousness and the view of the land, of the world, always relate to one another.*

The boundary in the outer world was the reflection of ego boundary, which walled off the domain of consciousness from the wild darkness of the unconscious mind. Within the analogous territorial boundary of the physical world was the homestead, village, or town. In short, civilization. Beyond the pale was wild nature, wilderness, dragons. Once, when consciousness was on the cusp of hardening, the boundary had taken the form of a *temenos*, separating profane and sacred space, but as all space gradually became profane, it became instead a defensive barrier.

This boundary between civilization (ego) and the outer wilderness (the unconscious) was thrown into sharp relief during the Middle Ages, with the Christian invention of witchcraft. Once upon a time there was the *myrkrida*, the night traveler. She would rub her body with ointments made from hallucinogenic herbs and "fly away" into the night, to the wild woods and the erotic meetings on "Venus Mountain." She would, in fact, fly away in trance into the vast spaces of the unconscious mind. But the night traveler became satanized, and she turned into an evil witch, a danger to civilization. She became the *hagazussa*, she who sat on, or crossed, the fence.[17] The person, the man, within the pale of civilization hated and feared the woman from the wilds, the hag, she who consorted with the devil. Gaps in hedgerows were viewed with suspicion, as places marking witchways through the barrier. Juniper was grown in hedges to dissuade night-flying witches from hedge-hopping or sitting. The drama of consciousness was played out in a literal fashion on the land.

So, when we visit a sacred site built or used in the prehistoric past, we are dealing with a place that comes from a different space of the mind, the archaic *chora* of the Greeks. We cannot apprehend its full essence by modern, civilized thinking, because it emerges into our rational worldview in just the way the fragments of a dream survive into waking consciousness. But if a place can organize our perceptions, feelings, memories, and imaginings, if it is expressive space, it may be able to speak to those dark areas of mind beyond the bounds of the modern conscious self; *perhaps information can pass between the place and our unconscious mind.* If we dream with open eyes, we may be able to include a greater range of information in our cognized model of the monument or sacred locale. The very nature of sacred places inspired "extreme states of topistic awareness," to use Walter's terminology,[18] and they often still can if their integrity has been left effectively unimpaired by the depredations of time and civilization, and if we use our full range of sensibilities and shift to the appropriate state of mind. A monument, after all, is for evoking memory. Such sanctified places can possess physical properties that "draw the believer into a meditative mood or even an altered state of consciousness," Walter declares.[19] Psychologist Julian Jaynes says much the same thing, referring to the hallucinogenic properties of certain places. He explains what he means in a particularly expressive passage:

> Oracles begin in localities with a specific awesomeness, natural formations of mountain or gorge, of hallucinogenic wind or waves, of symbolic gleamings and vistas, which I suggest are more conducive to occasioning right [brain] hemisphere activity than the analytic planes of everyday life. . . .
>
> Certainly the vast cliffs of Delphi move into such a suggestion and fill it fully: a towering caldron of blasted rock

over which the sea winds howl and the salt mists cling, as if dreaming nature were twisting herself awake at awkward angles, falling away into a blue surf of shimmering olive leaves and the gray immortal sea.[20]

Ruins are expressive places, and they can tell you about themselves, and the story they tell is the tale of mind, of your consciousness and that of your ancestors. It seems Sigmund Freud knew this at some level. He once confided to a friend that he had read more about archeology than about psychology, and his consulting room was packed with statuettes, effigies, figurines, and other ancient objects from Egypt, Greece, Rome, and other places of antiquity. One contemporary wrote that, "wherever one looked, there was a glimpse into the past." Another said that the room "immediately evoked a sense of the ages." One of his patients remarked that she looked at things in the room before she looked at him. Freud even used the history of the Eternal City, Rome, as a metaphor for the growth of the mind. Citing Freud's *Civilization and Its Discontents*, Walter notes that the great psychologist suggested imagining Rome "not as a human dwelling-place, but a mental entity with just as long and varied a past history," where all stages of development remained together. But he finally dismisses the analogy, because "the same space will not hold two contents." Walter protests that a city like Rome does indeed store all its past, and points out how the pioneers of the Renaissance were stimulated by the fragments of antiquity they found around them in Rome. J. A. Symonds has said that they were "excited by the very stones of ancient Rome."[21] The ruins were so expressive that in 1337 Petrarch could write that they "excited the tongue and the mind." Walter comments that Renaissance antiquaries found Rome to be a "theater of ancestral drama." He feels that Freud's collection, however, demonstrates the great psychologist's failure to recognize the value of place, for his objects were isolated from the places where they had been found, and that is how, in essence, he saw them and related to them. They were expressions of the human mind, and place did not come into his equation. Yet the artifacts, statues, and temples belonged together and carried a double meaning, Walter maintains: the temple related to the deity as it was expressed in the landscape, the statues were the god as imagined by humans. So having ancient artefacts on a shelf was only half the story, missing the context, the crucial element of place. "Freud experienced topistic reality but failed to understand and therefore ignored it," Walter claims. "Because of his influence, this specific ignorance helps us forget the old language of places."[22]

Certainly any form of psychology that may be fashioned worthy of proclaiming itself as "ecopsychology" (see the introductory chapter) will have to make place one of its most central concerns and references. Not only Freud, but most psychologists have overlooked place, and it does not yet figure very prominently in the language of even the aspiring ecopsychologists. Yet the relationship of mind and place has to be the cornerstone of our relationship with the planet. No grand, sweeping visions of ecopsychological harmony will be tenable without reference to that basic relationship.

How to apprehend place is possibly the greatest single lesson we have to learn from the archaic mind-set or worldview. We have to learn how to dream with open eyes. In terms of cognitive science, we will have to reprogram our neuronal processes to allow into the limelight of our consciousness the information received from place that currently falls outside the spectrum of our awareness. The informational model our brain-minds create of the world needs modification, or at least enhancement: we saw in the introductory chapter that we do not directly apprehend the world at all, but reconstruct it from electrical and chemical signals used in the vast processing capacity of the brain-mind, and that the product of this is shaped and modified by our own range of memories, associations, and cultural environment. What gets into our direct consciousness is a highly edited, selective view of the world. The environment we apprehend is a cognitive construction, built within the recesses of our brain-minds, and sacred space is therefore a division of that cognized environment.[23] But even if sacred space is made for us within the brain-mind, that does not mean that we can assume it is illusory—at least, any more than any other aspect of what we fondly think of as reality. Indeed, if we find ourselves engaged by a sacred place, and have our consciousness provoked by it, the reason such locations seem sacred, seem to possess a *numen loci*, may be precisely that we receive *more information* from them. The very fact that there are, and have always been, sacred places demonstrates their psychological importance. They may be where we get a greater glimpse of reality.

## BETWIXT AND BETWEEN: SOMEWHERE ELSE INSTEAD

Each year, the Nenets peoples (Kanin Samoyed) in the Arctic region of Russia south of the Barents Sea would follow the migrating reindeer herds. The migration route passed through what is now known as Kozmin Copse, a cutting through the narrowest strip of forest that separates areas of tundra. In spring the route was used northwards to the Kanin Peninsula, and southwards when the Nentsi returned to the mainland for winter. The trees on either side of the pathway were sacred, and were adorned with votive and sacrificial offerings. It was a "pathway shrine" and was used as a sanctuary up until the mid-nineteenth century. It was also the dividing line between the northern and southern extents of the Nentsi's migrational territory, and was a ritual threshold zone for them. To them, north was considered the female sphere of influence, and south that of the male. So in winter, when the herds and the people migrated southwards, the women had to abandon their sphere, the north and the tundra, and enter male space, the south and the forest. Kozmin Copse was on this boundary. The sanctuary provided an "in-between" space where this transition of status and context could take place, where the women underwent various purifications. In the spring, on the return migration, it was the men who had to carry out a sacrificial rite in the holy grove. As well as a division between north and south, and female and male, the pathway shrine also marked the change between raw and cooked food, reindeer husbandry and hunting, nature and culture.[24]

Such threshold places are known in anthropology as "liminal," a term coined by Arnold van Gennap in his *The Rites of Passage* in 1909, and developed later by anthropologist Victor Turner. The word derives from the Latin *limen*, boundary, from where we get "limit" in English. The Romans had household gods (such as Vestia guarding the hearth, as we saw in the previous chapter), and the doorway was the realm of the deities Limentinus and Limenting. The liminal condition is a phase of transition between different states of being, and can apply to a wide variety of circumstances—social, ritual, temporal, and spatial. Quite often, it involves a mix of these. The Romans also had a god of transition, the famous Janus, who faced both ways at once and presided over comings and goings.

This "betwixt-and-between" stage or place is remembered in surviving folk traditions like the groom's carrying his bride across the threshold of their new home, and also in apparently nonsense nursery rhymes such as that about the Grand Old Duke of York, who marched his men to the top of the hill and then marched them back. And when they were up they were up, when they were down they were down, but when they were only halfway up, we recall, they were neither up nor down. A. A. Milne put it more charmingly in his poem "Halfway Down" in *When We Were Very Young* (1924), in part of which he has Christopher Robin say:

> *Halfway up the stairs*
> *Isn't up,*
> *And isn't down.*
> *It isn't in the nursery,*
> *It isn't in the town.*
> *And all sorts of funny thoughts*
> *Run round my head:*
> *"It isn't really*
> *Anywhere!*
> *It's somewhere else*
> *Instead!"*

In an individual's life there are a range of thresholds that have to be negotiated, such as birth, puberty, marriage, parenthood, retirement, and death, as well as entry into a variety of social groupings and the attainment of changed social status. In traditional cultures, and to a very much lesser extent (where at all) in modern societies, these kinds of life thresholds were marked by ritual occasions—the rites of passage, in fact. In traditional initiation or puberty rites, boys might be taken by the (sometimes masked) elder men to a designated spot in the wilds outside the village. This location would be secret and otherwise unvisited, and if the place was in the open, the rites would often take place at night. The initiatory candidates would be stripped and subjected to various degrees of mutilation, and possibly circumcision. In the face of this, they had to be totally humble, accepting the actions and instructions of the leaders without question or complaint. They had died to their old life, but had not yet attained their new status. In this gray zone of nonentity, neophytes would often set up an intense companionship amongst themselves, a sense of profound equality and shared purpose that Turner called *communitas*.[25] Eventually they would return to the village (though in some cases initiates died during the rigors of the rite of passage), now men or initiates, with a new social status.

Geographical liminality can be expressed in certain places. A cave, for instance, is a typically liminal place, often used for initiation, being on the boundary between the sunlit open land and the enclosed, dark, subterranean world. The deep woods likewise provide a liminal situation, in which tree trunks and foliage take on eerie, ambiguous forms in the dim, green-filtered light. Crossroads were profoundly liminal to the Celts of old Europe. They were both the meeting and parting of ways, a zero point, a form of the *omphalos*, the mysterious sacred center we discussed in the previous chapter. A crossroads was an intersection but not a place in itself. Suicides would be buried and the gallows erected there. It was said that, if you stood at the crossroads at liminal midnight on liminal Hallowe'en, with your chin resting in a forked stick, you would see the spirits of the departed drifting by. Witches and demons were also thought to meet at crossroads, and at liminal New Year it used to be the practice in some regions to sweep crossroads clear of spirits. In contrast to these gloomy associations, it was also thought that the soil taken from a crossroads had curative properties. The

Romans placed altars at crossroads, and shrines can be found at them in other cultures even today.

In old Europe, the ground to the north side of the church was a liminal zone, for that was where the building's shadow fell. Suicides, transgressors, and unbaptized children would be buried in that part of the churchyard. Shadows were seen as liminal in many cultures, and the great German researcher of the Nazca lines in Peru (to which we shall return in chapter five), Maria Reiche, noted that the Indians would not walk where the shadow of a rock touched one of the mysterious desert lines, because it was hallowed or full of evil spirits.[26] A vestige of such kinds of avoidance probably survives in the childhood game of not stepping on the cracks in the sidewalk.

Land boundaries were by definition liminal zones. From at least the sixth century, the Christian church encouraged the Beating of the Bounds, the reaffirmation of the parish boundaries, by taking young boys from the parish and beating, bumping, or dragging them at various points along the parish limits, hanging them upside down, or throwing them into a boundary stream! In this way it was felt that the position of the boundaries would be ingrained into the memories of the upcoming generation. And rituals were enacted for secular boundaries, too. In Ireland, at liminal Beltane, the father of the house would light a candle and bless the threshold, the hearth, and the four corners of the house. At the same time of year, the boundaries of the farmstead might be marked by the woman of the house, who would carry a pail of well water around them or put sprigs of rowan in the four corners of each field.[27] In numerous societies, a land boundary might be reaffirmed by the carrying of a flaming brand or other form of fire along it.

Land boundaries also carried the mythic import of separating the human, lived-in land from the wilderness beyond, and as was mentioned earlier, the night-flying witch was thought to be able to penetrate this all-important boundary. The fear that the witch's spirit might enter the house was expressed in the use of the witch bottle, a container holding a jumble of threads placed over a doorway so that any entering wraith would become entangled and prevented from entering the dwelling. A witch was herself a liminal personality, as was the shaman, who could cross the boundaries between the human and spirit world. Turner also felt that jesters, clowns, and poets inhabited the border realm where outlaws and initiates sojourned temporarily. We can see what a liminal mythic figure Robin Hood is, being both an outlaw and the denizen of the wild greenwood.

Many kinds of sacred sites are themselves essentially liminal, being where contact with the world of spirits could be made, where the veils between this world and the otherworld are at their thinnest. A classic expression of this idea is the Hindu custom of calling sacred places *tirthas,* meaning "crossing" or "ford."

As with space, so with time. The Celtic festivals of Imbolc, Beltane, Lughnasa, and Samhain (represented by our Hallowe'en), discussed in the preceding chapter, were times when the threshold between the human and supernatural worlds was open, an idea that survives in our own Hallowe'en festivities today, only we have taken the dread and awe out of it. Samhain was the Celtic New Year, and the time of New Year is a threshold period in all cultures, as are other pivotal times in the year, such as the solstices. The day also has its liminal hours. Midnight is an obvious one, the "witching hour"; noon is another moment of "time outside time," when shadows are at their shortest but haven't commenced lengthening; twilight, or, to use the old-fashioned but much more powerful and expressive term, "gloaming," is a particularly potent example of a "crack between the worlds."

Perhaps the greatest threshold is dying—being at "death's door" (a door, like a window, is part of a boundary when closed, but becomes a threshold when open). If we look at funeral traditions practiced up until quite recent times in the Celtic countries of Europe's western fringe, we can see that a wide scope of liminality was involved, ranging from the social to the physical. In the first instance, the period between death and burial was profoundly liminal: the dead person had left the world of the living but had not yet physically left the community. Immediately after death, the deceased's face would be covered by a sheet or cloth. Next, the corpse would have its own boundaries defined: its eyes and mouth would be closed, and other orifices plugged, before being wrapped in a winding sheet and placed in the coffin. From the moment of death, the thresholds of the house took on special importance, and windows would be closed and drapes drawn. The door to the room where the body was laid out had to be left open, though in some districts it was customary to place the coffin on a trestle outside the front door of the house.[28] In many areas, friends and neighbors would show their respects by coming to the house of death but not crossing the threshold. They would be greeted by the chief mourner and receive a glass of ale or a cup of tea.

During this preburial period, a *sin-eater* would be summoned. This was usually a poor, solitary person, viewed as outside the pale of the village community. (One sin-eater in a Welsh border village was described as "a long leane, lamentable poor raskal" by the seventeenth-century antiquary John Aubrey.) But the boundary between this strange outcast and the community at large would be temporarily opened during the period of mourning so that he could come and take on the unexpiated sins of the deceased. This would be done in various ways, depending on the local custom. In some cases, the sin-eater would enter the house and consume a plate of bread and salt which had been laid on the breast of the corpse for some time, soaking up, as it were, the dead person's sins. This ritual food would be handed to the sin-eater *across* the dead body. In other versions of the custom, the sin-eater would arrive and stand before the door of the house of mourning. The deceased's family would come out and give him a stool or chair, and he would sit outside, facing the doorway, and receive a crust of bread and a glass of ale, which he would consume. He would then rise from his seat and pronounce, "with a composed gesture, the ease and rest of the Soul departed, for which he would pawn his own Soul."[29]

Caring for the body inside the house was primarily the work of women, but the outdoor association with the corpse—removing the body from the house and carrying it to the cemetery—was primarily the responsibility of the men. It was important that the corpse be carried across the threshold of the house feet first, and never by the back door. Ideally, its feet had to be kept pointing away from the house all the way to the grave. This was to reinforce the sense of a one-way journey to burial, to reduce the chances of haunting. Most country funerals in former times in Europe were walking funerals, with a procession of mourners carrying the coffin along specially designated pathways, known as "church paths" or "corpse ways." The procession would stop at certain points along the corpse way, which could be miles in length. These stopping places would be typically liminal locations, such as bridges over streams, ancient stiles, crossroads, and the boundary of the church-yard itself—as recalled by a church's "lych gate," or corpse gate. At these stopping points, the coffin would be rested on a special stone or the base of a cross to give the pallbearers a break, and hymns would be sung, or even a dirge, to advise the deceased how to navigate the hazards of the postmortem journey.[30]

Some corpse ways, or sections of them, still survive in rural parts of Western Europe, and can be traced leading to medieval churches or cemeteries. In Holland, these roads were perfectly straight and called *doodwegen*, or death roads. It was actually illegal to carry the corpse in other than a straight line to its burial![31,32] In parts of old Germany there were *Geisterwege*, spirit paths. These, like fairy passes in Ireland, were invisible, but also "dead straight," and linked cemeteries. Though they only existed in the folk mind, these spirit paths had definite geographical positions; it was thought unwise to cross or walk along them, for the chances of meeting a ghost along them were considered to be high.

Such death ways are liminal space extended in linear fashion. Not only were they associated with the carriage of the dead from home to burial, they were also seen as ways of the spirit through the land, a path along which the deceased might return from the grave-yard and haunt his or her survivors if proper ritual was not ob-served. In addition, they were the lines of least resistance through the landscape, along which general haunting or spectral traffic was most likely to occur. (This might be more complex than simple folklore: quite reliable reports exist of encounters with ghosts on old routes and death roads, as we'll see in chapter five.) To prevent unwanted encounters with ghosts in old Europe, old pathways were swept free of spirits, and "spirit traps" would sometimes be erected on the corpse ways; they were reminiscent of Native American "dream catchers," and consisted of threads crisscrossed over a hoop, which was then placed on a stick or staff and stuck upright in the ground.

(What is remarkable is that these liminal routes through the land, these usually—though not always—straight ways of the dead, are a *cross-cultural* phenomenon, with many similar ideas associated with them, and can be found not only in old European contexts but also in pre-Columbian America. This is most significant, in my view, and a matter to which we shall return when considering the mythologizing of the landscape in chapter five.)

What, then, are we to make of liminal space? It is place yet not place, occupying time that is outside time. I suggest that liminal space is *chora* without *topos*. It is where one can have "funny thoughts," just like Christopher Robin; where one can break through into numinous experience. In our effort to understand place, those liminal spaces, those *tirthas* where visions can be had, where hierophanies can erupt, where the boundaries between the human and spirit worlds can be breached, are the greatest teachers. In theory, all places possess the potential of being liminal, in that they can all be seen from the perspective of *chora* rather than *topos* alone, but in practice certain places are more expressive, and more able to provoke the mythic within us. It is a worthwhile if not urgent task for us today to reacquaint ourselves with the power of such places.

## EXPERIENTIAL

Before proceeding to outline some suggested experiential practices that can be used to explore the nature of place and liminality, I'll tell you about one of my own experiences, which I consider resulted from a combination of liminal place, time, and consciousness—in fact, see how many versions of liminality you can note!

It happened one evening in the early 1980s, when I was driving from London to a remote village in Wales, a distance of about 250 miles. I had been unprepared for the journey, but it was one I had done many times before. At around midnight, I passed through a Shropshire village virtually on the Welsh border. It had the last filling station likely to be open at that time of night for at least fifty miles in that sparsely populated region. To my concern, it was closed, and my fuel gauge was hovering at empty. I pressed on into the empty darkness of the mountainous Welsh border country to see how far I'd get, even though I knew I did not have enough fuel to reach my destination, which was still about fifty miles distant. Just beyond the village was a sharp left turn that led off into Wales, but the next thing I remember is driving along an unfamiliar length of road. It was a winding highway with high rock faces on either side, and ahead of me I saw the taillights of another car negotiating the sharp bends. Where the hell was I? What had happened? Eventually I emerged from the gorge. The car ahead sped off, but I pulled up at a country crossroads. I checked the map and found that I had somehow missed the turning I knew so well and driven straight on past it for nearly ten miles without any conscious recollection. Nowadays, it might be suspected that I had experienced "missing time" as a result of a UFO abduction, but I figured then, as I still do, that I had entered a trance state, caused perhaps by fatigue from the long drive and the monotony of driving on lonely roads at that late hour of the night. Possibly the sharp bends and the car lights up ahead had "awoken" me. I was angry with myself, not merely for driving in such a state, but also because I had gone miles out of my way, wasting what little fuel I had left. Rather than compounding the problem by retracing the way I'd come, I decided to take a very narrow country road leading from the crossroads and over a wild mountain area called Long Mountain, to get me into Wales. I set off into the inky-dark countryside, winding up the mountain slopes. Somewhere near the top of the ridge, I saw a white light ahead. As I got closer, I saw to my utter astonishment that it was the illuminated glass oval on top of an old-fashioned petrol pump. I could just make out the dark outline of an unlit house beyond. My elation at finding this unlikely object soon evaporated when I realized that

I had on me only charge cards and a fifty-pence piece. Even if I woke up the people in the house at this unearthly hour, it probably wouldn't help me buy any fuel. But as I pulled up alongside the old pump, I saw that it was automatic, and took only fifty-pence pieces! I have never found any other petrol pump that took this coin, which even then bought barely half a gallon of petrol. I was able to put just enough fuel in my car to get me to my destination. The next morning, the whole sequence of events seemed dreamlike, but there I was at my destination, with my car parked outside the window. I never went back to check if there really was an old-fashioned petrol pump, fitted with an automatic device to handle a next-to-useless coin, on top of an isolated mountain ridge on the Welsh border. I have preferred to leave the matter as ambiguous, because it was bizarre, whatever had happened: if there was no real pump, where had the fuel come from to power my car for the remainder of the journey? If, on the other hand, the unlikely pump really existed, how extraordinary could the sequence of events be to get me to it when I needed it? This perfectly true incident seems to me now like some episode out of TV's *Twilight Zone*. In a metaphorical, liminal sense, I suppose it was.

## Monumenteering

Surveys indicate that the visiting of ancient sites is mentioned by tourists as one of the prime reasons for vacation travel. When one considers that almost a million people visit a monument like Stonehenge in a single year, it is easy to believe this. It is almost as if the old places are calling us back again. More prosaically, it may be that, in a modern world of transience, speed, and uncertainty, it simply feels good to "touch base" with something that speaks of time and permanence, and of other ways of being in the world— something that utters the archaic whisper. Whatever the reasons, however, what I suggest as an activity here is not mere tourism but an approach more akin to the ancient Greek *theoria*, conducted in modern style. Monumenteering means not only visiting a sacred site and getting to know it physically, but also apprehending it through mythic means, allowing it to provoke memory and unsuspected associations.

So decide where you are going to go to visit an ancient sacred place. Take a special trip, or make it part of your vacation plan. You could visit one of the great prehistoric megalithic sites of Europe—say, Newgrange in Ireland (or, much better, the chambered cairns on the Loughcrew Hills thirty miles away); Stonehenge in England (or, again much better, the Avebury complex twenty miles to the north); the great rows of standing stones, dolmens or chambered mounds around Carnac-Ville in Brittany; or the mighty dolmens of Spain. You could visit instead one of the great Gothic cathedrals of Europe: any of them will do the trick, but it is difficult to better the mighty Chartres Cathedral in France for sheer power of place. Or you might visit the evocative, dreamy temples of Greece or Egypt, or the ancient marvels of Rome. Then again, there is a remarkable range of ancient sacred places in the Americas to choose from: the mysterious, two-thousand-year-old Serpent Mound of Ohio; the medicine wheels in the Rockies of Canada and the United States; the Cahokia mounds in Illinois; Chaco Canyon in New Mexico, or the many other extraordinary prehistoric Native American ruins and rock art of the Southwest. And so on and on—there is the whole world to choose from. Whatever your choice, for the purposes of this particular activity it needs to be sufficiently well known to have something written about it, and for its photograph to be reasonably accessible to you in books or brochures *before* you visit it for the first time. When you have chosen the site, and assembled data and picture, you are ready to begin.

First, just *say the name* of the sacred place out loud a few times. As Lage Wahlström has pointed out: "Hearing the name of a place often gives rise to certain associations."[33] Note any connotations that may arise. Then, after reading up on the place, study its photograph. How do you imagine the place to be from its picture and the descriptions you have read? Visualize your preconceptions strongly.

The next stage is to visit the site physically—the temple, the monument. Take a camera with you. Encounter the site with as few other people around as possible. Choose your moment. In that first encounter, try to catch the *difference* you *sense* between the place as you experience it and the place as you *imagined* it before you came. Play with that difference, both at the monument and afterwards. Try to identify what it is that is different. Is it the size of the monument? The area it encloses? The extent and nature of the surroundings? (I recall visiting the mystery temple of Eleusis and being shocked to discover that there were cement factories and housing hemming it in on all sides. Yet the site itself was picturesque and maintained its own quality. In fact, the unfortunate surroundings actually amplified the power of the place.) Don't *tell* yourself the difference; try to make yourself *feel* it. Remember that feeling.

As you move about the site, use not only your eyes but other senses and sensibilities as well. Are there any legends associated with this place? If there are, run them through your mind as you "take in" the site. How does your body feel; how does it relate to the space the site creates? How do you feel on an emotional level? A little fearful? Somehow enhanced and liberated? Awestruck? Disappointed? Don't analyze these feelings; simply be conscious of them. How does the site *smell*? There may not be a particular smell that you are readily conscious of, but sometimes there is. I visited Delphi for the first time on the sunny morning after a torrential rainstorm. As I walked up the Sacred Way, the smell of flowers, of freshened earth, and above all of cypress trees was noticeably strong. Now, whenever I smell the scent of cypress, I am instantly transported to Delphi; a sunlit picture of that powerfully expressive place is flashed into my mind. Smell is, of course, strongly linked to memory. It is a direct sense: it doesn't "cross over," as, for example, the information impinging on the right eye is "read" in the left brain. Smell connects to the limbic system, and can evoke emotion and memory in powerful ways. (And smell can be at work on you without your being aware: it takes only eight molecules of substance to trigger an impulse in a nerve ending in the olfactory lobe, but it takes forty triggered nerve endings for you to smell anything consciously.) So, if you have the opportunity, visit your selected site either prior to or just after a storm, when the smell rising from the soil is most noticeable, or during low pressure, when there is more moisture in the atmosphere and scents carry more readily. In the evening, too, ambient scents tend to be stronger. Perhaps it is the earth at the site that gives off a recognizable odor, or local plants, bushes, or trees. But if you can't detect a "site scent," come prepared to "cheat" by bringing a lump of incense, a sprig of herb, or an essential oil with you—any scent with which you have no prior personal associations, and which you feel is appropriate to the site. (So, for instance, I might take cypress to Delphi, frankincense or myrhh to an Egyptian temple, sage or copal to a Native American place of power.) As you walk around the site, quietly sniff the scent you have selected. Touch the place, too, where it is permissible to do so. Take many photographs, from many angles, distant and close up, including the surroundings viewed from the site, and perhaps a series of pictures to produce a panorama of overlapping shots. If you have even rudimentary drawing ability, take a sketch pad along, too: there is nothing like drawing a place or an object to make you see it. And spend some time just sitting or being at the place, not doing anything or thinking or concentrating on anything in particular. Before you leave, scan the surroundings so as to note visually and haptically how the site relates to its broader environment. If it is permissible and nonharmful to do so, go into the vicinity of the site (not the site itself) and take a blade of grass, or a leaf from a weed or other plant, a pebble, or a small handful of soil or sand (but take nothing if it would cause noticeable material damage to the site or its surroundings, and *never* take any archeological fragment from an ancient place).

Later, when you are back home, and back in your routine lifeway, put the photographs you took of the site, the associated scent of the place, and a tactile reminder (if you were able to bring one back) together in a box. On one or two nights every week, go through this material, looking, touching, smelling, remembering, immediately before going to sleep. If a scent is involved, then see that it is sprinkled on your bedclothes or in the air of the bedroom. Repeat this (perhaps for several weeks) until you recall having a dream about the place. However brief and inconsequential it might seem, make a written note of it and add that to your box of the site's memorabilia. Keep at this until your dreams about the place become more frequent and perhaps more complex. Note the imagery and associations that creep into your site dreams. Continue with all this until you get to a point where no fresh development in your dreamlife regarding the place seems to be happening. I hope that, by means of this process, which may take some months, you will develop a mythic relationship with the site you visited. Ponder the story that your unconscious mind tells you about the place (and, inevitably, about yourself through the medium of the place). In this way, you stand a chance of recovering some of the interaction that went on unconsciously between you and the site—the primal information superhighway that bypassed your conscious mind.

## Let's Go to Your Place

Monumenteering relates to specific ancient and sacred places, and for practical reasons cannot be a very frequent activity. The place you most often come in contact with is the one in which you live. What can you do to make that a more expressive, meaningful space? One quite devastating way of initiating this inquiry is to take photographs of the rooms you inhabit. Compare those views with your experience of *being in* the rooms. What is the difference? The photographs will show only *topos* (unless you are a gifted photographer). Try to identify what you feel is there experientially that the camera cannot show.

Next, the hearth. Do you have one? If not, then make some focal arrangement of natural objects, such as stones, soil, sand, pine cones, seashells, pieces of tree bark, and so forth. And a candle (though make sure it is situated in a safe manner). Spend at least a few hours each week with the electric lights off, using just the candlelight emanating from your natural focus, or, if you do have a natural fire, sitting by it and seeing your place in the glow from the embers or from the flicker of the flames. See and feel how the character of the space around you changes under this natural illumination. Note how much easier it is to drift into reverie, to daydream—and remember that we noted earlier Gaston Bachelard's suggestion that home was a place for daydreams. It has never been more important for us than now to experience natural illumination—only within the last smidgin of time, a mere hundred years or less, has a culture emerged that rarely sits in firelight or candle-flicker. Psychologically, this is a problematic development.

For increased daytime expression within your place, use sunlight. Observe how the sun's position changes through the day and year, and consequently the shifting pattern of sunlight through your windows. Select a key day in the solar year—midsummer, midwinter, the equinoxes, or one of the cross-quarter days, like the Celtic Samhain, Imbolc, and so on. Take sunrise, noon, or sunset on the day of your choice. Hang or fix a small mirror to intercept the sunbeam coming in through the window, skylight, or whatever at that time, and redirect the light into a darker corner of the dwelling, where you can place some object or image meaningful to you. In this way you will become more conscious of the greater cycles of time, and link your living space to the cycles of the heavens, to the larger order of time surrounding the small time of our human lives. If you want to develop this method, you could erect such devices in several places in your home to redirect the sunlight on many, or all, the solar stations of the year. This will literally give a cosmic background to your lifeway.

Thomas Bender has pointed out that "silence can be a vital tool of design."[34] He suggests that we listen to our surroundings, noting the half-heard music from someone else's place, noisy refrigerators, heating systems, and other unwanted sounds that subliminally pollute our personal environments. Do what you can to minimize these, and choose a time that is the quietest. Sit and listen to the place where you live. And if you have a special place outside somewhere—a tree, a rock, a bridge over a stream, or even a bench in a park—go there, too, and listen to it. Quite often.

### Entering the Twilight Zone (or Roaming in the Gloaming)

Although I have forgotten the details, I seem to recall that, in one of his books, the hapless Carlos Castaneda describes being told to sit at the edge of a clearing in the scrub at dusk by his mischievous mentor, don Juan. He is instructed to watch a huge iguanalike lizard that is standing stock-still in the clearing. Terrified of making a sound, Castaneda watches intently, seeing all kinds of frightening details in the creature. But it transpires that the "lizard" is just a gnarled section of tree trunk, taking on all kinds of ominous forms in the dwindling half-light. Whether his books are fact, fiction, or faction, this account by Castaneda can be recognized as a valid experience; many of us have had something like it. I recall my father telling me of an occasion in his youth in Ireland when he met the devil. He was walking home from a late-night card-playing session at a friend's house. His route took him along a path by the church wall. As he was approaching the church, he noticed in the dim starlight a movement underneath a tree overhanging the wall. He slowed his pace, then stopped in his tracks when he saw the movement was caused by a tall, manlike figure. Peering intently, he was sure the figure had horns on its head. My father was gripped with deep religious terror: here was the devil himself sidling by the churchyard wall! It took several rooted, terrified moments for my father to recognize that it was instead a goat on its hind legs, leaning on the wall and munching at the overhanging foliage. . . .

Make use of the gloaming as a tool to explore liminal states of mind. Go out after sunset into the woods, the fields, or even your back yard, when there is just barely enough light to see by. Settle down and focus in on some complex object—a bush, a rock, a tree trunk. Look "into" it; let its mythic aspect emerge. It may seem to move a little, or to take on other forms. Let your imagination play in the dusk, until the *imaginal* emerges from whatever object it is you are concentrating on. Try to be alert to the switches that are occurring in your cognition between seeing the object in its prosaic form and in its mythic or imaginal forms.

## Finding Your Warp Factor

I shall not tire of re-emphasizing throughout this book that we are engaged here on a study of mind, not the Earth; it is just that the Earth can lead us to a greater understanding of consciousness, of mind and soul, if we let it give us that healing. I am also suggesting

that, in a sense, the Earth itself is a state of mind. It is only to be expected, then, that the spatial and temporal expressions of liminality have their analogy within the workings of the brain-mind. The
biogenetic structuralists, whom we have met a number of times so
far in our inquiries, use the term "warp" to describe those transitionary stages between different states of consciousness. Warps are
brief experiential moments that have their corollary, the biogenetic
structuralists maintain, in neural transformations. "For example,"
they write, "if one is 'happy' one moment and 'sad' the next, then
somewhere between these two phases of consciousness is a warp,
involving the cessation of the 'happy' phase and producing the 'sad'
phase. The liminal aspect of the warp metaphorically implies a
threshold through which the stream of consciousness must pass
when it 'leaves' one phase behind and 'enters' another phase."[35]

It is an educational experience to try monitoring your varying
states of consciousness during the course of the day, noticing how
they arise and pass away, as do all phenomena that enter the scope
of your conscious attention. Most of the time, we are *unconscious* of
this ever-flowing process, the magic theater, that the brain-mind
keeps conjuring up before us. It is instructive, too, to become aware
how internal and external agencies can affect mind-states, sometimes subtly, sometimes quite dramatically. How different is your
mental state after a cup of coffee? How different is it, say, half an
hour after that? Does your mood change when you are wearing certain clothes ("power dressing," for example), or are in certain environments? The effects of weather, time of day, state of bodily
health, sounds, smells, electromagnetic fields, temperature, humid-
ity or lack of airborne moisture, and a thousand other factors can be
massaging your consciousness without your really being aware of
their influence. Close attention to your shifting daily mental range
might also reveal that you have unsuspected allergies that cause
changes in your consciousness or moods when you are near certain
materials in your immediate environment. (The effect of allergies
can be mental rather than physical, never forget.) Some workplaces
have unfortunate combinations of environmental factors that, under the umbrella heading of "Sick Building Syndrome" (SBS), cause

pronounced health problems and general discomfort in workers. But environments may be subtly affecting you if you are sensitive in certain ways, even if you never recognize them as exhibiting SBS. Pay attention, and try to track down the source of any problem by closely observing shifts in your mental state. Once identified, it might be possible either to remove the cause or to counteract it somehow.

But for the purposes of our work in this book, the most productive and dramatic warp to concentrate on is that which occurs between wakefulness and sleep. Most of us most of the time just nod off, crash out, or drift into sleep. We often know we have been asleep only when we awake! But the process of "falling" to sleep is one that repays conscious attention, for it will tell you much about your mind, and give you a firsthand experience of those magic moments of liminality. As you hover between wakefulness and sleep, sudden vivid flashes of imagery, or sometimes sounds, will dart very briefly before your awareness. This is the hypnagogic state (the corresponding state on waking is called "hypnopompic"). It is a miracle zone, a true crack between the worlds. If you can slow down and peer into this warp between wakefulness and sleep, it will open up into a whole universe of its own. Management of this warp can, ultimately, produce experiences on a par with anything that the Starship *Enterprise* warped its way into. In this warp you can enter into *conscious* dreaming, you can initiate apparent out-of-body states, and at the very least see an array of fantasia that you never suspected your brain-mind harbored. You will also start remembering your dreams more easily as a kind of by-product of this effort. But be prepared for a lot of trial and error; you will need patience and perseverance. All too often you will wake up hours later to find you missed the liminal moment of the warp. But your persistence will be richly rewarded: exploration of the hypnagogic (or hypnopompic) state is serious, practical consciousness-study. Masters of Tibetan dream yoga can pass into and out of sleep without ever losing consciousness. That is an ideal to aim for.

One of the best ways to start exploring this warp is to take a cat-nap during the day, for it is usually easier then to slip in and out of the sleep stage, allowing you more attempts at expanding the hypnagogic moment.

*Now that we have landed on Earth, have centered ourselves, and know our place, we are ready to start traveling. . . . The archaic whisper's talking 'bout an old way of walking—do you want to find your mind?*

# JOURNEYING

## Healthy Outdoor Exercise for the Soul

I T WAS ONE OF THOSE PERFECT, CRYSTAL-CLEAR spring mornings, and Gustav Fechner, the nineteenth-century German poet, physicist, and psychologist, just couldn't resist taking a walk in the country. As he wandered along, he became curiously entranced by the quality of the light; it somehow transfigured the world. A strange feeling grew within him. "It was only a little bit of Earth; it was only one moment of her existence," Fechner realized, "and yet as my look embraced her more and more it seemed to me not only so beautiful an idea, but so true and clear a fact, that she is an angel. . . . I asked myself how the options of men could ever have become so chrysaloid as to deem the Earth only a dry clod, and to seek for angels above or about it in the emptiness of the sky, and find them nowhere. But an experience such as this will be deemed fantastic."[1] Whether it is considered fantastic depends on the worldview of the culture in which such an experience occurs. As it happens, it would have been a perfectly acceptable observation in Mazdean Iran, for the *Avesta* refers to a liturgy in honor of "the Earth which is an Angel."

There are unique relationships with the Earth to be had, insights to be glimpsed, and moods to be experienced only when we are walking in special ways through the natural world. Walking is the rhythm in which the human being best relates to its environment. Running comes next, though even that tends to distract from the mental effects that relaxed walking—*sauntering*, as Thoreau insisted—can cultivate. Beyond that, land locomotion occurs at faster speeds, with horse and bicycle riding, and then becomes increasingly speedier, more technological, and more shut off from the environment—motorbikes, automobiles, trains. "By increasing the speed at which we pass through the landscape," warns geographer

Jay Appleton, ". . . [we] may greatly alter the time-sequences which are an integral part of our perceptive experience of it."[2] Though the deep mind-nature relationships and insights to which I refer cannot be obtained by speedy, let alone enclosed transportation, conscious walking can often provoke them more readily than can static locations.

This kind of special walking basically involves the act of carrying the center of one's being, the portable "here," along through nature, and breaks down into three essential forms. The first is simple walking, the emphasis being on *simple*—walking for its own sake, walking as a meditation. ". . . the walking of which I speak," Thoreau made clear in his "Walking" essay of 1862, "has nothing in it akin to taking exercise, as it is called. . . ." Nor is it utilitarian, to do with having to get from one place to another. The second type of walking is a development of simple walking, but is still not utilitarian in the mundane sense: it is the act of pilgrimage, primarily a foot journey to a sacred place. This, as I shall argue, is the classic liminal experience (see preceding chapter). Finally, there is that special type of walk, the vision quest, in the service of the soul. Let's look at all three a little more closely.

## TAKING THE SOUL FOR A WALK

Walking as an activity in its own right is considerably undervalued. It can be used as a tool for exploring our relationship with nature, with the Earth. To learn how walking can affect mind-states, hence worldview, we should listen to an expert, and what better expert than a vagrant? Philip O'Connor spent some of his life as a "wayfarer," and in his *Vagrancy* wrote remarkable accounts of his experiences, some of them touching upon the sort of visionary quality experienced by Fechner. The tramp, O'Connor contends, "drifts sensuously in the rhythm of walking" and enters "a sort of stuporous generalized existence, in which the ego progressively merges its sensible outlines into the environment." There is an "immense afflatus in the heart and soul towards evening, an incomparable feeling of being at home in the outside, as though one were a prayer winding along a road; the feeling is definitely religious, in that one feels blissfully at one with everyone and everything." (He adds pointedly that this feeling is helped if there is no one in sight!) O'Connor complains that the fascinating mental effects of walking can be likened to those of certain drugs, and have not been sufficiently researched. The prolonged act of "unproductive walking," walking that is not directed at exercise or destinations, produces cyclical alternations of thought, emotion, and sensation that are somehow linked. (This is, of course, the foundation for the apprehension of *chora* that we discussed in the preceding chapter.) He continues:

> At first the walker forms, like the wake of a liner, a train of associations typically attached to bodily sensations that must have some experiential connexion with them. . . . Once the flock of associations—gulls around the ship leaving harbour—have dropped off, more stable characteristics take over.
>
> The rhythm, eventually dominant over all perceptions, is poetic in its effects. All hard nodules of concepts are softly coaxed into disbursing their cherished contents. . . . Such dissolution of concepts induces euphoria of a kind augmented by practice. A thought may splutter up, but be drenched with emotion. . . . Maybe mental fireworks will gloriously light the mind—but quickly the world will attach the inner light to outer phenomena. . . . The speed of transit between inner state and outer appearance is a feature of tramping. . . . So one feel-thinks as a liquid fog contained in the vessel of the walking man, with sensitive frontiers, *until* the localized identity-sense is peaceably diffused into the landscape, which then becomes nebulous—colour-moods, but no lines. If lines there are, they become thoughts very quickly.[3]

O'Connor recalls an occasion when he walked past an uprooted tree by the roadside. "She has left me," he thought irrationally but mythically. He noted that a feeling of pressure at the back of the head accompanied "this perversion of thought, or insight of poetry." "When I rest, the front brain switches on, and I profoundly achieve the lie that 'a tree is a tree', etc. Superstition (an insight shrouded in a rationalizing folly) may be wiser than 'thought'. *Time* stops in such perceptions; a high sky, a statically spread landscape."[4] The tramp is mystical "by definition," O'Connor maintains.

It takes either heavy-duty walking of the kind O'Connor describes, or that rare happenstance of factors that gives the timeless mystical moment, as with Fechner, to produce these deep experiences of mind-nature relationships, but meditative walking can hurry the likelihood of such moments, and in the interim provides lesser but still informative and healing insights. G. Trevelyan, in his 1913 essay, "Walking," pronounced, "I have two doctors, my left leg and my right." The body's rhythmic action of walking, its natural pace and open contact with the environment it passes through, can help unravel mental knots. As the Latin tag has it, *solvitur ambulando*—"you can sort it out by walking." Theodore Roszak observes that psychiatrists are tied to cities by their careers and bank accounts, and that we have no psychiatry that calls for the specific use of nature as a healing agent, so most therapists are hardly able or likely to follow James Hillman's advice of prescribing nature. "Yet common experience," Roszak acknowledges, "tells us that a solitary walk by the river or ocean, a few calm hours in the woods restore the spirit and may produce more insight . . . than the best labors of the professional analyst."[5] The poet John Keats, who died so young, recollected in his last writings the healing joy of watching "intently Nature's gentle doings" while on country rambles, and remarked on a sense of "excited reverie" during such walks. Ralph Waldo Emerson famously reported in his *Nature* how, when crossing a snow-puddled common at twilight under a clouded sky with no particular thought in his head, he "enjoyed perfect exhilaration" and was "glad to the point of fear."

"The simplest way to explore Gaia is on foot," James Lovelock states flatly. "How else can you so easily be part of her ambience? How else can you reach out to her with all your senses?"[6]

Where enough people walk, paths will be worn. One of the glories of the English countryside is the number of old country paths that still survive, though their number diminishes every year. Kim Taplin has conducted a charming literary study of the subject in her *The English Path.* She suggests that, "because of their removedness from the human world and their closeness to nature, footpaths often induce that contemplative state which is the soil for visionary experience."[7] This may well be why pathways can themselves become shrines, as we saw in the preceding chapter with the pathway shrine in Russia's Kozmin Copse. Another example was a track called Yries in France, which was still being venerated with rags and old shoes as offerings as late as the seventeenth century, a pagan activity the church there finally stamped out, with difficulty. Walking a downland track in southern England, Richard Jeffries realized its origins went back into the "dimmest antiquity." A similar realization illuminated the Herefordshire antiquary, Alfred Watkins, when as a teenager he was following an old track through the Black Mountains in Wales. The track crossed a river, and as he splashed through the ford, the young Watkins saw something gleaming. Pulling the object out of the crystal water, he found it to be a Roman coin. Watkins was overwhelmed with the thought that perhaps a Roman centurion had walked this same route nearly two thousand years earlier. Indeed, there are tracks in Britain that were first worn by the feet of Neolithic travelers, thousands of years B.C., and medieval tracks are almost commonplace. In many ways, these rural footpaths are like time lines running through the landscape, and the act of walking them can trigger a sense of transpersonal memory. This, combined with what Edmund Blunden called the "sounds, scents and seeings" to be had along the path, provides a heady brew of conditions affecting the walker's perceptions and sensibilities. Such old paths are therefore expressive space in linear form, and can be used as tools in triggering unfamiliar perceptions of the environment and insights into mind-nature relationships.

The complexity of this expressive linear space is well explored in Bobi Jones' long poem, "Small Paths."[8] The paths "express the land and tell where / There's declivity and rise" and they define "The silence that's in the soil." By moving along them, "a civilized man smells the earth and enjoys / Recognizing its depth." There is a reference to the "secret walkers," those who had trod and therefore shaped the path before the present traveler. (This is that "transpersonal memory" I refer to above—a curious sense of companionship with previous users of the path, even those of remote antiquity, that the sensitive walker picks up.) The use of the paths gives the time "to teach the pupils of the eyes" about the wonder and detail of nature all around. And even if one follows the path on other occasions, it is different each time: "It isn't the same shout you hear across the hedge / Calling the cattle; it isn't the same breeze. . . ." Expressive space is meaningful space, and Bobi Jones tells us that the old pathways "write their meanings" on the land; unlike modern automobile highways, they do so quietly and in a different, deeper way—"before they had length / They had worth."

There is no more direct way of allowing the Earth to heal us than to use such footpaths; because of the expressiveness inherent within them, they can often provide a more powerful and focused effect than can wandering free across the land.

But not only are the numbers of these pathways declining in Britain; where they still exist, many are fading from the memories of people local to them, as Satish Kumar discovered during a personal walking pilgrimage to a selection of ancient sites around Britain—a journey that took him over two and a half months to complete—and reported in his autobiography, *No Destination*. He was nevertheless impressed with the number of long- and short-distance paths that still manage to survive in the countryside. "On these rural paths I met the trees, animals, rocks, rivers and birds, and realized the sacredness of all Nature," he recalls. "The churches, cathedrals, mosques and synagogues, shrines and temples are not the only holy places. . . ."[9] Kumar, a former Jain monk and now editor of the ecological journal *Resurgence*, first left India in 1962 on an eight-thousand-mile peace pilgrimage to the capitals of the four nuclear nations, Russia, France, Britain, and the United States. Apart from the crossings of the English Channel and the Atlantic, he traveled entirely on foot and without any money or logistic support across mountains and deserts to and through Russia, across Europe, and finally to America. Satish Kumar knows about walking.

To him, walking is a yoga, and this might be more than mere metaphor: the physiological effects of walking long distances, sometimes with little food, surrounded by the vistas of rural landscapes and deep wilderness, must have effects that prime the mind for shifting states. "Walking in itself was an end, a form of meditation, a way of being," he states. The outer journey became "a trigger for the inner journey."

There are old—pre-Columbian—pathways and "roads" in the Americas, too, but they are very little known about, and where surviving at all are disappearing rapidly. As different as can be imagined from the verdant, rural English footpaths, they are quite often to be found in wild mountainous or arid desert areas. Probably the most famous of these Indian "roads" are the straight line markings on the pampas above Nazca, Peru. What is not well known about these "Nazca lines," however, is that some of them contain well-worn, apparently prehistoric footpaths wandering along inside their precise, geometric outlines.[10] These paths don't seem to be going to or from anywhere. And perhaps they are not, as far as this world is concerned—we are looking at otherworldly paths relating to a profoundly altered state of walking, as we shall discuss in chapter five. There are many more sets of these curious straight tracks or roads in the Americas, such as the extraordinary features that radiate out across the desert for tens of miles from Chaco Canyon, a thousand-year-old cult center of the lost Anasazi people, in New Mexico. The Anasazi, "the Ancient Ones," had neither horses nor wheeled vehicles, yet they built thirty-foot-wide, mainly dead-straight roads. These were engineered features, not mere tracks. No one knows what they were for, especially since some run in parallel sections, making no rational sense to the modern investigator. They are hardly visible now, and it needs special lighting or seasonal conditions to reveal their presence visually at ground level, but dedicated, close observation to minor cues can reveal the course of an old road. To follow one of these is to feel an awesome sense of the power of the dauntingly vast and arid surroundings, a sensation all the more unsettling because the nature of the roads is not understood. They are expressive of something almost unutterably deep and alien. The Kogi Indians of northern Colombia also have ancient straight roads in their remote mountain vastness. These people, who of all Native Americans best preserve pre-Colombian traits, intensively walk these archaic tracks because they say that the Earth Mother told them long ago that they must always walk her surface. But we will return to these features later, and find that they are probably "mind lines" that are the product of a deeply different worldview and hence state of consciousness.

## PILGRIMAGE: WALKING THROUGH A HOLY LAND

During his British pilgrimage, Satish Kumar traveled for a while on the Pilgrims' Way to Canterbury. He had a flash of transpersonal memory that made him feel that "I was in the company of those people who had preceded me" on that medieval pilgrimage route. Pilgrimage is one of the hallmarks of religious devotion, cleansing, and healing in most of the great religions. Traditional foot pilgrimage is walking in the sacred sense, but with various ulterior motives. Essentially, the aim of a pilgrimage was, and is, to visit a specific shrine or sacred complex important to the religious life of the pilgrim, but apart from its being simply an act of devotion, the pilgrimage might also be undertaken to gain spiritual credit in the hereafter, to expiate sins, to seek healing, to be offered for the repose of dead relatives, not to mention baser motives such as pleading for greater prosperity and good luck. A strong underlying motive could also be the opportunity to "get away from it all." At its best, pilgrimage expressed "the human quest for a divine connection between man and the environment," as geographer and pilgrimage scholar Rana P. B. Singh has put it.[11] But the structure of pilgrimages was much more complex than just going to a shrine. There would be sacred sites en route, there would be the arduous act of traveling, often to remote and strange locations. And *the act of pilgrimage was liminal,* in that the pilgrim left his or her normal life and headed out for the sacred place, and while on the pilgrimage was neither here nor there. Because they were outside the normal social structure, pilgrims could strike up friendships with one another across social class, and a sense of comradeship, Turner's *com-*

*munitas*, was as much a feature of pilgrimage as it was of initiation. A pilgrimage could take days, weeks, months, even years, and would in many cases be the peak experience of a person's life, dreamed about, waited for, saved up for—a great "holiday of the soul," to use Satish Kumar's phrase. The thrust of perception and expectation was different from that in mundane life; the marvelous, the magical, and the spiritual were in the forefront of the traveler's mind. The set and setting of consciousness were therefore distinctly different for the lay person on a pilgrimage compared with his or her mind-state in everyday life. Pilgrimage was a physical act that moved the person out of the normal cultural domain and into nature, out of the routine levels of consciousness to conditions that exposed the mind to the possibility of sensibilities beyond the pale of civilized life, where mythic memory and visionary experience could be provoked.

The Pilgrim's Path along the spine of Glastonbury Tor.

The sacred places that formed the destinations of pilgrimage journeys had to be able "to absorb varieties of interpretation . . . capable of accommodating diverse meanings and practices."[12] "Why is it that exactly this place—Ephesus, or Lourdes, or Guadalupe—over countless centuries and through vicissitudes of religious form, retains its special qualities and its power to draw crowds?" Eugene Walter has wondered.[13] He marvels that "some sacred places never lose energy," drawing people even long after the religions that gave rise to them have long since disappeared from human knowledge. He further muses:

> In perennially sacred places—the sanctuary of Delphi in Greece, the base of Ayer's Rock in Australia, the Acropolis, Chartres, the top of Glastonbury Tor as well as Stonehenge in England—certain forces in the invisible world of spirit establish a location in the physical world of the senses. The religious program of sacred place engages or disengages the senses, edifies the mind, and leads the soul back to the world of spirit. . . . Any sacred place is a specific environment of phenomena that are expected to support the imagination, nourish religious experience, and convey religious truth. It organizes sight and sound, introduces light to present clarity and order, or makes things dark to suggest unseen presences and hidden power.[14]

The only way truly to appreciate the similarities and differences among pilgrimages is to look, even if briefly, at a representative range of examples worldwide.

I will start us off in Ireland, if only because that was where the liminal nature of pilgrimage destinations was first impressed upon me. I was driving with two companions one summer evening at dusk along the inland roads of Galway and Mayo. We were becoming slightly anxious, because we needed somewhere to stay for the night and there were no habitations in sight. The sky was overcast, with just a rim of soft orange light ahead of us to the northwest, where the sun had set. There was a strange, almost eerie light bathing the moody landscape all around. Turning a bend, we obtained a wider view of the sunset skyline, and we all gasped simultaneously. Far away across the plains of Mayo, silhouetted against

the late sunset glow, was a huge, solitary pyramid. It was clearly artificial, for it was so perfect in outline and symmetry, and yet it had
to be thousands of feet high! Was it some kind of optical illusion?
We all sought in vain for answers and really couldn't understand
what it was we were looking at. Some miles farther on we came
across a lone farmstead that let rooms for the night. Before entering, I asked the farmer's wife just what that mesmerizing object was
on the horizon. "Why—that's Croagh Patrick!" she said laughing. I
was stunned. I hadn't known quite where this famous sacred Irish
mountain was located, but I knew about the pilgrimage that centered on the peak every late July or early August, when sixty thousand people, some in bare feet, climb the mountain to the chapel
on the summit. Though now a Catholic pilgrimage, its origins must
lie in a pagan past. This is indicated by the date, Lughnasa, and the
fact that until the mid-nineteenth century only women were allowed to the summit during the pilgrimage. Childless women
would sleep on the summit during Lughnasa eve in the hope of encouraging fertility. Another indication is the legend of the mountain, which says that St. Patrick spent the forty days of Lent fasting
and praying there in 441 A.D., banishing the pagan spirits from the
place, as symbolized in the saint's removal of all the serpents in Ireland (it is a fact that there are no snakes in Ireland). All this I knew,
but nothing I had read had ever mentioned that this stunning
mountain was perfectly pyramidical when viewed from the east.
Now I knew why it must always have been a holy mountain, from
whenever human beings inhabited the region; the Christianizing of
the pilgrimage was undoubtedly a relatively recent gloss. Rising up
beyond any surrounding peaks, the perfection of Croagh Patrick
had seemed to us twilight travelers like some fabulous Cosmic
Mountain rising out of the golden light of the Blessed Lands of the
west. We had involuntarily experienced the mythic power of the
place, a power that had stirred human hearts down untold generations. The mountain rises dramatically from sea level on the shore
of Clew Bay close to Westport. "The power that draws us toward it
from the distant plains of Mayo is loric; we want to 'be there', to
participate in the transcendence afforded by its ascent. . . . We are
alone at Croagh Patrick, at the very westernmost edge of the world,

in a liminal position held there by the invitation to transcendence," writes scholar Walter L. Brenneman, movingly and accurately.[15]

Another current pilgrimage in Ireland is to St. Patrick's Purgatory at Lough Derg, in southeastern Donegal. Brenneman sees this also as powerfully liminal, though in a quite different manner from Croagh Patrick. He notes how the rust-colored waters of the lough are approached across "the emptiness, vastness and mystery of the bogland." The basilica on Station Island in the lough looks like "a castle in another world materializing out of the mists," and he recalls that the island in the lake is one of the mythic images of the Celtic otherworld. First documented in the twelfth century, the Lough Derg pilgrimage was famous throughout Europe, doubtless fulfilling "a dream that somewhere in the far western region of the world the impossible becomes possible."[16] Nowadays, it is little known outside of Ireland. In today's version of the pilgrimage, the pilgrim is ferried across to Station Island and there takes part in a three-day ritual. The pilgrim goes barefoot, drinks only tea or coffee, eats oatbread once a day, makes an all-night vigil in the church, and recites specific patterns of prayers around the so-called beds (low-walled circles of stone) of various saints while facing the water of the lough and standing or kneeling at various points. This is a much-reduced version of the original practice, which lasted nine days, after many days of preparation. The modern vigil in the church replaces what had been the core of the old pilgrimage—namely, entering a cave or pit which legend says had been revealed to St. Patrick. This was closed centuries ago, and descriptions of it vary; medieval accounts of those who spent time in the "purgatory" cave describe powerful visionary experiences in which both heaven and hell were glimpsed—demons, fantastic landscapes and buildings, nightmarish horrors, and terrifying journeys.[17] Though these are couched in Christian terminology, and may be somewhat embroidered, it is highly likely that they do essentially record altered states of consciousness caused by fasting, physical and mental stress, sensory deprivation, and lack of sleep. The pilgrimage seems to have grown up around an anchorite tradition at the lough, and it is thought that the "saints' beds" might be the remains of beehive huts used by the holy hermits. This tradition may in turn have supplanted an ancient pagan cult at the place, suggested by prehistoric monuments in the area, indicative place-names, and archaic chair-like rocks that are now named for saints (Brigit being one of them). It is even possible that the purgatory cave was in fact a prehistoric souterrain (underground chamber).[18]

Despite the almost certain great antiquity of both these pilgrimages, there is no actual documentation or currently confirmed archeological remains associated with either of them older than the twelfth century. Nevertheless, the tradition of the *turus*, the journey or pilgrimage, is archaic beyond reckoning in Ireland. Archeologists have been uncovering physical evidence of a very early Christian pilgrimage centered on the holy Brandon Mountain, near the end of the Dingle Peninsula, one of the five fingers of land that poke out into the Atlantic from southwestern Ireland.[19] So it, too, is a typically liminal place, at the edge of the ancient world. This pilgrimage was also almost certainly based on earlier pagan practice, for Brandon Mountain seems to have been sacred to Lug, the god of light to the pagan Celts, and was a site used for Lughnasa harvest festivities. Parts of a path known as The Saint's Road lead up towards the peak from the southern coast of the peninsula, and are one of two pilgrimage routes ascending the mountain. On the way are features that give an insight into aspects of the pilgrimage. These include occasional stone pillars and natural rocks carved with leaflike crosses and archaic ogham script. One of these scripts says simply, "Colman the pilgrim." Next to the marked boulders are small hollowed-out stones known as *bullauns*. The water that collected in them would have been considered holy, and passing pilgrims would have collected it for healing purposes.[20] Also on The Saint's Road is the now ruined twelfth-century church at Kilmalkedar, on the grounds of which is a stone carved with markings that have been interpreted as a sundial for telling pilgrims the hours of the day for their prayers. At this site there is also an oratory, a most ancient design of cell or religious refuge in the shape of an upturned boat, made of drystone construction. A similar but better-preserved feature, the remarkable Gallarus oratory, is set a short distance off The Saint's Road, farther along, at the precise point where the summit of Brandon Mountain is visible rising over an intervening ridge. This serves to emphasize that the geography surrounding the pilgrim was carefully planned to be full of meaning.

One of the most famous and important of European pilgrimages was and is that to St. James at Santiago de Compostela, in northwestern Spain. Here again is a site situated in a liminal position at a western extremity of the known Old World, emphasized by its proximity to Cape Finisterre—literally "land's end." When the pilgrimage began, in the ninth century, the location was on the borders of the world map. All roads led to Puenta La Reina, the starting point of El Camino de Santiago, the pilgrims' road, which cuts east-west across northern Spain. At the height of the pilgrimage's popularity, multitudes were drawn to Santiago de Compostela because of the claims of miracles associated with the relics of St. James, which were lodged there. The relics had been unearthed by a farmer who had seen a "field of stars" over a burial ground. Places where religious personages had been born or died, monasteries and convents, caves used by anchorites, and sites of miracles and wonders all developed into shrines along the pilgrims' road.

At the other extremity of the Eurasian landmass, a key pilgrimage destination from the fourth century in China was Wutaishan, one of the four sacred Chinese mountains, famous for its many temples, monasteries, caves, and shrines. It was associated with Wenshu (Manjushri), the bodhisattva of wisdom. The five-peaked mountain—a massif covering one hundred square miles—attracted pilgrims as a place of miraculous happenings. Even in quite modern times, strange light phenomena have been witnessed there,[21,22] and there are caves exhibiting bizarre curiosities such as shallow pools of water that can never be emptied despite having apparently no water source issuing into them. It was thought to be profoundly beneficial to go to Wutaishan: one would find the truth about oneself, and at that place alone did one stand a chance of seeing the bodhisattva. Stories of the experiences of early pilgrims abound. One relates to Wu Zhuo, a keen monk of the eighth century who had already achieved the "dharma eye" and had sought final enlightenment in springs and woods without success. He came to Wutaishan in desperation. While Wu Zhuo was in meditation one day, one of Wutaishan's mysterious lights wandered down from the heights and touched his head, making him feel cool, clear, and filled with happiness. The next day he set off in the direction from where the light had come, and encountered an old man leading an ox, who turned out to be Wenshu himself. But despite this exalted meeting, the keen monk didn't attain his full enlightenment, and remained at Wutaishan. In reality, many pilgrims never left the mountain, staying to have the visions and dreams that the place is said to encourage.

Mountains are a prime type of pilgrimage destination, and in Japan mountain pilgrimage was one of the first kinds to emerge out of the fusion of indigenous Shinto and folk religious beliefs with the incoming Chinese influences of Taoism and Buddhism. From the very earliest times in Japan, there was the tradition of the *gyo-ja*, austerity man, who was thought able to attain superhuman abilities by ascetic practice in the mountains. In the eighth century, Buddhism developed the "Nature Wisdom School," which sought enlightenment by being close to nature in the mountains. The indigenous shamans and healers who had developed their powers by mountain asceticism became loosely associated with this, and there emerged Shugen-do, the Order of Mountain Ascetics. The Shinto *kami*, or spirits of the mountains, were subtly transformed into manifestations of Buddhist divinities, and during the eleventh and twelfth centuries pilgrims flocked to the mountains, led by experienced mountain ascetics, to seek favor from the divinities there. This continued throughout the centuries, and by the end of the nineteenth century it was estimated that there were seventeen thousand "senior guides" to sacred mountains, which gives some idea of the vast numbers of pilgrims themselves.[23] Two other types of pilgrimage developed in Japan—pilgrimage to temples and shrines, based on faith in the divinities associated with them, and pilgrimage to places believed to have been hallowed by the visits of holy men.

We saw in chapter one that Mount Kailas, in the Himalayas, was a Cosmic Mountain, and sacred to Buddhists. Even to this day, a Tibetan pilgrim will encircle the base of this exceedingly remote peak in devotional fashion, using a most severe form of pilgrimage technique. From a standing position with hands held together in prayer, he kneels, bows down, then lies on the ground, touching it with his forehead. He marks a spot with his nose, rises again, and walks to that spot, then repeats the whole cycle. And so pilgrims proceed over the Himalayan terrain, in profound humility and literal closeness to the Earth.

Mount Kailas is also meaningful to the Hindus—to them it is the physical embodiment of the mythic Mount Meru. Hinduism has a great tradition of pilgrimage, and India can offer a huge number of examples: about 150 holy places in the subcontinent draw about twenty million people every year.[24] Varanasi (Benares), the ultimate sacred city of Hindu pilgrimage, has fifty-six pilgrimage circuits, of which five are the most popular and trace a sacred design or cosmogram on the landscape.[25] The circuits interlink a variety of temples and shrines. Some of these are sun shrines, *adityas*, and Rana P. B. Singh has discovered that these form alignments to sunrise positions on calendric or symbolic days in the year.[26] The pilgrims thus trace out a cosmically significant pattern during their devotional visiting of the temples, and it is most telling that the word for a cosmogram, *kashi*, was also the ancient name for the city territory of Varanasi. Singh calls such symbolic geography, strongly associated with pilgrimage centers in India, "faithscapes." A pilgrimage complex in India is called *ksetra*, meaning the concentration of cosmic influence in the topography. Braj, a *ksetra* in Uttar Pradesh, is a zone containing the River Yamuna, desert and hill country, and the ancient city of Mathura, where myth relates that the incarnated god Krishna was born and to which he returned. During the pilgrimage circuit at Braj, devotees experience the sanctity of the landscape as expressed through place symbolism associated with the life of the young Lord Krishna as he grew up in the region. In various places he demonstrated his divinity by subduing demons, other locations were where Krishna had amorous dalliances with cowherdesses, and so on. Since medieval times, oral tradition in India has yielded a form of dance-drama, *ras lila*, and at Braj elements of the Krishna mythology are imprinted on the landscape by such performances at the spots where the legendary events were said to have happened. "This occurs annually during monsoons when pilgrimage to Braj is most frequently undertaken," reports Amita Sinha. "For the witnessing pilgrim who is visiting the holy spots, the landscape thus comes alive."[27] The purpose of this particular pilgrimage is nothing less than for the pilgrim to experience transcendence through immersion in the Krishna mythos in the here and now. Sinha claims that a true altered state of consciousness is aimed for, and "probably occurs as a result of the combination of personal faith of the devotee and the powerful charge that the environment of the sacred place produces."

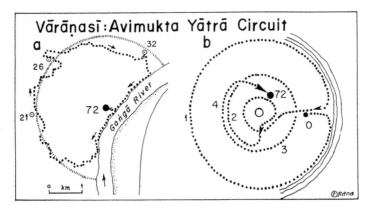

One of the Varanasi pilgrimage circuits. This relates to a zone said never to have been forsaken by Shiva, and is called Avimukta. (a) The edges of this mythic territory are marked by three mound shrines. The focus of the territory is the shrine of Avimukteshvara, 72. (b) The final approach to Avimukteshvara is by a spiral processional route. [After Rana P. B. Singh, 1993, p. 195.]

Something similar was aimed at in the Christian tradition of pilgrimage to Jerusalem during the period of Christian authority there, between 325 and 638 A.D. Although the Persians destroyed much of Christian Jerusalem in 614, until that point churches were continually being added to the sacred cityscape. Scholar Wendy Pullan has argued that the Christians were imaging in the physical Jerusalem the lineaments of the mythic celestial city, the Heavenly Jerusalem.[28] The place became liminal, a sort of Christian warp between revelatory image and physical reality. Such representation at Jerusalem involved no fewer than 326 churches plus three Constantine basilicas—the Church of the Nativity in nearby Bethlehem,

the Eleona Church on the Mount of Olives, where Jesus taught the
Mysteries to his disciples, and the Church of the Holy Sepulchre on
the Hill of Golgotha in central Jerusalem, the site of the crucifixion
and resurrection. This produced a spiritual geography, and the various sites were conceptually linked together in the form of the
Jerusalem Liturgy, developed by Cyril, the Bishop of Jerusalem between 349 and 386. This involved movement from one church to
another, with scriptural readings and prayers relating to the significance of each site recited at that place at the appropriate time of day,
week, or year. At Easter, for example, all the places involved in the
events of the Last Supper, Jesus' arrest, the interview with Pilate, the
scourging, and final Passion were linked in sequence by processions. Pullan describes how people would have thronged the
streets, the city being filled with songs and lamentations amidst the
flicker of candlelight and the smell of incense. Most pilgrims spent
far longer than one day traversing the sacred course through the
city, and some stayed years in order to experience the Liturgy fully.
Pullan points out that the symbolic geography of early Christian
Jerusalem was centered on Golgotha, which is linked by processional routes to many other sacred sites. She also stresses the delicate balance between mental and physical pilgrimage. A good
example of a mental pilgrimage is given by Sophronius, the Bishop
of Jerusalem in the early seventh century who composed poems
while in exile about walking through Jerusalem; it was a *pilgrimage
in memory*, therefore, a pilgrimage conducted in *chora* without *topos*.
But the delicate balance to which Pullan refers was exhibited by the
physical pilgrims. They saw and touched the places where they believed Christ had been present, picturing Jesus in the physical location. Sometimes this was stronger than just imagining: for instance,
St. Paula, who came from Rome, saw visions of Christ at the appropriate locations, so her contemporaries reported; Helena, mother of
Constantine, had a vision on Golgotha which revealed where the
cross of the crucifixion had been buried, which she authenticated
by raising a dead person there by her touch.

Mountain pilgrimages in the Holy Land were also conducted
during this period. Mount Sinai, the Horeb of Biblical record where
Moses saw the burning bush and received the tablets of the law, was

the focus of pilgrimage from at least 380 A.D., reaching a climax in the sixth century, when the entire topography of the area was peppered with hermits' cells and marked sacred or significant spots where the pilgrim might pause to pray. This pilgrimage site, with the (still-thriving) monastery of St. Catherine at its center, became a form of theology "fixed in space," say anthropologists Simon Coleman and John Elsner.[29] Pilgrims moved from one sacred site to another, "tracing a biblical narrative through the landscape." They visited mythologized places such as the rock where Moses struck water, the site of the burning bush, the spring where Moses watered sheep, the cave where Elijah fled from King Ahab, and the peak of Mount Sinai itself, where a small church marked the spot on which Moses received the Tablets of the Law. A series of prayer niches was built along the pilgrimage route up the mountain. "These marked significant spots," Coleman and Elsner state, "either places where the path joined another path, or places where pilgrims might glimpse a view of the distant peak (their goal)." The pilgrims carried out various activities on their movement through the sacred landscape, such as hymn-singing, praying, weeping, cross-carrying, and pious acts like hair-cutting.

Probably the most famous Middle Eastern pilgrimage is the *hajj,* Islam's great pilgrimage to Mecca. This has a central role in Muslim life, being included as one of the five pillars of faith. It is required that each Muslim make at least one pilgrimage to Mecca unless prevented by ill health or lack of funds. Mecca, the birthplace of the Prophet Mohammed, to which he returned and where he later died, is the key direction in the compass of faith for Muslims. Prayer has to be directed towards Mecca wherever one is situated, and this sacred direction, the *qibla,* also governs the orientation of mosques. The term *hajj* derives from an ancient Semitic custom and was used to describe a journey to a sacred place.

Fragments of evidence indicate that pilgrimage also occurred in the New World. Mount Tlaloc, for instance, was the center of an annual pilgrimage made by the Aztec kings of Tenochtitlán, Tetzcoco, Tlacopán, and Xochimilco. It took place in April or May, at the height of the dry season, and its purpose was to call forth rain from within the mountain. The richly attired kings proceeded in procession up the high-walled processional route leading to the temple precinct on the summit of the mountain, bearing gifts to the gods. Although empty now, the temple had stone idols in it, and these were dressed by the kings. Sacrificial offerings were made to these representations of the mountain gods, including fabulous dishes of food and the blood of a male child. The kings were perceived as active agents performing an essential part in the changing of the seasons. The Inca, too, had a range of pilgrimages, some associated with the mysterious *ceque* alignments that radiated out from the Coricancha, the Temple of the Sun, at Cuzco. These lines of sacred places, or *huacas*, seem to have served a number of functions to do with the ceremonial calendar, water sources, ancestor worship, sun watching, and ceremonial processions and pilgrimages. One such pilgrimage moved in a straight line from the sacred mountain of Huanacauri along a *ceque* passing through twenty-one sacred places to the village of Vilcanota, meaning "sun house." This particular *ceque* aligns to the midwinter sunrise position, and also points to the Island of the Sun in Lake Titicaca, over 150 miles farther on. Lake Titicaca was the birthplace of the sun, and the place from where the Inca believed they originated. Could the pilgrimage have extended that far? Some researchers find that the evidence hints it may have.[30]

Certain pilgrimages in various parts of the world were not for religious observance and devotion in the sense that we would readily recognize such practice today; rather, direct spiritual experience was the destination of the journey. In Greece, the Mysteries were centered on the initiatory temple of Eleusis, and were a ten-day affair in September each year. The climax was the pilgrimage from Athens to the temple at Eleusis for the Mystery Night, the revelation of the Mysteries themselves. The Mystai, the initiatory candidates, would proceed in joyful fashion along the Sacred Way linking Athens with Eleusis, stopping to make observances at various shrines along the route. The pilgrimage took all day, and the Mystai arrived at the temple by nightfall. No one knows what went on there, but the candidates certainly experienced a series of initiatory trials, and may have been given a hallucinogenic drink, before entering the huge

Telesterion, a curiously plain building where the revelation, the *epopteia*, took place. A similar example in the New World is the pilgrimage of the Huichol Indians in northern Mexico. For unknown generations, the Huichol have made an annual pilgrimage of several hundred miles from their mountain homeland to a high plateau region called Wirikuta, considered their sacred land of origin. They are led by a shaman-priest, the *mara'akame*. The journey takes some weeks, for it is highly ritualized: the Indians are mythically retracing the steps of the First Huichol, and they perform various actions attributed to those mythic ancestors at specific locations. "They rejoice, grieve, celebrate and mourn appropriately as the journey progresses," anthropologist Barbara Myerhoff writes.[31] *Primeros*, those making the pilgrimage for the first time, have their eyes covered on arriving at the edge of Wirikuta, the holy land, and the blindfold is removed only after proper ritual preparation. At Wirikuta, a hunt for and ritual consumption of the hallucinogenic peyote cactus takes place. This is the climax of the pilgrimage and the peak experience in the religious life of the Huichol. The pilgrim enters in on the inner journey to the paradisal realms of the mind and spirit. What the pilgrim sees and hears is not spoken about; it is for the individual alone, much as was the case in the Mystery tradition of Eleusis.

It is apparent from even this brief survey that huge numbers of people around the world were walking the land in the past, in a way few members of modern Western society experience. The landscape was rendered meaningful with mythic presences and events, and the pilgrimage routes provided vistas of such landscapes for people in liminal condition, outside their normal social structures and often in psychological and physiological states that laid the groundwork for visionary insight. Perhaps we need to teach ourselves how to journey like this again, even if we strip the process of specific religious contexts and just preserve the spiritual and psychological core of the matter.

As the Koran states, "And proclaim unto mankind the Pilgrimage. . . . That they witness things that are of benefit to them . . ." (Surah 22:27–28).

## VISION QUESTING

The "vision quest" involves solitary journeying in the wilderness in search of a guiding vision or meaningful dreams. Before there were religions in their names, Buddha, Christ, and the Prophet Mohammed all reportedly retreated into nature alone to achieve their definitive spiritual orientation. But we know mostly about the process of the vision quest from the archaic practices of Native Americans and Paleo-Siberian tribes. In a typical, traditional vision quest, the individual, around the time of puberty, journeys alone into the wilderness, perhaps to some special, sacred vision-questing site known to the tribe, and there fasts, prays, and goes without sleep for three or four days and nights. During this time, a vision—perhaps in the form of an animal that speaks to the visionary—or a set of visionary waking dreams may be experienced, which can give direction to the person's life. Such visions contain great medicine-power, which can be embodied in the medicine-bundle, the packet of natural objects—feathers, stones, etc.—the person finds meaningful and collects during the vision-questing period. The traditional vision quest is the celebration of the liminal: its wilderness location, its rite-of-passage status, and the state of consciousness involved. The vision quest is the central foundation of all Native American spirituality, originating in a remote period of prehistory.[32,33]

As with pilgrimage, mountains can often be focus locations for vision questing. An example is Ninaistákis, the Chief Mountain, sacred to the Blackfoot people (the Nitsitapii), in the Rocky Mountains, on the border between the Blackfoot reservation and Glacier National Park, Montana. The mountain dominates the landscape, standing just away from the main mountain mass. From one angle, Canadian archeologist Brian Reeves notes,[34] it does indeed look like a capped hat on a chief's topknot, while from another view it looks like a traditional upright headdress or bonnet. When the wind blows the mountain sings, and at sunrise and sunset it shines out and is visible for over one hundred miles in many directions. It is a mythologized place, for Blackfoot legend tells of a young chief who was killed in battle, causing his grief-stricken wife to climb the mountain with her baby in her arms and throw herself off. It is said that if one looks carefully at the face of the mountain the figure of a woman with a babe in arms can be discerned. Legend also has it that the oldest of the medicine pipes ("the Long-Time Pipe") was "visioned" here and given to the Blackfoot people by Thunderbird, the great spirit of the mountain. Ninaistákis is said to be a place of great spiritual power where exceptionally significant visions can be had, and it was and is a place of traditional Blackfoot spiritual activity. High on its ridges and buttresses, and on those of surrounding mountains, both ancient and modern vision-questing sites are to be found. These take the form of small enclosures of rocks, just big enough to sit or lie in, mounds or cairns of rocks, or platforms of flat stones. These sites are sometimes known as dream beds or prayer platforms, and are only to be found in locations from where the peaks of Ninaistákis or another sacred mountain, Sweet Pine Hills, are visible. Vision-questing structures oriented on Ninaistákis have been discovered up to fifty miles from the mountain and in spots up to ten thousand feet high. A person seeking to fast and pray for visions on Ninaistákis would often take a buffalo skull along to use as a pillow, and climbers have found several remains of these over the years, some of them of enormous antiquity.

Unfortunately, Ninaistákis is threatened by tourism, forestry, gas exploration, and other depredations of civilization. In July 1992, an earthquake shook the mountain, and this combined with heavy rains to cause a major rockfall and mudslide on the north face, the largest example of natural damage on the mountain in a thousand years. Blackfoot Elders view this with concern, feeling that it results from inappropriate activities on the sacred mountain.

Non–Native American forms of vision questing, "wilderness psychology," have become popular in recent years. Steven Foster and Meredith Little are amongst the pioneers in developing wilderness rites of passage for Westerners, and are the founders and directors of the School of Lost Borders in California. Foster tells his own story in *Vision Quest* (with Meredith Little). He pays homage to other pioneers who helped him find his way to leading others towards wilderness healing, and describes his own early, involuntary experiences in the desert, when his life seemed to be collapsing around him. He recalls "the awesome trumpet sound of the loneliness of the wilderness—the sound of *silence.*"[35] Like the pilgrims to Wu-taishan, he marveled at—and was a little afraid of—strange lights moving on the desert horizon. He learned that nature would speak to him only when he silenced his inner dialogue, and he saw "many powerful teachings" when his eyes were not governed by his pre-conceptions. He never had a vision in the true sense during that initial journey into the wilderness, but when he came back from it he nevertheless felt profoundly different, and he had made that critical realization that is emphasized time and again in these pages, that the outer and inner journeys are deeply and mysteriously interactive. Foster and Little go on to describe the details and experiences of modern-day vision questing. In the wilderness experience, nature can bestow teachings, moods, and symbols on the quester. The wilderness invades the body. It lets the quester's noise finally run down, disperse, until silent running takes hold. The authors stress the liminal nature of the experience, and point out that it is not necessary to learn as such while on a vision quest but, more accurately, simply to receive. And they add important practical points: a vision quester needs to be proficient in basic survival skills; an instructor, a "midwife" to help the crossing of the threshold, is required; and when one is actually out in the wilderness there needs to be an organized way of contacting support if needed—the "buddy system" in one form or another. As time for a quest draws near, the would-be initiate may become fearful, as if facing death. If these fears gain the upper hand, the quest has to be aborted. A vision quest is not to be undertaken casually or lightly. Preparation in wilderness walking and fasting has to be undertaken. Regarding any ceremonial activity while on a vision quest, Foster and Little point out that, once the quester is alone in wild nature, almost all actions have a mythic, ceremonial cast to him or her, and the practice of contrived cere-monies can interfere with or mask the actual, raw experience that is taking place. One's field of view enlarges both physically and metaphorically as time and space dilate beyond the pale of civiliza-tion. The best way to get to know the country is to go on foot, listen to nature all around, and "dream the dreams of the night wind."

These "dreams of the threshold" can sometimes have great clarity, and offer a name, a story, or a mission, Foster and Little inform. And, they add, quite often in these wilderness conditions dreams occur when the quester's eyes are open. This, surely, is something we should be getting used to by now in these pages. The vision quester comes to inhabit the chorography of wilderness more than its geography.

We need contact with wild nature in order to learn how to apprehend it and how to relate to it. We need to know wild nature, because we also are a product of nature and have that same essential wildness within us. Our unconscious mind is wild nature. We enter wild nature when we dream. And we all have to wander into wild nature alone at death—the ultimate vision quest. That is why, in ecological and cultural terms, if we exclude the experience of wild nature we shall lose the skills we need to relate to it and to understand it. We will become exiles from nature, in both its outer and inner forms—*and these are reciprocal*, one patterning the other.

## EXPERIENTIAL

### Learning to Walk

Let's go for a walk. What matters is not so much where as how. If you did the earlier "Drawing the Circle" activity (chapter one), then set off as close as is possible in your good-feeling direction, just as Thoreau did on his walks. On this occasion, it doesn't matter whether your walk is in the town, the local park, or the countryside, but it would be best to try to incorporate a range of environments. Arrange to go in a circuit of some kind, at least three miles in length, so you arrive back at your start and have no element of wanting to get somewhere in particular. Don't set out until you have time to walk it in a relaxed manner (no jogging; no "exercise" as such), and walk it alone.

Walk at an easy pace—Thoreau's "saunter." If the first part of your walk is familiar territory, make a point of noticing what you haven't previously, perhaps because you normally flash by in a car, or your eyes are fixed and you are preoccupied when you normally walk this route. I recall that for a two-year period I walked about a half-mile from a bus stop to my place of work. After about eighteen months, for no particular reason, I glanced upwards towards the rooftops, and I realized with some shock that I hadn't previously noticed anything on the walk that was higher than the ground floor of the houses and shops I passed by. My vision had been fixed at the horizontal, or even cast down to the sidewalk. From that day on, I experienced what was effectively a different walk, glancing up quite regularly, noticing the variety of apartment windows above the shops, the decoration of gable ends, the different design of buildings, birds, treetops, clouds, and so on. It is amazing what we miss, even on a route we travel regularly. On this walk, seek out those missing features; glance to your side, look above the horizontal, and if you look downwards, make sure you do *look*.

After a while, start shifting your consciousness from visual dominance to your other senses. Remember Edmund Blunden's "sounds" and "scents" as well as the "seeings." Listen to the sound of your breath as you walk, and the sound of your feet on the ground. The rustle of your clothing. The wind blowing through trees or around buildings. The buzz of insects. The hard dry scraping of dead leaves. The sounds of the day (or night) all around you: voices, vehicles, aircraft, dogs barking—or even blessed silence. Country parson Francis Kilvert recorded stopping on one of his regular nightly walks to listen to "the rustle and solemn night whisper of the wheat, so different to its voice by day." (It is instructive, indeed, to conduct walks along your selected route in the daytime and in the evening, to compare the different sensory impressions the same route can provide.) And as well as your feet, eyes, and ears, use your nose to walk—not literally, as in a Tibetan pilgrimage, but in the olfactory sense. What can you smell as you move along? The grass of lawns you pass? The smell of foliage or the scent of flowers in the hedgerow or the park? The stench of garbage, or gases from distant manufacturing processes? Or are there no smells you can particularly distinguish—are you in an olfactory desert? What does that tell you about the environment you are walking in?

Use your sense of touch as you walk as well. One way to do this is to become conscious of the air on your face or exposed arms and legs. Feel how your body cuts through the air; be aware of the direction of the breeze or wind.

Focus now on your rhythm of walking. Feel that rhythm. Is it comfortable and easy? If not, smooth off its rough edges—become conscious of your walking gait and your associated breathing. Meld them into one smooth entity. What do your feet feel as they touch the ground? And how is gravity today? Are you going up hill or down dale? Does the ground slope to your left or right—is it *really* horizontal? Notice forces of gravity on your body as you move, the subtle pull this way or that. Work it all into your gait and breathing pattern. Rhythm.

You should by now be purring along, with the bodily equivalent of Rolls-Royce locomotion. Now indulge in a "funny thought." Try to imagine that, although your body is moving in a rhythmic way, you are not actually moving through space; instead, try to feel that you are "walking on the spot," that space is passing through you— *that the route you are on is walking you.* Imagine you are the still center (you are still *here*, aren't you?) and the sensory world is just flowing on through and by. This mode of walking perception can sometimes have dramatic results. The first time it happened to me, I was hiking over heavy country far out on Dartmoor, in southern England, toting a hefty backpack. I had caught my "second wind" a long while before but was still stumbling along behind my two rugged, outdoor-type companions. Suddenly, I "clicked" into this mode of perception, and it was as if gravity had no further call on me. My breathing became easy and relaxed, and with the same effort I normally expend sitting in an armchair, I found myself moving over the moorland swiftly and easily. I felt like a feather in a breeze as I floated past my companions, their jaws agape in surprise. I felt that this must be what that weird Tibetan way of walking, *lung gom*, had to be like, when the adept bounds along the ground at an extraordinary rate while in a meditative state. And I was amazed at the state of physical relaxation I was experiencing as I moved; it made me recall Eugen Herrigel's discovery, recorded in his *Zen in the Art of Archery*, that his small, slight Zen archery master could pull back a powerful bow while his arm muscles remained relaxed (not to mention that he could hit the bull's-eye in the dark).

Zen in the art of walking—make it a habit.

## A Stroll Down Memory Lane

Another day, another walk. This time, let us take a walk aimed specifically at provoking memory and kindling the imagination—the putting together of physical and mental activities not normally associated with one another. Select a street in your town, a town local to you, your old hometown, or an accessible major city. Take a preliminary, conscious stroll along it. Then find an appropriate local library and do some local-history homework. Find out all you can about the history of the town in general, and your selected street in particular. If possible, find old photographs of the street in question. What did it look like in the 1950s? In the 1930s? At the turn of the century? In the nineteenth century? Study the pictures in great detail. What has changed? Perhaps more tellingly, what has survived through the decades? See the old cars and perhaps horse-drawn carriages in the street. Look at the people on the sidewalk, their old-fashioned clothes. Or they may just be blurs, because of the long camera exposures necessary in olden days. One of the most haunting photographs I've ever seen is Louis Daguerre's *Paris Boulevard* daguerreotype of 1839. It is said to be the first photograph of a human being. When Samuel F. B. Morse saw the daguerreotype he wrote: "The boulevard, so constantly filled with a moving throng of pedestrians and carriages, was perfectly solitary, except for an individual who was having his boots brushed."[36] The "moving throng" was too fast to register on Daguerre's plate, and only the fellow who stood still to have his shoes shined was destined to be the first human being to be photographed; he probably never knew of his immortalization. He seems to be standing in a deserted street—only his ghost survives to haunt us.

Armed with historic and, if possible, photographic information, take another wander along the street. Think of those old ghosts who had thronged this same street where you now walk. Imagine the noises that would have been in the street then—the clatter of horses' hooves on cobbled streets, a newspaper boy shouting the headlines, and so forth—and switch to be conscious of the noises you can actually hear now. Make an imaginary daguerreotype as you walk and see the people around you fade away, so that in your mind's eye the street becomes eerily empty, as did that busy Paris boulevard. The buildings leave their image, because they are in a different time zone from the humans who rush by. Explore these feelings and thoughts about time and transience. Look at the buildings, the physical definition of the street. What parts have changed relative to the old photographs you looked at? Which features remain the same?

If you were not fortunate enough to find old photographs of the street, then do what Freud did and use your acquired knowledge about the place. In Vienna, he loved to take meditative walks throught the city, sometimes late at night. Walking companions said he would sometimes analyze the city around him, reminding himself of its remotest past. "One sensed how easily such a re-creation of the past came to him," remarked a contemporary, "and one was reminded of the antique objects in his study and that the archaeologist had created the psycho-analyst in him."[37] In your work, you can more modestly re-create what your documentary knowledge tells you about the changes over time in the street in which you walk. Turn it into memory lane, and closely attend the processes of cognition going on within you as you do so.

### If You Go Down to the Woods Today . . .

In the course of recommending the virtues of country walking away from busy roads, the nineteenth-century rural writer William Howitt referred to "the dim solemnity of the wild wood." While walking in the Concord countryside, Thoreau saw "the setting sun lighting up the opposite side of a stately pine wood." He felt that its "golden rays straggled into the aisles of the wood as into some noble hall"; this prompted him to imagine invisible, mythical beings inhabiting the woods. Gothic cathedrals were raised, it is thought, so that their interiors would replicate the "dim solemnity" of the forest. Certainly, a similar sense of numinosity can be obtained in both types of environment. When exploring the Zen of walking, make sure one of your routes involves a woodland walk. The best time is when the day is overcast, for then an even, soft green light will filter down through the foliage. I well remember one early overcast evening walking through a woodland at Princeton, New Jersey. I had been making my way along a woodland path for about half an hour when I suddenly experienced a dizzying shift of consciousness. I realized it had been triggered by the liminal lighting conditions and the strong verticality of the slender tree trunks flickering in my peripheral vision. For a moment the woods did become a cathedral, and I felt what I can only call an *intelligence* emanating from the collective effect of the trees. I thought of the forest spirits the Lacandon Indians had laughingly told anthropologist Christian Rätsch about (see introductory chapter), and, a couple of years later, I was delighted to read John Perkins, in his *The World Is As You Dream It*, describe exactly the same feeling in the rain forests of Ecuador—"the incredible intelligence of the forest itself."[38] Down in the woods, your assured, late-twentieth-century Western cognition could be in for a big surprise. As you walk, concentrate on your peripheral vision. Pay attention to the margins.

## Medicine Walk

I do not suggest in this book that you attempt to go on a vision quest, because no book can prepare you for that or guide you on it. You need live, highly experienced teachers for a full-blown vision-quest attempt. (The appendix does, however, provide information as to where you can find out more about going on wilderness experience quests.) In any case, you might not be ready to undertake a vision quest as yet. It is not something to be forced. What can be done, though, is what Foster and Little call a "medicine walk," a single day's journey out on the wilder face of the Earth.

This activity needs careful peparation. Get yourself to an area of moderate wilderness—hill country, moorland, deeply rural countryside, or a national-park area. Take a backpack containing basic items such as water, weatherproof clothing if appropriate, a penknife, map and compass, a whistle, first-aid kit, and anything else you feel to be essential. But no food. Make sure someone will know where you are and how long you intend to be away. If you drive to the edge of the area that interests you, you might be able to persuade a friend or partner to have a lazy day staying around the vehicle. Set off alone early in the morning, ideally at sunrise, and walk into an area you have already studied on the map, even if you do not follow a precisely preplanned route. Make certain you do not journey too many miles from your starting point, avoid dangerous or exceptionally difficult country, be sure to avoid any known hazards peculiar to the area, and ensure that you have identified landmarks by eye and know where they are on the map before you start your medicine walk.

As you walk, use all the skills you have developed by practicing the activities described above. Keep your eyes, ears, nose, and skin surface alert. Let your movement and breathing get synchronized properly. Remember to let the country walk you. Don't have any hardened expectations; don't try to force the learning. Don't grab, just be in reception mode: keep yourself open to letting nature's intelligence make itself known to you. Be conscious of any unexpected images, thoughts, ideas that flash into your mind during your day's journey. Pick up a natural object—a stone, a feather, a piece of bark, whatever it might be—to bring back with you to remind you of the journey and any special insight, thoughts, or decisions that came to you. Return to your starting point, or a designated destination, by sundown.

*Now that we have started journeying from here to (t)here, it is time to unfold some road maps for the soul. . . .*

# MAPPING

## Move Over, Mercator (Finding Our Way in the World)

A FRIEND WAS PLANNING TO VISIT JAN DE-Blieu, who lived on Hatteras Island, in the North Carolina Outer Banks, so Jan drew a map for the friend, which, in addition to showing the road along the thin arm of sandy land, was embellished with amusing drawings of places and events that had meaning for her. Here was a heron, with its pink legs emerging from a tuxedo, where DeBlieu had stumbled across herons' nests; there was a crab waving a flag where she had witnessed crabs skirmishing; and so forth. A few days later, the friend phoned in puzzlement. "Are these amusement parks or something?" she wanted to know. DeBlieu realized that her map had shown places that were tied to her perceptions and memories in too personal a way to be translatable to someone else.[1] She recognized that places that we love or which have special meaning for us get mapped in greater detail than others. She noted a survey by Kevin Lynch and colleagues that had studied the perceptions of people living in Boston, Los Angeles, and Jersey City. Though the maps by these residents shared similar characteristics such as roads and major buildings, they were also largely idiosyncratic. Lynch concluded that even long-term residents of a modern, complex city had to simplify and order their environment by reference to a few places of personal meaning as navigational aids.[2]

This is the way with maps. Much of what we are discussing in this book revolves around that poorly explored margin between inner and outer geography, which is always the territory that all maps cover, no matter how technically advanced. There is no such thing as a map of the world; there can only be maps of worldviews.

And there are many kinds of map. There are maps of navigation through physical and mental spaces, and maps to establish boundaries—physical, political, ethnic. There are maps that show the movement and habitat of disease. Maps can be works of art in their own right—maps of feelings and meanings, private and public. We can make our own personalized maps, as did DeBlieu, of our environment; we can construct psychological maps. Gavin Flood has noted that what today would be considered a psychological, inner map can be similar in many respects to maps that had common, social usage in earlier times, maps of the physical world that were "imbued with mythological or religious meaning."[3] As we shall see in this chapter, maps can be on paper, on the ground, engraved on rock (even *be* the rock), verbalized in text and speech, written in the stars and the lineaments of the land, and wired into the neural architecture of the brain. But no one map can be used by everyone, for all maps contain symbols and conventions that have to be learned in one form or another. There is no such thing as a map that is neutral and accurate for all purposes and peoples, not even the fanciest, most technically advanced maps that Westernized culture prides itself on as an expression of its objective worldview. Lewis Carroll had no doubts on this issue: we may recall the Bellman's blank map of the ocean in *The Hunting of the Snark*—a map the whole crew could understand, after agreeing that poles and equators, tropics, zones, and meridian lines were "merely conventional signs"—or his ruminations in *Sylvie and Bruno Concluded* about a map with a scale of a mile to a mile "which has never been spread out yet."

Maps rely on links between place (and thus space), memory, myth, and imagination. Place and memory, as we noted earlier and shall further see, are particularly close bedfellows. Stephen S. Hall observes that both memory and geography are associative, and that we all carry a "personal atlas in our brains" with which we can cover vast distances in the switch of a synapse, or delve into, following its emotional latitudes.[4]

Volumes could be written on maps and mapping, and there is space here to touch on just a few aspects that relate to some of the strands that have been running through these pages, and to learn how people long before us—and some currently outside the pale of our culture—have mapped their world.

## BANISHING DRAGONS: MAPPING THE WESTERN MIND

"The story of maps tells a history of progressive rationalization," Eugene Victor Walter observes.[5] All maps are selective, and over the ages the nature of that selectivity has chronicled the hardening of the Western mind, mapping its journey out of dreamtime. Ancient maps were more naïve than modern ones, both mathematically and graphically, as Walter points out, but they were governed by different rules, which allowed imagination and myth to be mapped. Old maps showed fantastic monsters, mythological entities, magical islands. Herodotus declared that "the ends of the Earth" contained that which was most rare. The margins of the known world of ancient Europe were peopled with the entities, the fabulous places and creatures, that inhabited, and still inhabit, the unconscious mind. This was the zone at the edge of the map where "Here be Dragons" was written.

To the early historical European mind, the Atlantic seaboard was close to the edge of the known world, and journeys off into the ocean were effectively forays into mythic time and space. The Irish *immramma*, accounts of voyages to islands in the North Atlantic, included what we would recognize as real geography along with mythic material. The *immramma* material dates from the eighth to the tenth century A.D., and just four such texts survive, though there are references to three more. A slightly later work, the *Navigatio Brendani*, is based on the *immramma* form, and describes St. Brendan's seven-year voyage in search of the Land of the Saints. St. Brendan was an actual personage of the sixth century, who doubtless did visit monasteries on the islands off the Irish coast. There has been speculation that the *Navigatio* contains references to transatlantic voyages, perhaps as far as the West Indies, but Juliette Wood argues that St. Brendan's adventures are in fact imaginative tales rather than garbled versions of real voyages. "The Irish were very much at home in the Atlantic, and an extensive tradition of sea poetry developed which described the Atlantic in all its moods," she points out.[6]

One of the most famous of the magical islands off the coast of Ireland was Brâzil (Hy Brasil), named for Bres, the son of Ériu and the god Elatha. In John Purdey's Atlantic chart of 1830, the position of Brâzil was given as 51° 10' North, 15° 30' West; it was not struck off until 1865. Furthermore, the mythical island was considered to be visible from the Arran Islands, in Galway Bay, once every seven years. The antiquarian T. J. Westropp claimed to have seen it in 1872, even if it was no longer officially on the map, and to have made a color sketch of it. He records: "It was a clear evening with a fine golden sunset. Just as the sun went down a dark island suddenly appeared far out at sea, but not on the horizon. It had two hills, one wooded. Between these, from a low plain, rose towers and curls of smoke."[7] Westropp was accompanied by his brother and several friends who all saw the vision; one of them thought they were looking at New York. Strange things happen at the ends of the Earth.

The beginning of the map form as we know it was in the second century A.D., when Claudius Ptolemy wrote his *Geographia* in Alexandria, giving lists of places with their latitudes and longitudes. This was the standard work for many centuries. It made an effective distinction between geography and chorography (see chapter two), claiming that the two require different and separate modes of representation. Geography showed the world as a whole, a unity, whereas chorography detailed particulars, and had to use artistic representation. (In effect, this dualism related to the differing perspectives of the mathematician and the artist. The form of the map was the abstract, overall bird's-eye view; the contribution of the artist was the specific, ground-level, personalized viewpoint.) By providing the source of a grid and standardized information, Ptolemy's *Geographia* started the process of depicting the world as modern maps do today, but the mythic and expressive aspects of place were still acknowledged, if considered separate to geography. This separation, however, was to increase, so that the mythic and expressive elements were progressively pushed to map margins. By modern times, they had literally fallen off the map altogether.

The *Geographia* arrived in Europe in the fifteenth century, the same period in which Brunelleschi developed perspective geometry, which itself had a dramatic effect on the emerging Western worldview. The metrication developed from Ptolemy's lines of latitude and longitude meant that all points were commensurable; distance and directions between places could be established. Anywhere, known or unknown, could be granted coordinates. "It was the synthesis of perspective geometry and Ptolemy's work that enabled the imposition of a grid on the known world," David Turnbull states.[8] (Not that Ptolemy's grid was the first; it is thought that the idea originated in China, with Chang Heng, in the first century A.D. His biographer, Tshai Yung, says he "cast a network about heaven and earth and reckoned on the basis of it" according to R. Temple in his *The Genius of China* [1989]. But none of Chang Heng's mapwork survives.) "The significance of Ptolemy's *Geographia* was not just its use of a grid: it was also an atlas which enabled the co-ordination of maps of individual lands into one map of the world," Turbull further remarks. So the Western mind had developed a tool to image and enhance its worldview, and from which the emergent monoculture could ultimately be fashioned. This Western map, this worldview, this brand of consciousness, traveled over the Earth, bringing with it its attendant science and rationalism, history and linear time, and even, to a considerable extent, its Indo-European languages, encoding the very psyche of the West. The Americas were dreaming the last of their other kind of dreams when the new maps allowed Toscanelli to argue that the quickest way to the Spice Islands was across the Atlantic rather than around Africa, causing Columbus to sail westwards. The American dreamtime was effectively over, and the European clock was ticking on that in Australia.

The modern map of Western tradition is thought to be a highly accurate, completely objective depiction of the landscape, of the world. It has authority in our view because it is neutral and nonexpressive, except for hard, objective information. But all maps are expressions of the cultural milieu in which they originate, and our maps are no different in that respect from any other map. The assumptions that govern any map tend to be inherent rather than obvious. They are invisible to the user immersed in the same cultural context that produced the map, yet to someone from outside that milieu they can eclipse the information in it. The Western map carries all kinds of its own mythical material. The grid, for a start. You can go to Greenwich and see a brass strip in the ground marking zero degrees longitude, and stand with your feet on either side of it. But the map that shows this vertical line across its face isn't recording what is on the ground; the brass strip owes its existence, of course, to what is on the map. Lines of latitude are equally fictitious. (And we all know that the equator is a menagerie lion that runs around the middle of the Earth, don't we?) Contours are meaningless meanders unless one is trained in the convention of how they can be made to yield a profile of the terrain by means of cross-section. The infrastructure that makes these markings of the rationalizing myth possible, the benchmarks, trigonometrical points, and nowadays satellite technology, are physical pegs embedded in the environment by the mapmakers to allow their conceptual material to be added to their view of the world.

And then there is Mercator and his projection. This sixteenth-century Flemish geographer devised a method of geometrically projecting the globe onto a cylinder, so that the lines of longitude are meridians meeting at right angles with the lines of latitude, which are all the same length as the equator. The map of the world that resulted from this had immediate effect, for it showed a navigable northwest passage between Asia and America and the presence of a large southern continent, but the system of projection took many years to be adopted. (It is worth noting that even Mercator's maps had little boxes of information and legends of the kind that have subsequently not been approved for modern maps—a sort of last whimper of chorography.)

Because the Mercator projection portrayed compass directions as straight lines, it eventually became the most popular one in use. But the Mercator projection brought with it a set of distortions that many of us have grown up thinking are a true depiction of the relative sizes of the continents. So Greenland, for example, appears much larger than Australia, although it is only about a third of the size of that southern continent. In fact, all the northern countries appear disproportionately large compared with those south of the equator. And Europe sits happily in top center. There is of course no reason why north should even be at the top of the map: it could be any other direction. Even in the early Christian West, maps were oriented to the east (the meaning of the term "orientation"), for that was cosmologically the most important direction, as expressed also in the orientation of churches and graves. "That North is traditionally 'up' on maps is the result of a historical process, closely connected with the global rise and economic dominance of northern Europe . . . ," David Turnbull writes. "You may wish to ask yourself what interests are served in a Mercator projection. Is it a coincidence that a map which preserves compass direction (a boon for ocean navigation) shows Britain and Europe (the main seagoing and colonising powers of the past 400 years) as relatively large with respect to most of the colonised nations?"[9] In his *Maps Are Territories*, Turnbull takes the Peters projection, which maintains east-west, north-south directions and preserves the relative sizes of the continents, though at the expense of an elongated distortion of their shape, and turns it upside down, with its center on the eastern extremity of Asia. In that view, Europe is an insignificant appendage down the bottom right-hand corner. But the cultural reality was that, when the basis for the familiar Mercator projection was being laid down, Britain and Europe formed the world's dominant center, and they could draw the map in their image, and they lived the map they drew. Turnbull is right in challenging A. Korzybski's 1941 dictum that the map is not the territory: maps *are* territories, and they define the kind of Earth that is perceived.

## FOOTPRINTS OF THE ANCESTORS, AND OTHER MAPS

Other people in other times and places have mapped the world quite differently from the way we have, and no less truthfully in their own terms.

We saw in the last chapter how pilgrimage is a form of soul mapping, producing what geographer Rana P. B. Singh calls "faithscapes." It was noted how Christian Jerusalem was actually fashioned into a Christian faithscape, and the liturgy associated with it was effectively the map of that faithscape. The medieval *mappa mundi* (see chapter one), were not for physical navigation but for the spiritual journey of the Christian soul. They actually contained less "objective" information about the world than had Ptolemy's map a millennium earlier.

The Hindu pilgrim traces out patterns applicable to his or her devotions. D. P. Dubey and Rana P. B. Singh have studied the faithscape of Chitrakut, a celebrated pilgrimage destination sacred to Rama, west of Prayaga (Allahabad) in India. Eighty-four sites of significance are involved in the total faithscape, centering on the sacred hill of Kamadagiri. Pilgrims can obtain a map showing pictorial representations of the sacred places, plus depictions of major secular buildings for reference, the relevant routes, and the local river. Dubey and Singh comment:

> The pilgrimage-cognitive map of Chitrakut is an example of . . . cartography where faithscape is portrayed through the means of pictorial signs and mythological support concerning sacred topography. Most of the holy centers of India have such persuasive maps.
>
> Avoiding the sense of distance, the cognitive map of Chitrakut highlights various symbolic representations of mythology and topography. . . . The directional and locational contexts are not given consideration. . . . This map conveys the message about Rama's activities in this territory which ultimately help the pilgrims to follow on and get experience of those spots made holy by Rama's attachment there. . . .
>
> . . . The map also suggests the procedures of pilgrimage for the period of five days and the cluster of holy spots to be visited on respective days in the sequence of time and space. . . .[10]

Seven of the holy spots in the Chitrakut pilgrimage circuit are given prominence, and they form a geographical pattern of nested triangles based on the sacred hill: a cosmogram traced by the feet of the pilgrims on their circuit. And not only are there faith maps at pilgrimage centers; the centers themselves can form larger geographic patterns. So, for example, the five most sacred shrines of Vishnu form points on a star pattern that covers the whole of the Indian subcontinent.[11]

The Native Americans had their own way of spiritually mapping the landscape. The Wintu (Northern Wintun) of northern California live in a varied topography ranging from mountains to canyons and flat terrain. Features in this topography still have great significance for Wintu spiritual beliefs. The land is their bible, as it were, and so is part of their cultural and personal identity. (It follows that, when locales are altered, destroyed, or placed off-limits by non-Indians, there is damage to this identity.) The landscape is an outer expression of inner meaning for the tribal member who moves through it. The sort of places that attract specific spiritual meaning are mountains, distinctive rock outcrops, caves, springs, natural rock basins of water, whirlpools in rivers, and seepage holes, where the resident spirit can sometimes be heard as an audible buzzing. A Wintu on a vision quest might travel between such places in search of the special dream or spiritual guidance, for they are interconnected throughout the Wintu territory. This is effected by the use of "guide rocks," which operate between both sacred and secular places in the terrain. From a guide rock (usually a distinctive perched rock), the traveler informed in the conventions of this mapping system can understand the direction in which to proceed to the next guidance point. "Streams and rivers are also often used to determine the cardinal orientations," Dorothea Theodoratus and Frank LaPena explain, "and are thus part of the Wintu world-view. Rivers are sometimes named in a manner which includes the direction of flow."[12] The country is peopled with nature spirits and the souls of the dead. The newly deceased also has a map to follow: the spirit must travel northwards through the territory to the sacred Mount Shasta, or to a spring known only to souls. The soul then rises to the Milky Way, where it travels south and then east to a grassy plain where the Indians "are always having a big time." To assist in this postmortem traveling, the body is oriented towards the north at death. If a Wintu dies outside the tribal area, then the body is directed at Mount Shasta, in whatever direction that might be from the place of death. Wintu land is thus mapped for the body and the soul.

Mount Shasta, northern California, part of the spiritual geography of the Wintu Indians.

There are traditional maps of the sea as well as of the land. The South Pacific islanders employ a variety of techniques to aid their ocean navigation. These incorporate the use of stars, sun, landmarks, wave patterns, sea currents and swells, water-surface qualities, bird flight, fish, winds, and myth, all bound up with a sophisticated use of memory and profound knowledge of seacraft and boat construction. The Caroline Islanders, Emily Lyle tells us, move through conceptual worlds not exclusively concerned with the practicalities of navigation. "We have the real world of the ocean and we have what the navigator carried around inside his brain. His chart, as he goes on voyages, is a mental one, and the mind is responding to physical places on the earth or sea or to stars in the sky without an intermediary."[13] The Micronesians do produce training maps on the beach, though, which consist of sticks and stones or shells, collectively representing currents, lines of swell, reefs, localized wave patterns, and so forth. Their thirty-two-point "star compass" can also be represented as a beach diagram of pebbles for the training of young navigators. All this subtle information is consigned to memory—as one Micronesian song puts it, "When one is down, another rises / He remembers those stars / Deep within him. . . ." There is a variety of other navigational mnemonics. In one scheme, Puluwat navigators use the shape of the triggerfish as a mental "chart." In this, the navigator imagines his base as the center of the fish's backbone. He envisages himself when sailing west to be traveling towards the tail and the setting position of the star Altair, then back to the backbone or center of the imaginary fish, and south following the Southern Cross to the ventral fin, back to the center, north to the dorsal fin, and finally back to the center. A mnemonic system extended from this, called "triggerfishes tied together," contains named information on physical places such as reefs and islands and sandbanks, as would appear on a Western naval chart, but also includes the name of an imaginary frigate bird seen in rough water, a mythical vanishing island (somewhat like the Irish Brâzil), names for big waves, a large and mythical destructive whale, and a place where a figurative whale with two tails can be seen. Systems like this not only encode a great deal of information about the ocean environment that would be missed by the average Western observer, but can also serve a wider purpose, according to Per Hage, who suggests they can be used "for the storage and retrieval of other kinds of cultural information—myths, spells, ceremonies, chants, recitations, etc."[14] In another system used by the Caroline Islanders, each inhabited island is envisaged as having imaginary lines radiating out from it towards twenty-eight of the navigational stars. These lines are "marked" every few miles in a variety of ways, sometimes by physical features like a reef or islet, but often by mythical items.

A Pacific Island navigator will know the direction from his own house in which each navigation star sets, and will mark it by some feature on land. As he leaves his island, he will use a back sight

along two landmarks there to set his initial course, and can maintain direction by the use of characteristic wave patterns, which master navigators can detect by sticking an arm into the water. The
Puluwatans picture the boat as stationary, with the world moving
past (see "Learning to Walk" in the preceding chapter). They can
conceptually mark an invisible island over the horizon to left or
right of their course and picture its relative "movement" against
their mental star maps so as to judge speed and distance. All in all,
Micronesian navigation represents one of the great feats of human
cognitive mapping, and one, moreover, in which both physical and
mythical references provide information.

Ancient cognitive sea charts could also be carved out of wood.
The Greenland Inuit skimmed coastal waters in their kayaks, using
what to the uninitiated eye appear as nothing other than pieces of
whittled wood to guide them. These are actually coastal charts,
however, mapping the bays and capes of the coastline and marking
offshore islands.

And when not wood, maps could be written in stone. Some rock
carvings (petroglyphs) at Valcamonica in Italy, dating from around
2500 B.C., depict human figures and animals amongst what seem to
be fields, houses, and trackways. These we can easily imagine to be
maps, but other prehistoric rock markings are more enigmatic, and
are beginning to be seen by archeologists not so much as maps in
themselves as *elements in* a mapping of the landscape. One example
of this is in Galicia, in northwestern Spain, where Richard Bradley,
Felipe Criado Boado, and Ramón Fabregas Valcarce have studied
markings on natural boulders and rock outcrops. These petroglyphs
include abstract designs, simple pecked dots, hollowed-out "cup
marks," and circular motifs, with interconnecting wandering lines.
In addition, there are several representations of deer, horses, and
human figures. No one knows the meaning of these patterns, especially the abstract ones (over ninety theories have been put forward
for cup-and-ring markings alone), so the researchers chose to ignore their stylistic aspects and concentrate instead on the relationship to the local topography of the rocks on which the designs were
engraved. One of their findings was that the rock-art motifs were
aligned and repeated in various parts of the landscape in such a way

that they marked rocks whose distribution reflected the routes taken today by free-ranging horses over the terrain, which has changed very little since prehistoric times. This meant that the carved rocks mapped out the best grazing and shelter during the late-summer drought. Deer would have been equally likely to follow these same invisible routes through the landscape in the past. But the researchers were also alert to the probability that the petroglyphs had spiritual and symbolic meaning for their makers; sometimes the images of animals would appear next to the strange abstract markings, and "even the distinctive behaviour of the red deer . . . may also have provided a vital source of metaphors and symbols."[15] It is hard for us to imagine a world where the very boulders were charged with meaning.

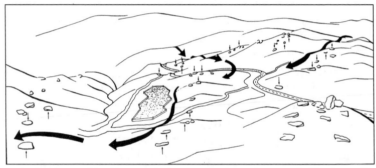

The distribution of boulders inscribed with prehistoric rock art (marked by the small vertical arrows) at Chan da Lagoa, Campo Lameiro, in Galicia, Spain. The heavy black arrows show the paths across the modern landscape taken by free-ranging horses. [Drawing by Anxo Rodriguez Paz, courtesy of Richard Bradley et al.]

Bradley has also studied prehistoric rock art in the British Isles. Here there are only abstract cup-and-ring marks or circular motifs and the connecting lines, a type of motif that seems to have commenced with the incredibly ancient passage tombs and chambered mounds of the early Neolithic period (New Stone Age), which seem to have been associated with ceremonial, funerary, and probably ancestral rites. "All is not lost if we are prevented from reading these

Example of prehistoric cup-and-ring–marked stone, Coilsfield, Scotland. The "cups" (hollowed-out areas of stone) are depicted as dark circles in this old drawing.

symbols," Bradley comments. "Even their organization in the landscape sheds light on the ancient mind."[16] He found that they were carved on rock faces and boulders that occupied the margins between lowland areas of year-round land use, and upland regions of seasonal use—in other words, between areas occupied by farmers and hunter-gatherers respectively. The carved boulders and outcrops occupied the liminal zones, therefore, between culture and nature. The rocks were at places near ancient routeways where there were good views. The carvings were meant to be seen, and there are indications in Bradley's analyses that the complexity of the rock art (the number of and spacing between motifs) varied between those rocks that would be seen by the lowland farmers and by the upland herders and hunter gatherers. They were meant to be read and interpreted by different populations who lived on the land in differing ways. "Farmers define agricultural territories by enclosing them, but hunter-gatherers perceive their territories in a very different way, by monitoring paths running between specific *places*," Bradley explains. "Those places overlook the surrounding land, and hunter-gatherers define their territories by the views seen from them. For hunter-gatherers, tenure is . . . 'one-dimensional' because it is based on places and paths respectively. Among agriculturists it is 'two-dimensional' because it works by delimiting an area of ground."[17]

Pastoral nomads, like certain animal species, have migratory routes. The Bedouin of the Arabian Peninsula migrate with their herds of camels and flocks of sheep and can travel as much as six hundred miles on their circuits; Norwegian Lapps traditionally migrate over a 250-mile range. Others, such as the Fulani of western Africa, or the tribes that circulate on vast routes through the border regions of southern Russia, Iran, Turkey, Pakistan, and India, cover even more ground, herding and raising beasts, or following the migratory routes of animals, or seeking rain and food. "Pastoral nomads, like all other humans, learn the positions and directions of landmarks and routes, using when necessary the sun, moon and stars as compasses," zoologist Robin Baker writes. And there are specialist elements, so that the Bedouin, for instance, assist their mapping by the observation of cloud-bank positions and even lightning. "All of this information is stored in some form of spatial memory and can be used at any time to find the way from one familiar place to another."[18]

Of all the traditional wanderers on the Earth today, the Australian Aborigine is probably the generally most known about. Although the imposition of the Western worldview has played havoc with it, enough fragments of the Aboriginal lifeway survive to provide us with a time telescope so we can peer back to the remote past of human consciousness.

The Earth was featureless, flat, and uninhabited in the long ago, in the time before time, at the timeless time of the *tjukuba* or Dreaming. During this Dreamtime (this is a European term dating from 1927, but the Aborigines say it approximates the meaning well enough), giant totemic beings emerged from within the Earth—or came from some vague upper region of the sky, in some traditions—and walked the land, the country. In the course of their meanderings they created the topography, the landscape that now exists. They left their tracks across the surface of the world, they camped, made fire, defecated, dug for water, fought, copulated, conducted rituals, and so forth. Everything they did left on the country a mark that can still be seen to this day. When these world-creating beings left, they turned into rocks or re-entered the ground. Aborigines, for unknown generations, have traced the footsteps of their Dreamtime ancestors. These routes are variously known by non-Aborigines as "songlines," "dream journey routes," or "dreaming tracks." The Yolngu of Arnhemland refer to them as *djalkiri*, a term often translated as "footprints of the ancestors."[19] Some of these dreaming tracks are, or were, followed by whole tribes, often as part of their seasonal, nomadic circuits over the Outback, but they can also be followed individually by tribal members—the "Walkabout," so misunderstood by non-Aborigines. Sometimes information on dreaming tracks previously unknown by a tribal group can be transmitted to a tribal member through the medium of a dream, and new rituals and songs are produced. A track newly discovered like this may have a hundred or more verses associated with it.[20]

Australian author James Cowan points out that, with the dream journeys,

> . . . we are not just dealing with an unending journey back and forth across tribal territory solely in pursuit of food. Instead we are looking at a sacred journey in which each stage is imbued with sacred significance.
>
> . . . the land they [the Aborigines] cross is part of themselves. The Dream Journey on the ritual level is a way of renewing contact with themselves, since they and their land are inseparable. It is at this point that the Aborigine enters into a Dream world where the land is transformed into a metaphysical landscape saturated with significations. . . .[21]

The "country" in general and specific features in particular are charged with meaning—with *djang*, or numinous power. The Dreamtime was the long-ago creative era, but it is also a timeless zone of perennial presence. Hills, ridges, trees, water holes, rocks, caves—these are not mere topography but also a real and present spiritual, mythic landscape to the Aborigine.

The presence of dreaming tracks became fully clear to non-Aborigines through the discoveries of anthropologist and explorer C. P. Mountford. In nearly two decades of ethnological traveling over the central regions of Australia, he noted, he kept encountering certain myths, which he came to realize had a linear geographical distribution over large distances. Then, in 1960, he was led along the approximately two-hundred-mile route of the dreaming track of Jarapiri, the Snake Man (a version of the Rainbow Serpent), and his companions. Mountford's guides were elders of the Ngalia and Walbiri tribes of central Australia. The elders trusted Mountford and felt that the course of the dreaming track would be best preserved with him: the normal succession of knowledge to the young men of the tribe was being disrupted by the influence of non-Aboriginal culture. The birthplace or emergence point of Jarapiri was Winbaraku (Blanche Tower), a twin-peaked hill in the western Macdonnell Ranges. From there, the route stretched northwards through thirty-five sacred sites. These included a heap of stones where the spider Mamuboijunda appeared, a pavement of white quartz that was the burnt-out leaves of Wanbanbiri's fire-torch, caves that were the vulvas of the Nabanunga women, and a line of rocks that represented the track of Jarapiri and his party. At one of these sites, Ngama, a rocky outcrop, is a rock shelter where a huge painting of the snake is located. Mountford was able to map the course of the dreaming track, and noted that a precise route was followed, apparently known to the tribal peoples for unknown ages. At a certain point on the route, Mountford's Ngalia guides became uncertain about the position of the next sacred site and the words of its associated chants. When he inquired as to the reason, he was told:

> . . . their 'line of songs' finished at Walutjara, and that those belonging to the remainder of the totemic route were the property of the Walbiri tribe to the north. . . .

> This evidence suggests that the finishing place of the 'line of songs' of a mythical creator is a tribal boundary . . . because the mythical stories of the tribe, and the

topography, art, songs, and ceremonies associated with them, which dominate all aspects of aboriginal life and thought, could also determine the boundaries of the tribe.[22]

Each of the significant places along a dreaming track (the whole route in itself also being significant) would have its song, its dance, its ritual. There also would probably be secreted *churingas*, ritual objects of flattened stone, wood, or bark. These would be marked with motifs which in effect would be a map of their part of the song line.[23] A *churinga* also told the legend of the place, the story of the Dreamtime being associated with the site. It was a mnemonic, in that it told the initiated elder what songs and dances were associated with that spot. In the 1940s, T. G. H. Strehlow gave an account of a visit to a sacred site in the Ulamba region, northeast of the main western Macdonnell Ranges, by North Aranda tribesmen. Apart from Strehlow, the party consisted of young Aboriginal men being led by an elder of the tribe on a day's pilgrimage to the site area, which consisted of an opening in a rock where the Dreamtime being had first emerged, and a heap of rocks marking his night camps. Finally, they all came to two great boulders, one on top of the other. The lower one was the body of the Ulamba ancestor who had collapsed there, mortally wounded, after various encounters and adventures. Strehlow describes the elder removing stones blocking a cleft between the two boulders, from which he took out bundles of *churingas* that had been carefully wrapped with hair string. He took each sacred object one at a time and chanted the part of the myth depicted on it. The objects were carefully passed around the group and handled with great respect. After all the songs had been chanted, the *churingas* were cleaned and wrapped up again and put back in the crevice.[24]

The vast desert and wilderness regions of Australia may look desolate to non-Aborigines, but they are crisscrossed with the dreaming tracks of myth. These gave much spatial information to the Aborigine, always linking one part with another, one site to another, and were integrated with the overall tribal lifeway. Helen

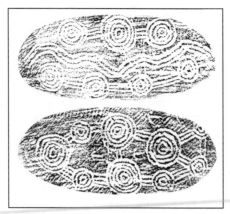

Markings on a *churinga* stone, both sides displayed. [Collection of John Michell.]

Watson, from her work with the Yolngu, calls this collective system a "knowledge network," each person responsible for his or her part of it, and constantly requiring activity, such as singing, dancing, and painting, for its maintenance.

Many non-Aboriginal observers have commented on the Aborigines' exceptional sense of direction and location. "I have often been struck," wrote an early Australian settler, "with the exact position each tribe takes in the general encampment [a major intertribal gathering], precisely in the position from each other their country lies according to the compass (of which they have a perfect notion). I have found this invariably the case, and latterly could form an idea, on the arrival of blacks, what part they came from."[25] When researching nomadic travel, David Lewis traveled a total of almost eight thousand kilometers with Aborigines in the Simpson and Western Desert areas between 1972 and 1974, and he witnessed many instances of the Aborigines' highly developed sense of location. He was unerringly led to water holes across trackless terrain. "All my preconceived ideas about 'land navigation' turned out to be wrong," writes Lewis. "In place of the stars, sun, winds and waves that guide Pacific Island canoemen, the main references of the Aborigines proved to be the meandering tracks of the ancestral Dreamtime beings that form a network over the whole Western Desert."

He found that his Aboriginal guides were particularly accurate if asked to point out the direction of distant locations when they were standing at sacred places. Lewis found, time and again, that their general sense of orientation was a mental "dynamic map, which was continually being up-dated in terms of time, distance and bearing, and more radically realigned at each major change of direction." On one occasion, in the midst of a gently undulating but "remarkably featureless" stony desert, one of Lewis' guides drew a cross in the sand to represent the cardinal directions. Lewis confirmed by his compass that the Aborigine's directions were accurate. "North, south, east and west are *like this in my head*," the guide explained. "I know them because we were traveling west and circled back south until we were heading south-east when we made camp." Lewis also had an instructive experience when he and his Aboriginal guides hunted a wounded kangaroo for half an hour on foot through featureless terrain covered in mulga and spear grass, which reduced visibility to a hundred yards. They returned without error to the Land Rover. Again his guides explained to Lewis how they had constantly updated their position relative to their starting point, the Land Rover.[26]

The dreaming tracks are thus primarily mental lines embedded in the landscape. The land itself is the map (Lewis Carroll's map with a mile-to-a-mile scale), sharing an interactive relationship with the mind, body, and soul of its native inhabitants in a way that is quite unfamiliar to modern Westerners.

In one notable instance, the dreaming tracks managed to preserve that unique relationship when it was threatened. As part of his personal research, Kingsley Palmer of the Australian Institute of Aboriginal Studies, Canberra, mapped the dreaming tracks of the southern portion of the Great Victoria Desert with the aid of Aboriginal helpers. When the work was completed, the Aborigines "immediately regarded the map as an item of great cultural importance."[27] It was decided that, since it contained some information secret to the tribe, they should place it in a bank vault in a nearby town. A short time later, the tribe entered into protracted land-right negotiations concerning the return of the Maralinga lands to the community. When parliamentarians flew up from Adelaide, the map was withdrawn from the bank vault, unrolled on the sand at the agreed meeting place, and used successfully to demonstrate to the parliamentarians the sanctity of the land from the Aboriginal perspective. The lands were subsequently handed back to the community.

## SPACED OUT

Mapping, in all its multitudinous forms, is a spatial way of storing information. (And a very effective method it is, too: it is estimated that the amount of information contained in even a medium-sized map of the United States is one to two hundred million bits.) This underlines the curious fact that place and memory are inextricably welded together within our cognitive processes, a relationship that has long been recognized. In the classical world it was celebrated by "the method of *loci*," or places.[28] In this memorizing technique, a person commits to memory the visualized layout of a building, or any geographical location that provides a suitable number of separate spots, like rooms, or houses and shops down a street, or even islands in a bay. If the person wants to remember a set of items or a list, he or she "walks" through the memorized location and mentally assigns each item on the list to a separate spot within the imagined scene. The spot and the item are linked visually in the imagination. When the time comes to retrieve the list of items, the person simply "walks" back through the memorized locale, "seeing" the items that had been "deposited" earlier in their various places. It is a proven method for recalling material that is otherwise difficult to retain. A variant on the system is to think of abstract items linked with imagined objects; so, to remember the number 39,762, for instance, one could visualize, say, three apples, nine grapefruit, seven lemons, six oranges, and two plums laid out in a greengrocer's boxes. Or a number like 7,529 could be visualized as a giant figure seven painted on a familiar clockface where the hands are showing five minutes to nine o'clock. We saw the same basic principle in action with the Pacific Islanders' use of the triggerfish for their navigational purposes (and also the placing of mythical islands at specific spots in the ocean where currents change, etc.). The·

Aborigines sometimes make use of a similar system, in addition to their other methods: the Gumatj people of northeastern Arnhemland visualize their home territory—near Biranybirany, by Caledon Bay—as a crocodile, an image that encodes specific geographical information.[29]

The well-known astrological zodiac is a similar device, emerging from the archaic Middle East, only here the places are in the sky, each star pattern linked with time, the planetary environment, and whole sets of divinatory information.

Place boils down to space, for all places (and objects) inherently define space: they occupy space, and there is space between them. When an object is moved, it leaves the space it occupied behind, yet carries its three-dimensionality with it. Space is a nothingness which is at once both unmovable and portable. A nothingness, and yet it defines our perception, our world, and how we organize information. (One can imagine an object disappearing, but not the space it was occupying disappearing.)

To this conundrum has to be added *psychological space*, how our minds represent this mysterious but essential nothingness. In what is known as the naïve view, most of us most of the time do not examine how we see things, and we assume that there is space "out there" around us, and space inside our head. But a moment's thought advises that this simply isn't the case. In the introductory chapter, we reminded ourselves how the head is, in fact, quite solid, and isn't a little room with windows (eyes) and doors (ears) and so forth. There is no little person inside looking out. Even if there were such a homunculus, what would be happening inside *its* head? The whole problem would simply extend like a corridor of mirrors. But the matter does not improve if we consider the "outer" environment. The physicists tell us about a vast array of energies zapping around, and that we ourselves are part of that energy matrix. Even light is just a tiny slice of the electromagnetic spectrum, with colors simply being different wavelengths of that energy, fading off into wavelengths we are not biologically tuned to perceive. Pressure waves of certain frequencies in the air (or any other medium, such as water) somehow become transformed into what we know as sound; smell and taste involve the recognition of molecules. Even touch, the most grounded of the senses, is, according to physicists, only a response to variable concentrations of energy patterns. We simply do not experience the world in the way physicists describe it—we see blue sky, rainbows, sunsets; we hear Mozart, birdsong; we touch the grain of wood, the coolness of marble, the velvet of a lover's skin. We smell fresh-mown grass, a bouquet of flowers, and taste the salty breeze of the ocean, the silent explosions of a gourmet meal. Yet "all" that is "out there" is what has been described as an "n-dimensional energy soup." More than that, there is no evidence that anything that impinges on our senses has anything inherently three-dimensionally spatial about it. We may map the outer world with various geometries, but this, too, is the application of mind. The experience of space, like every other representation (or "intuition," to use the philosophical term) of that energy matrix we call the physical world, seems to be generated in the brain-mind. We can demonstrate this easily enough to ourselves. Take those 3-D viewers, for instance, where two slightly displaced slides of a scene or object can be optically merged so that we "see" the depth, the space. Or, again, those flat, mathematically jumbled patterns called "stereograms," which, when looked at in the right way, suddenly spring into three dimensions. And we also now have cyberspace generated in virtual-reality headgear and glove sensors. In all these cases, we are perceiving space that isn't there (wherever "there" is ). Space is the unseen specter that haunts our perception. Our brain-minds produce a smooth, stable psychological space from spaceless data that shimmer, bombard, flicker, or pulse into the sensors at the thresholds of our senses, then reach the spaceless arena of our brains in analogue form by electrical and chemical changes.

So where does the space come from, and how is it held together in our minds?

For centuries philosophers have argued about the nature of space, and how we perceive it. Two distinct strands of thought developed, one that saw space as *absolute*—a stationary void, a unitary spatial framework, which contains all things—and one that considered space as *relative*—that is, it exists only as the relation between objects, a line of thinking that was strengthened by the discovery of non-Euclidean geometries. But it is perhaps best to think of space not as "something" *to be perceived*, but as an *inborn organizing principle* of the mind that is used to construct the perception of the world from the data received through the senses. In the late 1970s, two brain researchers, John O'Keefe and Lynn Nadel, started to develop on this essentially Kantian idea.[30] They suggest that the ideas of relative and absolute space could be synthesized. There are, they claim, numerous neural systems within the brain that handle relative space, plus one that does the cognitive mapping involved with absolute space.

Relative space is essentially *egocentric space*, centered on the eye, the head, and the body, which we encountered in chapter one. We saw there how deeply rooted the expression of this kind of space had been throughout human history, across all cultures, and the "Experiential" section of the chapter dealt with the idea of consciously seeing the world in that way: space radiating out from the ghostly center of the self to the all-encompassing horizon. Objects were relative to that center, and to one another from that viewpoint. As we move, movement parallax causes objects to move with regard to one another and our moving center. To put it in simplistic terms, O'Keefe and Nadel suggest that we carry our egocentric space with us; in turn, it is mapped against and within a framework of non-centered, absolute space, giving us an integrated mental model of the environment.

Piaget, whom we referred to in the same chapter, saw a progression in which the way a child moves and acts (reflexes of grasping, sucking) helps it form an understanding of the spatial environment, starting out from this egocentric stage in infancy to a learned understanding of three-dimensional Euclidian space at about the age of ten or twelve years. O'Keefe and Nadel argue, along with other researchers, that Piaget may not have taken into account the whole picture, and give reasons for thinking that the ability to map absolute space (that is, a given, "on-board" sense of space that does not have to be learned) exists from an early age. This may be instinctual and only come within the range of conscious awareness in the sort of time frame suggested by Piaget. The researchers also point to the spatial behavior of other creatures. We have seen a variety of human mental mapping traditions in this present chapter, and animals likewise have the capacity. Prime examples of this are provided by migratory bird species, not to mention homing pigeons. Much effort has been expended on *how* birds receive the data that can guide them over hundreds and in some cases several thousands of miles, and it is now generally agreed that they can incorporate numerous cues. These include the position of the sun, the Pole Star and star clusters (a particular cue not, apparently, used by pigeons), and the Earth's magnetism. In some cases of local navigation, landmarks may operate as well. (For instance, research has shown that the Arctic tern uses these global cuing mechanisms for its mighty pole-to-pole migration, but uses local visual cues when homing in on its nest.) Birds work out their compass direction by calculating the height, say, of the sun at a given time of day according to their internal biological clock. Other animals use other cues. Wolf packs, for example, can split up and regroup at distant points, beyond the effective range of howling, and wolves can take intentional shortcuts and return from any direction to where pups were left. Sophisticated cognitive mapping is clearly taking place, and is probably heavily dependent on the sense of smell. A great deal of laboratory work has also shown that rats can devise mental maps to explore complex environments in which they are placed. In all these cases, the crux of the matter is not so much the cues that are used but the use the animal makes of them. The cues are not the map. The animal is orienting itself in some framework of space, as indeed are human beings who migrate, go on walkabout, or sail long distances.

"This conclusion has several implications. . . . It ought to be possible to discover the neural correlates of unitary space perception, in as much as this 'concept' is not built up from others but rather is built into the brain," write O'Keefe and Nadel. ". . . there must be a pre-existent spatial framework in order for organisms to experience the world coherently. Objects could not be identified, nor localized, nor even seen as extended [three-dimensional] in the absence of this framework."[31] They accept that concepts of space can vary in different cultures, and that species are attuned to different slices of reality, but insist that the universality of the way members of a species spatially relate to one another indicates that there has to be some underlying structure organizing perception.

Though asserting that much of the brain's processing handles information from head, eyes, and body, and thus organizes the sense of egocentric space, O'Keefe and Nadel identify the hippocampus as the seat in the brain where the overall, unitary spatial processing takes place. The hippocampus is a large, complex brain structure, curved in shape and somewhat reminiscent of a sea horse; hence its name (*hippo* means horse, *campus* a sea monster!). It is connected to the limbic system (consisting of old parts of the brain, the exact function of and relationship between which is not fully understood) and is associated with olfaction, visceral function, learning, emotion, motivation, and probably long-term memory. O'Keefe and Nadel claim that it handles input of sensory data and the body's positioning, and can send output to motor areas that control an organism's behavior. This, since the hippocampus is creating a perception of space and thus place, can guide the organism and promote exploratory activity based on curiosity, which is how a creature acquires its information for mapping. The researchers suggest that arrays of neurons within parts of the hippocampus are the "mapping space," and even go so far as to suggest that "each neurone (or group of neurones) would represent a place in a given environment." At last! A place of our own . . .

This mapping system is constantly updating, modifying, or overlaying earlier maps but not erasing them (thus, no known place is lost to the brain-mind, even if it is destroyed in the physical world), so that *difference* can be noted, keeping the organism alert to changes in its environment. It needs both place and *mis*place detection systems. The researchers acknowledge that the meaning a place has for a person affects his or her perception of it, but suggest that such value-feelings are laminated, as it were, by other neural systems onto the essential mapping information. (This of course begs questions regarding how a people recognize a *sacred* place: What is the data input that relates to that value? Where are the neurons for sacred space, the sensors of sanctity?) "The cognitive map is *not* a picture or image which 'looks like' what it represents," O'Keefe and Nadel emphasize; "rather, it is an information structure from which map-like images can be reconstructed and from which behaviour dependent upon place information can be generated."

Finally, we come to the long-term-memory aspect of the hippocampus, and its relationship to the whole matter of perceiving and understanding place and the lie of the land around us. As will be explored in the next chapter, this is potentially a more profound matter than it might seem on the surface: *the mapping system, it seems, possibly underpins the processes of language and imagery.* It is recognized in psycholinguistics that long-term memory is required for connected discourse; the meaning of a narrative is embedded in the wording and syntax. And we have seen in the "method of *loci*" that linking verbal and other abstract data with imagery is effective in the process of memorizing. In other words, placing information in a spatial context seems to enhance memory recall or reconstruction. For some time, investigators felt that imagery was distinct from language and involved different forms of mental processing. Now, however, it is thought that a *deep structure* underlies both imagery and language—a neuronal information network that subserves both. This network contains neither words nor pictures but is, rather, "some deep structure which captures the relationships embodied in the image and from which the image can be reconstructed." O'Keefe and Nadel locate the *semantic mapping* in the hippocampal structure in the brain's left hemisphere, and the representation of nonverbal physical occurrences with the right hippocampus. Put simply—words on the left, imagery (thus spatial mapping) on the right. Together they form the basis for a "long-term, context-specific memory for episodes and narratives." In their major work, *The Hippocampus as a Cognitive Map*, the researchers go on to test this idea usefully against the clinical data that have been collected on amnesia involving hippocampal damage.

It is not our concern here to go into this neurological and clinical work in any greater depth, but simply to outline it so we can grasp the deep nature of our sense of space and the significance of how we map within this mental construct, and because it will be suggested in the next chapter that the hippocampal mapping of space and language—or some similar brain-mind system—could be the mechanism nature has supplied to allow us to hear the actual voice of the Earth.

## STRANGE SPACE: MAPS OF THE OTHERWORLD

As one reads the work of cognitive scientists, especially the philosophers, it is easy to be drawn into the web of the extraordinarily fine-textured intellectual arguments that are spun about the problem of consciousness. I suppose it is necessary in our culture for this detailed reasoning to be conducted. But one is struck by how little considered are states of consciousness other than the monophasic condition in which the debate is being carried out. Even though altered mind-states are so relevant to the very problems the philosophers are investigating, they never get properly addressed in the debate at mainstream level. Yet the effects on time-and-space perception in altered states of mind could be profoundly pertinent to the understanding of how we cognize the world around us. By whatever means one effects a shift from the monophasic state deemed as normal in our culture, whether deep meditation, yogic practice, breathing exercises, the ingestion of hallucinogenic substances, sensory deprivation, fasting, trauma, or spontanous mystical rapture, three sensations are prominent in heralding the changing worldview that accompanies the mental shift. First, the quality of *light* appears to alter. It becomes dynamic and self-luminous, and a golden glow can even illuminate what to monophasic eyes is the darkness of night. Occasionally one hooks on to species-illegal wavelengths like X-rays and can see into the interior of plants, people, and objects. In cases of synesthesia, colors can be heard or tasted, thus proving that the experience of the world is quite definitely constructed within the brain-mind. Second, *space changes*. The walls of a room don't fit together the way they used to, and the ceiling is somewhere away "up there." Outside, in nature, it is easy in these altered states to see how the sense of three-dimensional space is a sort of fairground illusion. Many types of space may unroll before the amazed gaze. What is happening, then, to the spatial mapping of the brain-mind? One is clearly seeing a few extra dimensions of the "n-dimensional energy soup," so systems must exist within the brain-mind that can map these extended realms even if they lie dormant within the culturally locked monophasic state of mind. Sometimes representations of the energies rippling through that soup are presented to consciousness, not edited out as usual. These can look like flickers or rays of light, shimmering nets of energy, or even exotic spectral human or animal forms. Third, *time* plays tricks. It is even possible to experience space without time, and to watch with unspeakable awe as eternity settles over a scene, and movement is frozen in the amber of Great Time. This can affect hearing, so that even the sharpest and loudest of sounds do not break a primordial, ringing silence, "the peace that passeth understanding." The ghost of the self is revealed as insubstantial, and can become mobile. It is no longer in the head, it is somewhere else instead, perhaps even outside the body looking back at it.

It is thus a pity that the mind side of the brain-mind equation isn't studied by mainstream cognitive scientists with quite the same intensity as is the brain. Where the question of altered states does get referred to, it is subordinated to monophasic models of perception and worldview and so is treated as hallucination, a remodeling of the picture of the world, a creative reconstitution of memory images. This may well be true—there is no need to shy away from the wonders of our neural architecture—but the important point is that in these exotic mind-states the brain-mind has volumes to tell us about how our assumed "real world" is presented to the consciousness, for the same mechanisms are in play. The "real world" is, in a sense, a hallucination, too. The block to coming scientifically to grips with this range of experience is cultural. At the broad level, it is difficult (not always impossible, though) for researchers to get funding and approval to use substances that alter consciousness for research purposes. Legal issues and peer disapproval cloud the situation. The bulk of what research work is done in this regard is conducted in a gray zone between the wilds of psychedelia, or the frowned-on domain of parapsychology, and the academic mainstream. At a more specific level, there is a cultural block within the mainstream itself against raising this work to full status, probably because of the bad press "drugs" have in the popular culture. Some of this attitude is justified, but much of it is based on selective ignorance. And there is an almost willful failure to acknowledge the difference between a research usage of mind-altering substances and their indiscriminate availability at public level.

Yet, in other cultures, older and in some ways perhaps wiser than ours, quite different mental states were well known and well mapped. The shamans of various societies made maps of their otherworld journeys. One map from the Nyurumnal clan in Siberia shows how the shaman sent disease to another group, and depicts the track of his spirit and his spirit helpers through the tribal landscape.[32] A Chuckhee drawing shows a shaman being led to the otherworld by the spirits of the hallucinogenic fly-agaric mushroom, and another shows the shamanic three worlds (upper heaven-world, middle Earth-realm, and lower underworld) as concentric circles with figures and tents around the edges and the Pole Star in the center. (This is just one of many examples of how a society's cosmology maps its religious mind-states.) An Altaic map from Siberia shows the shaman's route from the site of a sacrificed horse and tent to the World Tree, then maps his route after he climbs the tree and goes up to the upper world, crossing nine thresholds before finally reaching the glorious presence of the god Ülgen.[33] A Koryak map even shows the journey of a sacrificed dog's spirit to the otherworld![34] And shamanistic tradition mapped altered states of consciousness in richer and more detailed ways than these graphic versions. It must be remembered, too, that the prevailing, communal phase of consciousness in some archaic and traditional societies would be at considerable variance with our own culture's idea of a normal mind-state.

There are also other than strictly shamanic maps of the otherworld (though all archaic knowledge of altered states of consciousness derives originally from the shamanic tradition). There are archaic texts, for instance, that describe the otherworld. The *Elder or Poetic Edda* (*Codex Regius*) was a collection of writings by unknown poets in Norway and Iceland dating from around 1300. In fragmentary form, they describe the Norse otherworld, a series of realms which were all attached to the axis formed by the World Tree, Yggdrasil, the cosmic ash. In the upper realms was the divine kingdom of Asgard, the central world was Midgard, the "Middle Earth" of Tolkien's *Lord of the Rings*, and below, around the roots of the tree, was Jotunheim, realm of the giants, and Hel, the underworld of the dead.

A quite different kind of mapping occurs in Tantric initiation, involving the use of the mandalic form—a form that can be similar to that of the labyrinth. Mircea Eliade describes such a usage for initiation in his *Yoga*. A piece of ground is selected, smoothed, and spiritually cleansed; then the *mandala* is drawn on it by means of two cords. The first, which is white, is used to trace the outer limits; the second is composed of threads of five different colors. Alternatively, the design can be laid out with colored rice powder. The center of the concentric circles is divided into triangles, where offerings of aromatic substances, vases of flowers or branches, and so forth are placed in honor of the gods who will descend there. The initiatory candidate sleeps outside the mandalic ground-drawing, lying on his right side (the Buddha's "lion posture" as he entered nirvana). In the morning, he tells his guru the contents of his dreams. If these are auspicious, the initiation ceremony begins. The candidate undergoes various purifications and consecrations and is finally blindfolded and thrown into the mandala. The section into which he falls determines the divinity who will be specially favorable to him during his initiation. "Entrance into the *mandala* resembles every 'march toward the centre . . .' " Eliade explains. "Since the *mandala* is an *imago mundi*, its center corresponds to the infinitesimal point perpendicularly traversed by the *axis mundi*; as he approaches its center, the disciple approaches the 'centre of the world'. In fact, as soon as he entered the *mandala*, he is in sacred space, outside of time; the gods have already 'descended' into the vases and insignia."[35] The candidate then enters meditation, and interiorizes the design of the mandala in all its cosmological meaning and symbolism.

As a final example of "other maps," we might consider what has been called the oldest travelers' guide in the world—the Chinese *Classic of the Mountains and Rivers*, written around 600 B.C. This describes the "Nine Cauldrons of Hsia," metal surfaces covered with pictures that represented the nine provinces of the country. In this manner people were instructed so that they could recognize both good and evil spirits, allowing them to avoid encounters with any nature spirits or genii when traveling through the mountains and forests, so such spirits as the Chhih, the Mei, and the Wang-liang were not offended by their intrusions and did not attack or otherwise accost them. Thus, harmony prevailed between the worlds of humans and spirits. Just imagine a modern map giving instructions on how to deal with the spiritual population of a region!

So what is being mapped in all these examples, and countless others of their general kind? "In some shamanic cultures, the path of initiation is an invisible one," writes Joan Halifax. "Scrolls, labyrinths, meandering trails, and straight lines, all roads of varying meaning, denote the 'orientation' of the neophyte's direction. Certain forms, such as the labyrinth, represent explicitly the experience of initiation—entry into the abyss of the mysteries, the pilgrimage of the spirit. The journey is in fact an expression of the evolution of the human spirit out of worldly time and space."[36]

Outside one of the ages-old stone towns built by the ancestors of the Kogi Indians of northern Colombia stands a stone crisscrossed with lines. It is a "map stone," partially relating to the stone-path systems that cross the Sierra Nevada de Santa Maria, the territory of the Kogi. These paths are integral to their spiritual life. As we noted earlier, Kogi tribal society preserves strong pre-Columbian traits, and is ruled by a shamanic elite called the *mamas*, the "enlightened ones." Over footage of this strange stone, the BBC producer Alan Ereira, who had unique tribal permission to film the Kogi, says: "The *Mama* has to walk in a world visible only to the mind's eye, the world of *aluna* [the spirit version of the physical Earth]. . . . The stone paths of the ancestors are traces of the spirit paths which the *Mamas* walked, in a space we do not understand. These are the paths in the Map Stone. . . ."[37]

It has already been briefly noted that there are several regions of the Americas where strange, straight desert lines, tracks, and "roads" laid down in pre-Columbian times map another world on the surface of the physical Earth, where "strange space" is mapped within "mundane space." It is a crucial matter in the understanding of former worldviews, and one we shall touch on again in the next chapter.

**EXPERIENTIAL**

### Home Ground

Relax and close your eyes. Create in your mind's eye what you see when returning home to your dwelling. Imagine yourself walking up to the entrance door. Note the details of the exterior of the building. Open the door and enter. Re-create in your memory every step you take to get to, say, the kitchen, the bedroom, or the den, including going along the corridor, up or down stairs (or elevator) as appropriate. Visualize coming into the room, finding a seat (perhaps where you are now—let your memory ghost merge with your present body image). Do all this slowly and in as much detail as possible. Not only will it strengthen your visualization capabilities, important for later experiential activities, but it will allow you to inspect how your brain-mind treats space as it conjures memory information. Become *aware* of the process.

### Life Line

Create a map of your life (always a useful exercise) in the form of a line. The overall structure of the map could be in any form—horizontal or vertical linear, or a variation on a mandala, and so forth. It could be based on a geographical map, plotting along a line where you have lived at different points in your life, or places you have visited on vacation—everywhere you have been in physical space. It could even have a "grid" based on years. Take some time to devise what you find to be the most useful form and scale. Punctuate the life line you draw with little notes of what to you were major incidents, life-changing experiences, important events. These could be external matters—like the death of a relative, meeting a new partner, the birth of a child, or key developments in your career—or they could be inner events—when you decided to give up smoking, or to change the way you were living your life, and so on. These events could be noted against dots or within little boxed areas along the life line. Use simple sketches or photographs and memorabilia as well to enhance the legends you apply to your map.

If this takes up a large area, well, why not? Cover a wall, or a large sheet of paper or board!

Primarily, this memory map is *associative*, linking your life events to time (the line), and also to places, if you map your life line over a representation of physical geography. It is surprising how "taking stock" like this can show patterns in your life, including redundant and unhelpful ones, and even indicate new directions—the real function of a map. It could save you a fortune on psychotherapy!

## Mapping the Territory

Draw a map of your home area—the position of your block in the general locality of the landscape or cityscape. Draw your own sketch map from memory but using a style based on a geographic map. Mark a route through it. Later, walk or drive that route and make sketches, take photographs, or do both. Attach these to your map at the appropriate places, along with any written observations, thoughts, poems, etc. Revise your sketch map as necessary, having noted in your walk or drive what you missed or placed incorrectly in a geographical sense. *Query yourself about these omissions and "mistakes."* In this way you will be combining two different approaches to mapping—geographic and chorographic. The geographic map is the bird's-eye view, the "neutral view" preferred by our culture; the other is the personal view—that is, a study of the locale from a human, interactive viewpoint. In *Maps Are Territories*, David Turnbull wisely comments that navigation requires such personalized elements, memory of place and so forth, and is not possible by the sole use of a "proper," neutral map. Believe it.

## Orienteering

This requires a trip to your local bookshop or library. Obtain some maps, either of your locality or of some area you wish to visit, and a book on orienteering. Since orienteering—following a route by skilled use of map and compass—is practiced as a sport, there are orienteering societies and groups as well as written information. Learn how to read a modern map in some detail—not just a road

atlas. Learn how to translate compass direction onto the plane surface of the map, how to rotate the map so you look along it in the
direction you are traveling, and how to make cross-sections to understand contour conventions, so you can see the information
coded in the contour imagery on the flat surface of the map "come
to life" as a profile of the terrain, with all its ridges, hollows,
canyons, and mountains. Orienteering is a specialist subject and
cannot be taught here, but I recommend that you try it if you are
not already familiar with map-and-compass work. Who knows, it
may one day save your life!

## A Personal Compass

This activity is designed as an antidote to the previous one. Modern
maps are part of the problem in some people's opinion, giving us
an abstracted, "off-Earth" worldview. Stephen S. Hall says that he
likes to revisit an area already known to him and see it in different
ways. He recalls streets in Greenwich Village and Rome he knew
well, "where history, memory and the street plan share a single set
of coordinates."[38] By making a personal compass, you can exercise
this chorographic element.

Base your compass on the *luopan* or *lo'pan* of *feng shui. Feng shui*
was (and is) the ancient Chinese art of "wind and water," and governed the layout of dwellings and ancestral tombs. Nowadays, it is
also applied to the layout of offices, bank buildings, and the like
in Singapore, Hong Kong, and elsewhere—even on Wall Street and
in the City of London! This is not the place to go into the subject in
depth (there is considerable literature on it), but we can note here
that the *feng-shui* diviner or geomant would use a special compass,
the *lo'pan*, to help him make his deliberations about a site. Essentially, this instrument consists of a central compass needle (one of
the first uses of the magnetic compass needle, incidentally) surrounded by rings of correspondences. So one ring would mark the
directions, another would give the colors and elements associated
with the directions, a third the astrological and astronomical associations with each direction, a fourth the characteristic topographi-

cal forms (flat-topped peaks, etc.) associated with the directions, and so on. A full-sized *lo'pan* can be a daunting, incomprehensible object, especially for Westerners not familiar with Chinese characters. But there is no need to learn *feng shui* other than for historical purposes: though there are some universally valid elements associated with the old geomantic system, most of it has relevance only to old Chinese culture. It will be of no use to you unless you become very expert in it. But you can create a simplified version of the *lo'pan* tailor-made for yourself.

A *luopan* or *feng-shui* compass in use.

Obtain a thin, flat cardboard box, or a thick sheet of cardboard or equivalent, a square or a squat rectangle. Insert in the center of the topside a small (ideally liquid-filled) magnetic compass. Draw a series of radiating circles, centered on the compass. Mark off the four directions related to the compass dial and the intercardinal directions. Run these lines out to the edge of the surface you have inserted the compass into, dividing it into eight segments. In the first circle, block in the segment that is "your" direction (as determined from the experiential work in chapter one). In the second circle, color the four main directional quadrants in colors you feel appropriate. Meditate on this, and follow your instincts (for this purpose, it is better to do this rather than simply adopting the color-direction codes used by traditional peoples, such as the Native Americans). In the third circle, name the moods or qualities you (again instinctually) associate with the eight directions your compass board is divided into. In the fourth circle, write in each of the eight directions the tides of the day, perhaps using the old Northern European system indicated in the "Drawing the Circle" exercise in chapter one. On the outer or subsequent rings, put in any further associations you find meaningful (they don't necessarily have to be "useful").

Equipped with your personal compass, go on a *wander*, a non-goal-oriented walk, when you are not constrained by time—your "medicine walk" (chapter three) would be an ideal opportunity for this, or even an afternoon in your local park or another open space. Take some cue in your environment—the direction the wind is coming from (or blowing to), for instance, or the course a bird takes as it flits across your field of view, or a cat, dog, lizard, or whatever is underfoot. Start out in that direction, and orient your compass so the north point of the magnetic needle is aligned with the north of the compass board you have drawn out. What is the direction you are traveling in? What are the associations that follow from that according to your compass board? Check how you feel as you walk in that direction. Pay attention to moods, subtle changes in consciousness, feelings, and so forth within yourself that you usually do not take time to notice. Treat this outer walk as an *inner adventure*! Wander with the winds; look for different cues to pull you into other directions, checking all the associations on your compass as you do so, and working on yourself as you walk. Terminate this when you are ready to, but try to maintain it for at least a half-mile, which is probably enough to develop a real sense of this flicking in and out of your attention, from inner mood to outer directional cue and back, giving unusual, poetic, nonrational lateral associations for your intellect to struggle with.

## Blind Man's Buff

You will need a friend to help out with this (choose someone in sympathy with the principle of challenging the culturally given worldview!). We all recall adventure tales in which the heroine or hero is abducted and is blindfolded or placed in a car trunk and taken to the villains' hideout. After escaping, the person is later able to find the hideaway location by remembering nonvisual cues, during the abduction journey. This activity does not require you to get yourself abducted, but is an exercise in nonvisual mapping. Have someone lead you around an unfamiliar environment, indoors or out, while you are blindfolded or wearing a sleep mask. (To make the task extra difficult, spin around a few times before setting off.) Take note of any sounds (including those of your feet on the ground), smells, changes in orientation, rough or smooth ground, steps, slopes, and so on. Get your friend to stop you at certain appropriate points so you can touch objects in the immediate environment. Afterwards, map this route by jotting down in order all the nonvisual cues you can recall. With your helper's assistance, retrace the route, this time with your eyes unmasked (or, to make it more gamelike, see if you can work out what the route was from your nonvisual information). Compare what you see with the mental impressions you formed from the nonvisual cues. Also, be conscious of the different ways you feel about the same environment when masked and unmasked.

This activity may sound particularly bizarre, but it is surprising how much fun it can be! And, should you ever be kidnapped . . .

## Haptic Mapping

Now use a deeper nonvisual sense to map your environment. Often called "dowsing" or "water-witching," this method uses various kinds of implement to amplify muscular changes in the body, which themselves may be amplifications of subtle responses to information received by the unconscious mind. The traditional tool for accomplishing this is the "dowsing rod," a flexible forked branch or twig (typically a hazel twig, but any will do). Towards the end of the nineteenth century, the pendulum (any small, suitably weighty object tied to a length of thread) started to be used for dowsing as well, a method that came from psychic research. Dowsing was first historically recorded as being used by late-medieval miners in Europe seeking mineral veins, and the early literature also refers to the finding of water sources by this method. Later, it developed into the finding of lost objects, or divining illness and places that were dangerous to health. Some research has seemed to show that some human beings can register very slight changes in the electromagnetic environment (probably everyone feels these subliminally, but only certain people can express them as a dowsing response without training).[39,40,41,42] *But be warned*, the term "dowsing," or "energy dowsing," is now often used in ways that verge on pure fantasy; claims made for it are as ridiculous as they are unverifiable. Unfortunately a great deal of "New Age" literature exists that promulgates such nonsense. There is a great difference between attempting to expand your worldview subtly by employing different sensory modes and becoming engulfed in rubbish. Here's how to avoid that trap.

First, select your dowsing tool. I find the good old-fashioned flexible forked twig the best. Pendulums can all too easily be made to produce the responses you secretly want, "angle rods" (rods of metal bent to form handles, often held in short plastic sleeves) even more so. If you have no dowsing tool, then hold your hands in front of you as if you were praying, the palms just barely separated; when you pass over your target, you may find that your hands will gently press together. Then obtain, say, ten plastic or paper cups, and ask someone to fill them all with water, but to dissolve salt in one and sugar in another. Your helper should mark each of these on the bottom in such a way that only he or she knows which is which. These are then spaced out across the ground or the floor. Using your dowsing tool, approach each cup, seeking, as consciously as possible, the cup that contains salted water. If you are holding a forked twig, hold it by the splayed ends, with your palms uppermost and your fingers and thumbs slightly clenched. Hold the twig in such a way that there is a degree of tension in it by pulling out the splayed ends, enabling it to flip up or down (it doesn't matter which) readily and firmly as a response. Repeat the exercise seeking the sugar. Make a note of which cups are which in your opinion, and check with the person who prepared the cups. (This helper should not be in sight or earshot while you are conducting your dowsing, because it is easy to pick up subtle cues from a person even when no one is trying to cheat.) If you identify both substances correctly the first time, you are a good natural dowser. If you get one out of the two right the first time, you are pretty good and will soon be expert with a little practice. If you get neither, you'll need to work at it, like most of us. I often do a version of this activity as part of my workshops, and only twice have I seen anyone get it right completely and repeatedly. One was an elderly English gentleman who had never tried dowsing before, and the other was a middle-aged American woman who had dabbled previously. But quite often people will find one of the targets. Keep at it until you get reasonable results. If you just can't do it, then don't worry, abandon this activity. We can all knock a tennis ball over a net, but there are only a certain number of professional tennis players, and most of us drive cars without becoming good enough to be racing-car drivers.

If or when you establish a modicum of expertise, then put it to use. Get someone to bury a target object somewhere in a large area of ground, and use your dowsing tool to find it. And try to map the underground streams (or pipes) of water in a given area. Use markers (sticks or colored thread) to map out your findings. Compare your results with those of other dowsing friends, or, better still, check against any piping or hydrographic charts, if such exist for the area.

As you become more proficient, you can begin to use your dowsing sense to explore the environment in all kinds of ways. You might even use it to find "your place" when settling on some location in an area you are unfamiliar with. Or you might "ask" if the space in a building is harmful or beneficial (where you work or live; or if you are an architect). This can be particularly useful, for architectural space is haptic space, it is something we feel and sense around us, and this method is haptic sensing. But start pragmatically before launching off into these more exotic uses of your newfound skill—ungrounded dowsing is worse than no dowsing at all, and is a waste of precious time.

### Space in Your Face

When you think about it, space always *is* in your face, but most of us very seldom pay it any mind (literally). But if *places* can have different qualities, which we all consciously or unconsciously recognize, then what about space itself? Do regions of space have characteristic qualities?

A useful first approach to developing space awareness is a simple drawing exercise. When I was at art college, I used to hate having to draw rows of bottles—a standard exercise. It was boring, and, quite frankly, I just couldn't get one side of a bottle to match the other! Then, one day, a bright tutor suggested that I look not at the bottles but at the spaces between them. Revelation! By forgetting about the bottles, and just looking at and drawing the *spaces*, not only was I able to get the proportions of the bottles pretty accurately as a kind of by-product, but the whole exercise became new, fresh, and exciting. I do recommend this. Set up three or four different-shaped bottles in a row and draw them, with the tallest bottle extending the full distance from the top to the bottom of your sheet of drawing paper. Focus only on the gaps between the bottles, and when you have finished their outlines, shade in the spaces heavily, leaving the bottles blank.

Carrying out space-awareness activities simply requires you to become more sensitive to space as you find yourself in different places. For instance, when you have been away from your home for a while, and especially if you have been out of doors for a period, catch that initial sense of the space inside your home when you first come back. It will be quite distinctive and curiously unfamiliar, yet within a few minutes you will find it hard to be aware of that initial sense at all. Practice space awareness by arranging to go fairly quickly from an enclosed space (say a tent) to a place outside with extensive views. *Feel* that difference: space exploding in your face. What *is* it that you are feeling? Another classic exercise is to revisit the school you attended as a very small child. This is always a space trip, and creates classic space-memory associations. Immediately you will be astonished at how small the playground seems to your adult eyes, likewise the schoolroom desks, exercise bars, and so on.

Your experience of space in the school when you were small is powerfully evoked in your memory and creates a most instructive dissonance with your present experience of the place. Space becomes almost tangible. Also take note if you find the quality of the space anywhere to be depressing for no particular reason (such as having a bad memory associated with it). When you are in a place you find sacred or otherwise powerful, be sensitive to its space. In particular, spend a little time just feeling the space at ancient sacred sites. In Gothic cathedrals, the space is especially powerful.

But in the end, this is not something I can really write about—you just have to do it. Give space its due. And when you have done this kind of thing for a while, on and off, check to see if your *memory* improves. You may find that it does.

*Now that we know (w)here we are, and have our maps, it is time to try to find our way home. . . .*

# DREAMING

## Soul-to-Soul with *Anima Mundi*

I am She-Who-Loves-Silence, emerging from the Western Mountain, provider of spiritual nourishment and the authority of sovereignty. I was here from the time before time. I was recognized, given names and worshipped by the earliest people, then, later, as Hathor by those who built temples at my feet: as cobra I guarded the pharaoh and denoted the right of kingship; as divine cow, the sun rose between my horns and I suckled the kings. Though these people passed, as all people do, I am still here, older than known ages and dwarfing the temples left behind. Yet now unseen, for the people who come and go here no longer dream. . . .

"THE . . . MIND IS A PART OF THE NATURE of things; the world is a divine dream. . . . Behind nature, throughout nature, spirit is present . . ." wrote Emerson.[1] And that was the kind of world the ancients inhabited. It was greatly different from the world we think we look out onto today. Yet, even ancient dreaming leaves its monuments, as we shall see in this chapter. I will suggest that in the remnants of those dreams left in the land is the most profound and important message the archaic whisper contains. That message concerns the nature of mythic consciousness, the subject that has interwined itself throughout the pages of this book.

### DREAMLAND

The valley of Deir el-Bahri extends into the Theban mountain range for about a mile, and ends in a large natural ampitheatre or bay. The mountain massif stands on the western side of the Nile opposite present-day Luxor, the ancient Thebes. The massif is dominated by the Theban Peak, called "el-Qurn," ("the Horn") in Arabic. This

The remarkably symmetrical Theban Peak (el-Qurn, "The Horn") dominates the Valley of the Kings, Egypt.

startling natural feature of striking pyramidical form was perhaps what inspired the architects of ancient Egypt to create their monumental pyramids. Certainly people seem to have been drawn to this western mountain for tens of thousands of years, long before dynastic Egypt. The Egyptians similarly gravitated to the mountain complex, and within its folds built the tombs for their kings and queens, digging them deep inside the limestone walls of the mountain. Deir el-Bahri was sacred to Hathor, the goddess who was Mistress of the West, often shown as a cow, or a woman with cow's ears and horns, an aspect that betrays her origin in the prehistoric cults of nomads and pastoralists.[2] She emerged from the western mountain to receive the souls of the dead kings. She it was who nurtured Horus, and so was deeply involved with the divine kingship of Egypt. This association is further emphasized by the Aten, the sun disk, between her horns, an aspect of the supreme creator, Re (Ra). She was also depicted as a cobra, the symbol of royal power. In this, she was an extension of Meresger, "She Who Loves Silence," a cobra goddess of popular worship, who was identified with the Theban Peak. Both the bovine and serpentine aspects of Hathor were displayed at Thebes. In the shrine of Hathor within the temple of Thutmose III in Deir el-Bahri, a statue was found showing Amenophis II being brought forth by the goddess in her cow form and being suckled by her, and across the Nile, in the Temple of Karnak, Amenophis II is shown with a cobra wearing horns and the Aten rearing behind and over him (this statue may also have originated in Deir el-Bahri). Hathor had priestesses in her cult, and she was mainly identified with joy, music, lovemaking, and general gaiety, in addition to her funerary and royal roles.

Within the bay of Deir el-Bahri is the vast New Kingdom temple of Queen Hatshepsut. This has three successive terraces set into the cliff wall behind it and has long been admired as one of the great

The highly eroded "statue group" in the cliff face behind the temple of Hatshepsut, Deir el-Bahri, Egypt. The head of the pharaoh, with headdress and ceremonial beard, can be easily distinguished; the cobra, with distended hood, rises behind. [Drawing: N. Griffiths, courtesy of V. A. Donohue.]

achievements of ancient-Egyptian temple architecture, especially as one that adapts superbly to its physical surroundings. In particular, the temple's structure is focused on a column of rock that obtrudes from the cliff face and reaches up to and beyond the cliff edge. No one saw anything special about this column until the winter of 1990–91, when Egyptologist V. A. Donohue of Oxford's Griffith Institute was conducting fieldwork at the site. He suddenly perceived that the forms constituting the rock column "simulate the configuration of a statue-group in which the cobra, its eyes and the lateral markings on the underside of its distended hood clearly observable, rears to the full height of the cliffs behind a standing anthropomorphic figure, either sovereign or deity, who wears the head-dress and beard."[3] This colossal figure group, hundreds of feet high, is heavily eroded but still discernible for those who have the eyes to see. Further technical investigation is needed to determine whether this is an untouched simulacrum (the chance likeness of a natural form to another figure or object), or whether the suggestive natural features have been enhanced by human sculpting. The implications are intriguing. In either case, there had to be human recognition of the forms in the column, which means that people must have looked at the natural topography for symbolic meaning. Either they projected into the natural forms an expression of their own religious ideas, or, more startlingly, the western mountain, with its pyramidical peak and goddess column, may have promoted royal and religious iconography in the minds of the Egyptians. Donohue feels that other temple locations along the Nile also incorporate such rock-face simulacra.[4]

A similar case has been discovered in a completely different context, that of the Externsteine rocks, a group of five weirdly weathered fingers of sandstone, each around a hundred feet in height, located in the Teutoburger Wald district, near Detmold, Germany. Remains have been unearthed around them suggesting the presence of reindeer hunters as far back as 10,000 B.C. Some researchers have maintained that the place was a center for pagan worship until Christianization by Charlemagne in 772 A.D., whereas other scholars have suggested that very early Christian worship took place at the rocks. Whatever the truth of these conflicting claims, the site presents a bizarre appearance today, with steps, apparently going nowhere, carved out of some of the sandstone pillars, an apparent

The huge simulacrum of Odin or Christ with arms out-stretched on one of the rock pillars at the Externsteine rocks, Germany. Note the hole in the figure's side. See text.

sarcophagus hewn out of a giant boulder, and caves or "rooms" honeycombing the lower reaches of some of the pillars. (These may have been used by hermits or anchorites at some remote period.) Surmounting one of the pillars is a rock-hewn chapel, either pagan or early Christian, which has a round window through which the midsummer rising sun shines. On one of the rock columns is an overhanging segment that from certain angles looks strikingly like a man with his arms raised, as if tied to the rock. This phenomenon has long been noted, and there have been suggestions that it represents Odin hanging on the World Tree. Recent technical examination has confirmed that this natural simulacrum was in fact worked with tools to enhance its anthropomorphic appearance. But still the pagan-Christian ambiguity exists, for a hole has been made in the side of the figure. Was this to "Christianize" the Odin image? No one knows.

This remarkable simulacrum of a head, complete with cheek-bones and lips, is to be found on the summit of Carn Brae, a major hill in Cornwall, England. (The summit of the hill also harbors the remains of a Neolithic encampment five thousand years old.) Legend states that the head is that of the Carn Brae giant. He faces St. Agnes' Beacon, another hill, six miles away. The giant on that hill was known as Bolster, and he and the Carn Brae giant threw rocks at one another until Bolster ran out of ammunition. That explains why St. Agnes' Beacon is smooth and Carn Brae littered with rocks. This is, of course, very similar to the sort of topographically related creation myths of the Aboriginal Dreamtime in Australia.

Ancient and preindustrial people often saw gods, goddesses, and heroes in the lay of the land, in just the same way that today we sometimes incorporate external stimuli into our dreams. The shapes of mountains, already associated in ancient times with spirits and the abode, or seat, of the Earth Mother Goddess, the Mountain Woman,[5] were particularly important elements in this mythic, dreamscape perception of the topography. One example with roots at least four or five thousand years old is to be found at Callanish, a group of remarkable stone circles on the Isle of Lewis, off Scotland's west coast. The Callanish stones seem to have been associated with the observation of the moon. At their latitude during the major standstill period—a period reached every 18.61 years in the long and complex lunar cycle when the moon rises and sets at its most northerly and southerly extremes—the moon just skims the horizon between its most southerly rising and setting points. (Indeed, the moon cannot be seen to rise at all at this time from positions all that much farther north than Callanish.) At this time the moon appears to rise out of the Pairc Hills, which, from the area of the Callanish stones, resemble the form of a woman reclining on her back. This formation, sometimes called the "Sleeping Beauty," has the Gaelic name Cailleach na Mointeach, the Old Woman of the Moors, a pseudonym for the Hag or Earth Mother. She is well known to the present inhabitants of the Callanish area and was doubtless so to their distant ancestors. The moon, then, skims the horizon, passing up the body of the Sleeping Beauty and finally setting into the Clisham range on a nearby island, but what is seen by an observer standing at the end of the Callanish avenue of stones at the main Callanish site, the "Stonehenge of the North," is the moon setting within the stones of the central circle. Symbolically, then, every 18.61 years in its great cycle at Callanish, the moon is born out of the Earth Mother and dies into the stones. This event came around again in the major-standstill year of 1987, and was actually witnessed, photographed, and drawn.

Something similar happened farther south down the Western Isles of Scotland, but this time involving the sun. A row of three gaunt standing stones and a burial kist form a site known as Ballochroy, situated on the western coast of Scotland's Kintyre Peninsula. The middle one of the three standing stones is a flat slab placed edgewise to the line of the stone row, and looking along its flat face directs the eye towards the midsummer sunset position amidst the mountain range called the Paps, on the island of Jura, some nineteen miles distant across the sea. The word "paps" means "breasts," and the Paps of Jura are so-called because the central peaks do indeed look like two rounded breasts. Celtic scholar Dr. Anne Ross has remarked that place names can be of incredible antiquity, and we can be sure that the mountains looked like breasts to the megalith builders, too, to whom they would have represented the Earth Mother, in just the same way that the Pairc Hills would have looked like a goddess in the landscape to the prehistoric users of Callanish. When the midsummer sun sets behind the Paps of Jura as viewed from Ballochroy, a ribbon of sunlight dances across the intervening water like an umbilical cord connecting the viewer with the old Earth Mother, whose breasts stand out starkly silhouetted against the golden sunset sky.

The importance of these breastlike mountains in prehistory has been further confirmed by an archeological discovery in 1994 on the island of Islay, close to Jura. Geophysical investigation of the ground around a standing stone by the shores of Loch Finlaggan, which was itself the focus for ceremonial activity by different cultures for thousands of years, revealed the remains of a former alignment of stones leading up to it. This alignment pointed to a gap in the local skyline in which the two main, breastlike peaks of the Paps of Jura are perfectly framed.[6]

Near Killarney, in Ireland, are two peaks that stand out distinctly from the hill country around them and are profoundly breastlike in their symmetry and roundness, an impression enhanced by teatlike cairns on their summits. They are known as the Paps of Anu. Anu was the mythical mother of the last generation of gods who ruled the Earth, the Tuatha De Danaan. Anne Ross writes that the hills "personify the powers of the goddess embedded in the land," and remarks that Anu is still regarded as the local fairy queen, and people still gather there at Lughnasa and climb the heights nearby.[7]

Seeing mythic beings in mountains was a cross-cultural phenomenon in the ancient world. In Greece, for instance, this was intriguingly revealed by important observations on the part of architectural historian Vincent Scully in the 1960s.[8] Gods or goddesses housed in Greek temples were the manifestations of spirit or "atmosphere" of the physical surroundings of the temple—a special case of the *genius loci*. "The landscape and temples together form the architectural whole," Scully writes.[9] Similarly, Rachel Fletcher has observed that Greek theaters, located in temple complexes, "ex-

The Paps of Anu, Ireland.

pressed an intimacy and continuity with the immediate physical site unparalleled in Western theatre."[10] (Performances could be held at dawn, so a rising sun in the events of a play would be synchronized with sunrise in the actual surroundings.) Working from earlier German research, Scully noted that many ancient Greek temples were oriented on or within sight of distinctive cleft-peaked mountains. The cleft-peaked mountain was a symbol of the Earth Mother. "These features create a profile which is basically that of a pair of horns, but it may sometimes also suggest raised arms or wings, the female cleft, or even, at some sites, a pair of breasts," Scully states.[11] In fact, the "raised-arms" salute or sign of the goddess was well established throughout the eastern-Mediterranean world by the Bronze Age: Mycenaean figurines, predynastic Egyptian pottery motifs, Sicilian pot handles and tomb slabs all refer to the sign. In some cases, there are profound ambiguities between arms, horns, and breasts.[12]

At the Minoan palace of Knossos on Crete, the court opens to the distant, cleft-peaked Mount Juktas. At Knossos, of course, is a great sacral-horns sculpture and a mural showing the Minoan bull-cult ritual in which young men and women seized the horns of a charging bull and somersaulted over its back. A seal found at Knossos shows a woman on a mountain with sacral horns in the background. (The great archeologist of Minoan Crete, Sir Arthur Evans, also noted that Juktas looked like a man's head gazing skywards when viewed from the direction of Tylissos, and discovered that the locals there called it the "head of Zeus.") Elsewhere in Crete, the palaces of Ayia Triadha and Phaistos are in view of the twin-peaked Mount Ida, in which are caves that were used even prior to the time of the palaces for goddess worship. It was in Kamares, the main cave

Mount Kerata ("Horns"), Greece, rises above the site of the Temple of the Mysteries of Eleusis and the surrounding factories.

there, that the legendary Cretan shaman figure Epimenides fasted, went into trance, and became master of "enthusiastic wisdom"—in other words, became expert in the techniques of inducing altered states of consciousness. The palace of Mallia is directed at Mount Dikte, which also has a split peak. The caves there came to be dedicated to Zeus. On the Greek mainland, the great Temple of the Mysteries at Eleusis, mythically the spot where Persephone (Kore) was abducted into the underworld and where her mother, Demeter, mourned for her, has a clear view of the dramatically cleft peak of Mount Kerata ("Horns"). Moreover, the cross-axis of the Telesterion, the initiatory temple where the Mysteries were revealed to the Mystai with a secrecy that has survived the ages, aligns to another prominent skyline saddle or notch on the offshore island of Salamis. And from the summit of the Acropolis at Athens, the eastern horizon is dominated by the saddle between the sacred twin peaks or "horns" of Hymettos.

In the Americas, similar ancient dreamtime visions within the topography are to be found. Hovenweep National Monument, for example, is situated forty miles west of Cortez, Colorado, and strad-

The Sleeping Ute mountain viewed from Hovenweep National Monument, Utah.

dles the border between southeastern Utah and southwestern Colorado. This atmospheric site consists of six groups of buildings approximately eight hundred years old which are situated in small box canyons. They weren't documented until 1874, and are still very much off the beaten track. Very little archeological work has gone on there, and the buildings are today much as they were left by the lost Anasazi, except for the depredations of time. Nobody knows what these structures were all about: theories abound, but there are no firm answers. The site complex looks out to the east, towards a prominent mountain now known as "The Sleeping Ute," which looks very much like a sleeping chieftain beneath his blanket. Legend has it that he will awake at the time of greatest need. If this mountain has insinuated itself into Ute mythology, we need have no doubt that the Anasazi saw something very similar.

Far across today's United States, in New England, an even more arresting simulacrum exists in the White Mountains. There, to the east of the Connecticut River, is a rock face with the startlingly convincing profile of an Indian chief. We can be sure it was seen as a god or a hero before the Europeans came, for the land was mythologized throughout the Americas. "Almost every prominent rock and mountain, every deep bend in the river, in the old Cherokee country had its accompanying legend," James Mooney points out, for instance. "It may be a little story that can be told in a paragraph to account for some natural feature, or it may be one chapter of a myth that has its sequel in a mountain a hundred miles away."[13]

The Australian Aborigines, we noted earlier, wandered their country following the routes of their Dreamtime ancestors. They walked through a landscape that was a topographic myth. The land harbored the dreamtime; it enriched the inner lives of the people. The dreaming tracks were both outer and inner journeys, the two aspects exquisitely interactive. The sites of significance along these routes had their songs, their dances, their legends. Each was a mythologized place. "The bond between a person and his (or her) country is not merely geographical or fortuitous, but living and spiritual and sacred," wrote the anthropologist A. P. Elkin in the early decades of this century. "His country . . . is the symbol of, and gateway to, the great unseen world of heroes, ancestors, and life-giving powers which avail for man and nature."[14] Similarly, ". . . the native cannot look around him anywhere without feeling in a very vivid way that here, there and everywhere some supernatural power, some mythic being, has at some time made his presence felt, and indeed may still be present in the place," Lucien Lévy-Bruhl wrote many years ago. "Earth and sea are to him as living books in which the myths are inscribed. . . . *A legend is captured in the very outlines of the landscape. . . .*"[15] One settler, Olive Pink, was inducted into the myths of the land by an Aborigine in the 1930s. She was shown *arumba arunga* (literally "spirit doubles") within the land. Two pieces of blue stone, one large, the other smaller, were pointed out to her as "that mother and baby blue kangaroo"; another was a low hill which was said to be the heads of two Dreamtime women who had gone back into the ground. "To the spiritually blind eyes of a non-native, this was simply a low hill, though remarkable because of its isolated white limestone cap on the bronze country. . . . When one's spiritual eyes had been opened by the totemite's explanation one could quite well imagine it as the decorated heads of two *altjira* women," Pink admitted.[16] The landscape was being seen with Blake's "double vision."

All these are just a few cases of simulacra that represent the nature of mythologized landscapes of many different peoples around the world and in former times. They tell us that the whole body of the Earth in the ancient world was permeated by mythic meaning. Where peoples have disappeared or lost their heritage, the dreaming of the land has been abandoned, too. Today, we think of these things as curiosities, as features that "look like" something, but we must not make the mistake of thinking that is how the ancients perceived them. To them, these landscape elements were truly powerful mythic entities, as powerful as features in our dreams are to us *at the time we dream them*, not after we wake up and dimly recall them as the passing phantasms of an unimportant phase of nighttime consciousness that we use alarm clocks, showers, and cups of coffee to shake off—which is in microcosm a daily replay of the historical psychological process that James Hillman refers to when he says, "As the Gods died, the Self emerged."[17] The Dreamtime peoples of the world did not share our current cultural phase of consciousness, which brings with it linear time. They were awake to prehistory but hadn't "woken up" to history. Having awoken ourselves, we cannot now readily experience a state in which the land was in a real way the equivalent of the environments in our dreams. We should tread lightly in the wilderness, therefore, lest, unaware, we disturb the dreams of the ages.

## THE SPIRIT EARTH

In the early years of this century, anthropologist Paul Wirz noted that the native peoples of New Guinea recognized *Dema* or spirit sites. "In most cases such spots have a striking outward appearance in consequence of some strange or unexpected aspect . . ." Wirz remarked. "Curious noises may be heard in them. In the rivers the *Dema* cause unpredictable currents and eddies, in the sea they raise waves which are dangerous for canoes. Occasionally people catch sight of strange apparitions, the *Dema* themselves, rising out of the earth, though mostly such visions are but fleeting and uncertain. . . ."[18]

Spirits could take many forms, well beyond our imagination today. The Ajumawi of the Fall River Valley in northeastern California, for instance, had a gigantic spirit that took the form of a shadow. The solstices and equinoxes were deeply integrated into several aspects of Ajumawi life, and were important times in the ceremonial calendar. The five-thousand-foot-tall Simloki (Soldier Mountain) was and is a sacred being to the Ajumawi. At the solstitial and equinoctial sunsets, the tip of its shadow reaches the Big Valley Mountains, about a dozen miles away to the east. On each date, it points out a sacred place in the mountains—at equinox, for example, it touches a sacred spring inhabited by many spirits; at midwinter it points to the rocks where Jamul, the Coyote-Man, left his footprints, and so forth. It takes up to one and a half hours for Simloki's shadow to creep from its base across the valley to the Big Valley Mountains. Jamul and Kwahn (Silver-Gray Fox-Man) were creator-heroes, and they had raced Simloki's shadow in the time before time to settle a dispute. The Ajumawi developed a tradition of racing the shadow in remembrance of this Dreamtime duel. Only those Indians who beat the relentless progress of the shadow to the eastern mountains gained power, and it was essential that the runners not look back: the advancing shadow was actually a spirit being in its own right, and to look back at it while racing was to invite instant retribution, often in the form of sudden death.[19]

This type of mythic thinking alerts us to the fact that in earlier worldviews the land was inhabited by spirits in all sorts of forms. Indeed, the extent to which the human and spirit worlds met on the face of the Earth in former times is probably underestimated by us today. People still see apparitions today, of course, but such events are ushered out of any official worldview as "unreal."

So extensive was the perception of the ancient spirit world that it had its own geography, which is only now being revealed to our gaze as a result of research into "spirit lines." I have written at length on these elsewhere,[20,21,22] providing detailed references, and I will be writing further on the subject, so here I will simply summarize the matter. It does have a strong bearing on alternate worldviews and states of consciousness, even though it is one of the least-heard aspects of the archaic whisper.

In the Americas, spirit lines are still a visible phenomenon if looked for in the right places. The famous example is the complex of lines on the pampa near Nazca in Peru. Here a wide range of dead-straight lines are scored into the desert pavement, crossing, re-crossing, or running parallel with one another, and radiating out of what have been termed "ray centers," or piles of rocks on slight natural rises. Amongst the lines are ground drawings of animals, insects, spirals, and other abstract designs, traced in a unicursal line, so the drawings can be "entered" and followed on foot without the path's crossing over itself. The Nazca lines are, however, only one example of many similar types of features left by prehistoric Native Americans. In the United States, for instance, the two-thousand-year-old Hopewell peoples left remarkably geometric earthworks and straight ceremonial roads in Ohio and adjacent states; the Miwok Indians of the California sierras made tracks so straight that one researcher in the 1930s described them as "airline in their directness," running tens of miles without deviation from one mountain ridge to another; the Anasazi of the American Southwest left behind engineered "roads" up to thirty feet wide that also run re-markably straight for tens of miles, especially from (or to) the Anasazi cult center of Chaco Canyon in New Mexico, as we noted in chapter three. These people had neither wheeled vehicles nor horses, so it is a mystery why they needed such roads. The mystery has deepened with the results of infrared photography carried out by NASA in the Chaco area, which has revealed as many as three parallel thirty-foot-wide sections of some Chacoan roads. These roads pass through ruins of "Great Houses" which seem to have been ceremonial buildings, their architecture accommodating the passage of the roads. Farther south, in pre-Hispanic Mexico, similar though older straight causeways and roads proliferate around the ancient temple or citadel of La Quemada.[23] Some of these have al-tars along their center lines, and others just run into cliff walls. Still farther south, in the Yucatán, the northern domain of the ancient Maya, there are *sacbaob*, straight and level ceremonial roads linking the temple cities of the Maya. The longest of these currently discov-ered runs between Cobá and Yaxuna for nearly a hundred kilome-ters. The Maya also had mythic, invisible *sacbeob* that ran beneath the ground or through the air (these were called Kusam Sum). In Costa Rica, NASA infrared aerial surveys have revealed straight tracks cutting through mountainous rain-forest country.[24] In South America, there are the stone paths of the Kogi Indians in Colombia, already referred to in the preceding chapter (and later in this one). New ethnological work is revealing the existence of previously un-known "song lines" running through the Amazon.[25] In Peru, be-sides the Nazca lines already mentioned, there are straight-line complexes on desert surfaces in numerous places along the Andes chain. The Inca had apparently invisible alignments called *ceques*, also noted earlier, running out through sacred places, *huacas*, from the Coricancha in Cuzco. Spectacular old straight tracks occur on the altiplano of Bolivia. They run up to twenty miles in length and are perfectly straight, regardless of the terrain. These features link Ayamara Indian sacred places. Straight tracks or desert lines have been noted as far south as Chile.

So why were pre-Columbian Indians marking the land with straight lines? There is evidence that some of the *roads* were multipurpose, so there was military use of some of them in state-type Native American societies, such as that of the Inca. But equal evidence exists that there were ceremonial religious functions associated with them as well. The old straight tracks and desert lines are even more mysterious, and what we know about them suggests a definite religious association. In 1977, anthropologist Marlene Dobkin de Rios noticed that these large-scale land markings occurred in the territories of Indian societies that were known to be shamanic, and in some cases still are. It is known that the Hopewell people were essentially a shamanic-based group of societies, and shamans' graves have been excavated, revealing such items as wooden models of hallucinogenic mushrooms. The Miwok took the powerful *Datura* hallucinogen, Jimsonweed, as did the Chumash, also in California. It is not known if the Anasazi took hallucinogenic plants for their ceremonial purposes, but the pueblo peoples, whom the Anasazi probably dissolved into, certainly did: a pre-Columbian wall painting in the Zuñi Indian Kuaua kiva, near present-day Albuquerque, depicts a medicine man holding Jimsonweed. In Mexico, the surviving Huichol Indians practice a peyote religion that seems to have originated in remote times. Throughout Central America there is evidence of the ancient use of hallucinogenic psilocybin mushrooms. Numerous "mushroom stones" have been found that date back two or three thousand years, and modern ethnobotanical research has revealed the continuing practice of mushroom-based shamanism. In South America, a bas-relief at the ancient religious center of Chavín de Huántar in Peru shows a deity holding a San Pedro cactus, also a powerful hallucinogen. And throughout the Amazon rain-forest areas, the use of *ayahuasca*, the "soul vine," is widespread. Ethnobotanist Weston La Barre has noted that these Native American plant hallucinogens specifically induce the sensation of spirit flight[26]—the "out-of-body" experience, in modern parlance. Leading ethnobotanists Richard Evans Schultes and Robert F. Raffauf have noted petroglyphs in the Colombian Amazon depicting winged beings, and comment that "this use of wings may be the result of the experiences of ancient Indians who made the engravings—experiences of flying through the air, a very frequent initial symptom of intoxication with hallucinogens."[27] Dobkin de Rios similarly noted winged creatures and winged humans depicted by large-scale effigy mounds in the Americas. She felt these, along with the lines, related to the "aerial journey" of the entranced shaman.[28]

There is no doubt that the trance of the shaman was pictured by ancient societies as a journey, very often a flight, of the shaman's soul to the otherworlds of spirit, during which time the shaman's body was slumped unconscious and deemed temporarily dead. Only in this way could the shaman meet the ancestors. Consequently, there is a worldwide abundance of bird symbolism associated with shamanism—bird-claw shapes cut out of mica and hung on shamanic robes, ceremonial shoes in the form of bird claws, iron effigies of bird skeletons hung around the neck, bird masks and costumes, bird-headed sticks, feathers tied at the ankles, and so forth. The arrow, too, figures prominently in shamanic spirit-flight symbolism.

"As the crow flies," "as straight as an arrow"—these phrases are synonymous with straight movement or structure. Could the straight landscape lines be symbolic depictions of the spirit flight of the shaman? Researchers in Britain, Switzerland, and Germany had independently come to conclusions similar to Dobkin de Rios' by the late 1980s, and her rather obscure paper was uncovered during the later stages of that research process. I have elsewhere termed areas containing such lines or "roads"—often associated with ground drawings or effigy mounds—"shamanic landscapes" to indicate their nature.

The European research has further determined that the same basic "straight-path" pattern occurring in the Americas can also be found in the Old World, but obscured by deeper and more numerous cultural overlays. In Western Europe there are Bronze Age stone rows, usually associated with burial sites. In Britain there are even older earthen lines, known as "cursuses," linking burial mounds sometimes a mile or more apart. These features, four or five thousand years old, now show up mainly from aerial survey, and whatever their function was isn't known. Moving into medieval times, in Holland, we have already noted (chapter two), there are surviving straight paths called *doodwegen*, or "death roads," that terminate at cemeteries, and it was actually illegal to carry a corpse in anything other than a straight line to burial. In parts of old Germany, we recall, there were *Geisterwege*, spirit paths, which were invisible but were considered to be dead straight and had geographical locations in the folk mind. They linked cemeteries, and because it was thought that ghosts could be encountered upon them, these linear strips of spirit geography were shunned by the peasantry. Similar spirit geography, though not specifically associated with death or cemeteries, occur in Celtic countries as fairy paths—or "passes," as they are called in Ireland. These are straight, primarily invisible paths that link fairy mounds or "raths" (prehistoric earthworks of poorly understood purpose). In England, work is under way reappraising church paths, corpse ways, and "coffin lines," which seem related to the *Geisterwege* and *doodwegen*.

What is most intriguing is that investigation of the Costa Rican rain-forest paths mapped by NASA show them to date from around 800 A.D., and to have been used for carrying the dead to the burial grounds and for the transportation of special stone used for funerary purposes. This coincidence tells us that we are dealing with a cross-cultural phenomenon, which usually indicates some social development of a pattern common to the human mind. An equally cross-cultural phenomenon is shamanism, which arises out of common characteristics of the human central nervous system in trance states. It was this cross-cultural aspect to the investigations that gave the European researchers their clue as to the shamanic origins of the lines.

Eurasia is the home of classical shamanism, and the tradition of the *myrkrider*, the night traveler, which became satanized as witchcraft by the medieval church, was probably the tail end of a Western European version of the old shamanism. The night traveler, the "witch," of Western Europe used hallucinogenic herbs to produce a special salve or "flying ointment," based on belladonna and other psychotropic herbs and plants. When applied to the skin, these caused the woman to collapse in trance while her spirit went wandering through the wild night—the wilds of consciousness, as discussed earlier. It may yet be discovered that there are mythic lines of witch flight still discernible on the landscapes of old Europe, awaiting identification. The Harz Mountains of Germany, for instance, were infamous as the gathering place of witches on their night rides, and on one of the mountains—the Wurmberg, or Dragon Mountain—there are prehistoric stone circles. Some of these are linked by a straight *Steinweg,* "stone road," that pollen analysis has shown to be medieval. Its purpose is unknown.

The *Steinweg,* a medieval spirit path linking prehistoric sites of the dead in the Harz Mountains, Germany.

It is clear that the inhabitants of medieval Europe were obsessed with the idea of spirits roaming around the land, and were fearful of meeting them. We saw in chapter two that standard protective procedures included spirit sweeping and witch bottles. Another common procedure was the erection of spirit traps (somewhat like Native American dream catchers). Such "traps" reveal a form of logic in the old way of thinking: straight lines facilitated spirit movement, so jumbled or convoluted lines bound spirits. This is seen in Asia as well, where the sacred geographical and divinatory system of *feng shui* was based, amongst other things, on the idea that spirits traveled in straight lines. Any straight feature in the landscape would be made sinuous, or masked off in some way to protect a tomb or house from infestation by troublesome ghosts. Similarly, in Ireland, a house blocking a fairy path would be subject to problems.

Unraveling the full complexity of the old straight path in the Old World will take a great deal of time, but the origins of the old European landscape line seem essentially the same as that of the shamanic lines in the Americas, where there has been less cultural flux, so that the form of the surviving spirit paths in many cases remain closer to their original form. I had myself proposed that the lines in the Americas must have been seen, essentially, as traces of spirit-journey routes by the disembodied shaman (this would quickly have become associated with spirits of the dead, too, for the shaman was thought to be temporarily dead when he went on his "journey"). This was to some extent confirmed by questioning BBC producer Alan Ereira, who had filmed the rarely seen Kogi of northern Colombia. We have noted that these Indians have maintained pre-Columbian traditions better than possibly any other Native American group, and are governed by a ruling elite of shamans or *mamas*. These are selected at birth by divinatory means, and are brought up from childhood in conditions involving extreme sensory deprivation. Eventually the child begins to see the spirit world, *aluna*, and is able to converse with the ancestors, developing a strange, singing "language." For the rest of his life, the *mama* is able to see the spirit world, the spirit version of the Earth, superimposed on the physical world. When he sings himself into trance, the *mama* travels on certain routes through *aluna*, and some of these routes are partially traced by stone paths in the physical world. On one occasion, Ereira saw a straight stone path leading up from a river to the men's ceremonial house, which was being swept and cleaned by tribal members under the direction of the *mamas*. It was explained to the filmmaker that the maintenance of the physical path was mirroring the upkeep of the corresponding spirit way in the spirit world, in *aluna*. Further, it was impressed on him that the spirit way continued in a straight line from the ceremonial house to another river, but that that segment was not marked by a physical path. Here was that selfsame, worldwide belief that sweeping and clearing a physical path could affect its spirit condition. We noted earlier that recent research has shown that the fifteen-hundred-year-old Nazca lines were also ritually swept.

That the straightness of the spirit lines was *symbolically* associated with spirit flight and movement was now as certain as could be, but a *neurological* explanation for it was also to emerge. This lay at the heart of the cross-cultural nature of the archaic straight landscape line.

The realization emerged through a revolution of understanding that was taking place at the same time in archeology with regard to certain types of abstract imagery in prehistoric rock art—dots, crosshatching, zigzags, and half-human, half-animal creatures known as "therianthropes." The understanding of these features began to dawn primarily because of the work of archeologists J. D. Lewis-Williams and Thomas Dowson in studying San (Bushman) rock art in southern Africa.[29, 30, 31] Reappraising earlier anthropological research on the San, and interviewing surviving Bushmen, made it clear that many of the markings in the rock shelters related to altered states of consciousness experienced as a result of trance dancing in earlier times. (This is still practiced by the Kalahari !Kung, when they experience *kia* and leave their bodies.) One recurring Bushman rock-art image is of a half-man half-deer creature flying along with lines trailing out behind it. This was found to represent the out-of-body spirit of the trance dancer, and in some cases, possibly, the spirit of the deceased. In the context of all this, the abstract imagery was recognized by Lewis-Williams and Dowson as "entoptic" imagery—that is, characteristic geometric patterns produced in the central nervous system during the earlier stages of trance. These entoptic patterns, categorized by neurologists by the 1970s,[32] consist of specific groups of visual patterns, such as curves, spirals, dots,

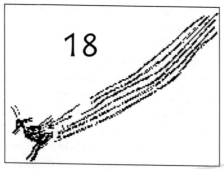

The therianthropic "flying-buck" or "trance-buck" type of image, which recurs in Bushman rock art, and depicts spirit flight. [Harold Pager.]

zigzag lines. These seem to hang before the closed eyes as glowing imagery, and if seen with open eyes appear as if projected onto surfaces in the physical world, as if painted by spirit hands. Rock art linked with ethnological and neurological research revealed the same explanation for similar rock-art patterns elsewhere, such as that belonging to the Coso Indians in America.[33] The Coso rock engravings resulted from the imagery experienced in trance states by Indians on vision quests, and the rock-art sites were themselves considered places of supernatural power or *poha* and so the rock art at them effectively mapped the Coso perception of the distribution through the landscape of *poha*.[34]

It became apparent to those of us studying the phenomenon of landscape lines that we were looking at entoptic patterns on a huge scale: the spirit lines were a mental geography; mind lines marked on the ground. They were the terrestrial equivalent of the rock-art entoptic patterns, only more organized and formal (as they would have to be on that scale). It was found that the Tukano Indians of Colombia, in the area where the winged petroglyphs mentioned above are found, still maintain a practice in which entoptic patterns seen during their *ayahuasca* trances are used as the basis for their decorative art. Certain patterns are "owned" by particular kinship groups, and the Tukano have developed techniques to prolong the entoptic state so as to manipulate the patterns more effectively.[35]

In later stages of trance, the geometric entoptics become iconics—that is, memory images start to become grafted onto the geometric forms, so a zigzag line might turn into a snake, for example. It is here that the therianthropes begin to appear as well.

Lewis-Williams and Dowson have now been able to categorize Bushman rock art into the appropriate stages of trance.

One of the key entoptics is the spiral-tunnel-vortex, which heralds a shift from merely observing the entoptic and iconic imagery to participating in it. There is a sense of the self's becoming mobile, leaving the body, and rushing down a tunnel or being sucked into the eye of the spiral or vortex. This effect is frequently reported among those in *in-extremis* cases of altered mind states now referred to as "near-death experiences." It is with this specific entoptic that the out-of-body or spirit-flight sensation is associated. This entoptic tunnel could be the neurological blueprint for the straight line on shamanic landscapes.

These linear markings are vast monuments in landscapes across the world testifying to a worldview in which the Earth had a spirit dimension. That they are only now just beginning to be discovered results from a series of accidents. The features are studied at the junction of many disciplines, such as archeology, anthropology, neurology, psychology, and more esoteric study areas, and consequently there has never been an overview of the phenomenon as a cross-cultural whole. This fragmentation has been made worse because of the association of what has been known as "ley hunting," a heretical area of pseudo-archeology in which ancient alignments between sacred sites have been postulated since the 1920s. Valuable research has come out of this area, powerfully contributing to the discovery of spirit lines, but so has a fantasy-based idea of "energy lines" discoverable by dowsing. This "energy" view, as discussed in chapter four, belongs to modern New Age notions in which landscapes are seen as kinds of circuit boards with unspecified energies running through them, rather than being based on genuine archaic worldviews. Because of this New Age element, academics and serious researchers have tended to shy away from the whole question of ancient landscape lines, leaving it languishing without sufficient research attention.

Nevertheless, that is now changing; we are beginning to see the scale of the spiritual heritage left on the landscape by former peoples, and we are starting to look earnestly at the whole question of how altered states of consciousness, such as occur in shamanism, allowed different views of the Earth to be perceived.

We can see these lines as being "nothing more" than the product of altered mental states, but we ought to exercise caution, in case they relate to information about the world that our culture simply edits out (see Christian Rätsche's experiences with the Lacandon Indians, described in the introductory chapter, for instance). As an example, we can consider the experience of Arthur Grimble, a British colonial officer assigned to the Gilbert Islands in the Pacific during the early years of this century. On those islands there was a ceremony called Te Kaetikawai, Straightening of the Way, which was conducted over the recently deceased so that the soul could travel on a straight course through the archipelago, safely leaving for heaven across the ocean from a sandspit on the northernmost island. The positions of houses in villages were arranged so that anyone dying in any one of them could travel on this straight-line course without passing through another house. Any deviation off the straight line by the soul could result in its being caught by an evil supernatural being. Grimble insisted on visiting the sandspit, known as "The Place of Dread," against the advice of the locals. On his way back, he walked south along a path that marked that segment of the course of the souls to the dreadful place. It didn't bother Grimble that he had been strongly urged not to do this. On his way, he passed an islander with a limp, going in the opposite direction. He greeted the fellow, who ignored him. When Grimble arrived at a nearby village, he encountered a Straightening of the Way ritual taking place. The body the participants were standing around was that of the man Grimble had just seen on the path.[36] Other examples would be the ghosts that are reported as being seen traveling over certain stretches of ground on separate occasions by different witnesses. For instance, Cheryl Straffon, editor of a local Cornish magazine, reported her sighting of a line of spectral Cornish miners in old-fashioned helmets crossing the road ahead of her and disappearing into a hedge near Gunnislake. She told no one. Some years later, the selfsame phenomenon, at the same place, was reported in the local newspaper by another woman, and two more women wrote in to say they had seen the same apparitions at that spot also.[37] What are we to make of such reports? These are not all lies or silly perceptual errors. Perhaps, after all, the Earth *does* harbor spirits—or there is something in the nature of certain places that can interact with the mind to produce visual imagery of a characteristic kind. We do not have to accept old explanations for phenomena, but that doesn't mean we should dismiss the phenomena themselves.

## LAND AND LANGUAGE: VOICES OF THE EARTH

Ancient peoples saw the Earth as animate. We do not; the idea of having a conversation with this great being is anathema to scientific, rational thought, and even the Gaia scientists shy away from such a notion. But once, in cultures older than ours, it was a mainstream idea, and various mechanisms existed that allowed the land to stimulate language. This can happen to us today, if we let it. Nature writer Barry Lopez has powerfully written of this in his *The Rediscovery of North America*:

> I remember a Kamba man in Kenya, Kamoya Kimeu, a companion in the stone desert west of Lake Turkana—and a dozen other men—telling me, you know how to see, learn how to *mark* the country. And he and others teaching me to sit down in one place for two or three hours and look.

> When we enter the landscape to learn something, we are obligated, I think, to pay attention rather than constantly pose questions. To approach the land as we would a person, by opening an intelligent conversation. And to stay in one place, to make of that one, long observation a fully-dilated experience. We will always be rewarded if we give the land credit for more than we imagine, and if we imagine it as being more complex even than language.[38]

I had precisely this experience, beyond metaphor, during my study of the Neolithic landscape of the Avebury complex over a number of years in the 1980s. The complex is situated in southern England, about eighty miles west of London. Avebury Henge is the largest stone circle in the world, covering some twenty-eight acres, with stones weighing up to seventy tons. About a mile to its southwest is the enigmatic Silbury Hill, a mainly artificial mound 130 feet high, the tallest man-made structure in prehistoric Europe. The whole landscape around it is much as it was nearly five thousand years ago, in the Late Neolithic period, with monuments and the natural lay of the land subtly melded together into one sacred geography. I visited the complex over several years, at all times of the day and night and in all seasons and weather conditions, attempting to understand something of the way the builders of Avebury might have thought, and what their monuments might have meant to them. It was all there in this ceremonial landscape, yet for years I just couldn't come to grips with the meaning of the place—and neither could anyone else, for that matter. In one moment of frustration, I actually fell on my knees within the great avenue of standing stones called Kennet Avenue, which snakes southwards from the henge, and invoked the spirit of the place out loud, imploring that it let me *see*. After this momentary lapse of rational control, I felt a little embarrassed and was relieved, on looking around, to see that nobody had been there to observe my bizarre actions. Over the following several months, I *did* learn to "see," and some important insights were made that are now in the mainstream archeological literature.[39] These have been recounted in depth elsewhere,[40] and so I will not detail them here but, rather, describe the process I experienced, for that is what concerns us in this book.

Because the charming Wessex village of Avebury sprawls around and even into the henge circle, that is usually seen as the focal point of the whole complex. However, I started to become powerfully aware that Silbury Hill was the true focus of the ritual landscape; the hub of the wheel. As soon as I became aware of this, a curious relationship seemed to develop between the great mound and myself. I distinctly felt that it was *sentient*, but I couldn't rationalize the experience. It seemed to me that Silbury was somehow communicating with me, but I wasn't sure how it was doing this or what it was trying to communicate about. It came to assume the role of a teacher to me. I also became acutely aware that this was a nonrational way of thinking, so I made it a rule that whenever I entered the Avebury complex I would click fearlessly into this animistic mode of consciousness, but that when I left I would revert to my normal, twentieth-century mode of thinking, which passes for rational. I realized that what had been holding up my perception of this special, ancient landscape was my twentieth-century worldview and my incessant questioning. Did the sun rise on midsummer's day over there? Is there an alignment through these sites? What happens at Beltane from this, that, or the other monument? I kept coming with theories and making so much mental noise that I couldn't hear what the place was telling me, much less see it. As soon as I adopted a more passive approach in an animistic mode, the situation changed. At every visit I learned some small piece of information that I could never have predicted. This could take the form of suddenly noticing how one site was visible from another at a very narrow angle through the natural topography of the area. One day I noticed a subtle, eroded ledge or former walkway that runs around the otherwise smooth slopes of Silbury Hill about seventeen feet down from its flat summit. I found that this was recorded in archeological texts but little commented on. I moved around the whole sacred landscape, looking up periodically at Silbury, which from some angles dominated the landscape like a giant plum pudding, yet from other places disappeared into the folds of the land. Until 1970, Silbury had been assumed by archeologists to have been Europe's largest Bronze Age burial mound, but excavation showed it to be considerably older (Late Neolithic, around 2700 B.C.), and to the disappointment of the BBC, which was poised with its new color-TV cameras, there was no central chamber, no burial of some gold-clad Bronze Age chieftain. Nothing. Nothing in the heart of the mound but . . . *green grass*, miraculously preserved from nearly five thousand years ago. Amongst the blades of grass were the intact bodies of flying ants, so that though not being able to tell the exact year when construction of Silbury began, experts could state that work on the monument had started either at the end of July or in the early part of August. The mystery deepened as to why, then, the ancients had built this great monument, uniquely constructed out of twelve million cubic feet of chalk in the shape of a stepped cone, then covered and smoothed with earth except for the top ledge. And people were equally puzzled as to why anyone should have built anything so tall as this mound at the lowest spot in the valley of the little River Kennet and alongside a natural ridge, Waden Hill, of about the same height. Silbury was the mystery that beat in the heart of the ancient ceremonial landscape formed by the Avebury complex of monuments.

View of Silbury Hill from the East Kennet long barrow. The eroded ledge can best be seen on the left slope, a little way down from the flat-topped summit. Note how the horizon coincides with the mound's summit.

Then, one day, while standing on one of the oldest monuments in the complex, the West Kennet long barrow, a chambered earthen

mound some three hundred feet in length, I *saw*. Silbury Hill was to
the north, and I noted that the distant skyline passed behind the
mound's profile at just the point where the ledge interrupted the
smooth slopes. This happened only when Silbury was viewed from
the western tip of the long barrow, which archeologists believe was
extended long after the rest of the barrow had been built. I was sure
that had been done to afford this sightline to Silbury. The skyline
beyond Silbury was in fact formed by Windmill Hill, a natural hilltop where people had gathered for unknown purposes around
4000 B.C., before any monuments had been built around Avebury.
Windmill Hill was the grandmother of the whole sacred landscape.

I realized that Silbury had indeed been communicating with
me—visually. I went on to discover that, when one was viewing Silbury from all the major surviving Neolithic monuments in the
complex, the far horizon appeared to pass behind the profile of the
mound somewhere between its ledge and the flat summit. The view
of Silbury from within the henge circle at Avebury was particularly
dramatic: if I stood at the site of what had been the tallest stone
within the main circle, the same top segment of Silbury between
summit and ledge was just visible rising up in a cleft formed by a
dip in the distant horizon and the angle of the lower slope of
Waden Hill. But just before harvest time, when the cereal crop on
Waden Hill was at its tallest, the view to Silbury was blocked by the
height of the crop. It was a *harvest-dependent sightline*. The significance of this exploded on me like a revelation. Harvest time was
early August, the cross-quarter day of Lughnasa in the old Celtic calendar, or Lammas in the Christian one—the very period when Silbury had started to be constructed. Harvest home: it became
transparently clear to me that Silbury Hill was a huge harvest
mound, a representation of the bountiful Earth Mother. I felt that
Silbury had *told* me this, revealing an open secret that had been
there unnoticed for thousands of years.

After this set of observations, I visited Silbury itself regularly, at
all times of the day and night and periods throughout the year. I
used to sit on its flat, platformlike summit, gazing around at the
deeply interrelated artificial and natural landscape beneath. What

was the mystery? Why did this top segment of the mound have such significance? One morning I got to the site before sunrise. Although there was a low mist clinging to the land, when I climbed Silbury I found that its summit rose above the mist like a grassy island poking out of a cotton sea. Dawn started to break, and delicate rosy hues tinted the mist. I was sitting in a quiescent, possibly light-

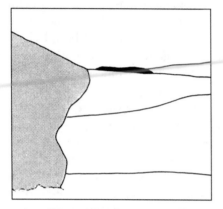

The sightline to Silbury Hill from the Obelisk, within the great stone circle at Avebury Henge (see text). The top segment of Silbury (in silhouette) can be seen, showing exactly where the far horizon and the middle-distance slope of Waden Hill intersect. Shaded area at left is part of a standing stone within the henge.

trance state. Suddenly, a bell-like voice spoke into my right ear. "In this Mystery shall we dwell," it said. Startled, I turned my head, knowing even as I did so that no one would be there. It had been what a rationalist would call an auditory hallucination, but to me, there and then, it was as if Silbury itself had spoken to me. There followed a curious sensation in which I *felt* a flow of language, but below the threshold at which I could verbalize it. It was as if subliminal activity was occurring in some primary language structure in my brain-mind; I was convinced that a communication was going on between the place and parts of my mind where my conscious attention could not or did not operate.

On a later visit to the summit, I witnessed a glorious Beltane sunrise, and in a flash I *saw* what I had only looked at dozens of times previously: the eastern horizon viewed from Silbury was *double,* in the sense that the far-distant skyline of the Marlborough Downs exactly mimicked the contour of the nearby ridge of Waden Hill in the foreground. From Silbury's summit the two skylines were visually barely separated, the distant one appearing fractionally above the other. But there was a slight dip in the middle of the span of the distant horizon, and I realized this meant that, if the sun was seen to rise in that dip while being viewed from the summit of Silbury, it could be seen to rise a second time shortly afterwards from the ledge seventeen feet below, because the slight dip was just obscured by Waden Hill when the viewpoint was lowered to the ledge. (It will be recalled from the "Experiential" section of chapter one that the distant skyline always seems to move up or down with the level of one's eye-line.) This dip in the skyline was where the Lughnasa sun would also rise, for sunrise occurs at the same point on the horizon at both Beltane and Lughnasa. By now, the sun had risen too far actually to test this effect, and I had to wait two more years for an opportunity actually to witness the Beltane/Lughnasa "double sunrise." That came about on August 1, 1989, and I had an archeologist along to witness it. Sure enough, we saw the Lughnasa sun rise in the far distance; then we immediately slid down the grassy slope to the ledge, where, a couple of minutes later, the sun's rays broke over the huge bulk of Waden Hill. I had little doubt that the builders of Silbury Hill had skillfully engineered this visual display as a celebration of fecundity (the sun as well as the Earth was seen as feminine in old Europe). The height and location of Silbury had been exactly worked out to unite the various monuments round about, the natural lay of the land, and the seasonal movements of the sun. Silbury Hill was a symbolic summation and a celebration.

But it did not end there. The following daybreak, my wife and I were on Silbury to photograph the double-sunrise effect. After doing this, we turned to go, but a remarkable and glorious sight stopped us in our tracks. To the west, as the Lughnasa sun rose behind us, the long shadow of Silbury was thrown across the fields. Issuing out of the top of the shadow was a golden light that shimmered across the countryside. My mythical consciousness knew instantly that this magical light was Silbury's—the Earth Mother's—blessing on the land. Later, in rational mode, I discovered that it was an optical effect known as a "glory." If a person stands in a field at sunrise, a glow will appear around the head of

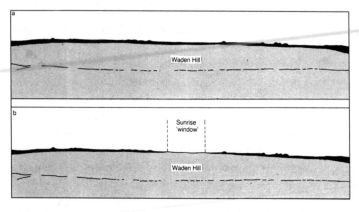

A diagrammatic representation of the view eastwards from Silbury Hill. Top: view from summit, showing how the distant horizon (shown in black shading) just "skims" the nearby ridge of Waden Hill. Bottom: view from ledge, showing how a segment of the horizon appears to dip behind Waden Hill, providing a "window" in which the Beltane and Lammas sunrises can seem to occur twice. See text.

his or her shadow, caused by a refractive effect in the dewdrops on the grass or other vegetation. On Silbury, the spectator's shadow is thrown across the flat top of the mound as far as the shoulders, but the head part of the shadow is cast hundreds of feet below, into the main shadow of the mound, causing a greatly enhanced glory effect. This can only happen at sunrise, while the dew is fresh.

These various discoveries demonstrated to me that, if one learned to listen to the sacred landscape that is the Avebury complex, to let it speak and display itself, information locked away from human knowledge for thousands of years could be again released. I could no longer doubt that the land really is a repository of memory. In this specific case, it was possible to translate some of the message into the language of academic archeology, but many other things included in the message, in the revelation of memory, were not amenable to such translation. The whole complex revealed its mythic nature in a depth I cannot summarize even here. I can still feel but not articulate it. I am unable to bring all of it into the limelight of my conscious mind.

All ancient and traditional cultures had this cognitive closeness with the land, a psychological intimacy with Earth we have lost. Everywhere the land promoted myth, memory, and language. This relationship with the Earth has lingered just long enough in the Americas for anthropologists to grasp some knowledge of it, before the archaic whisper dies away back into the land forever. Learning from the Apaches of Arizona, Keith H. Basso found that for them the land stalked the people, telling them stories to make them live right.[41] The way this "stalking" worked was powerful and subtle. Place names were "pictures," and stories related to them were "arrows." Everyone had learned the names of all the places. "White men need paper maps," said one informant. "We have maps in our mind."[42] Sometimes the Apaches would say out the name of a place two, three, or more times while pointing to it, because "those names are good to say" or because "that name makes me see that place like it really is." Basso, who had heard some Apaches reciting long lists of place names quietly to themselves, mapped the region around Cibecue and recorded the Apache names of 296 locations. Usually these place names would take the form of whole sentences, such as "big cottonwood trees stand spreading here and there" or "coarse-textured rocks lie above in a compact cluster." If a person transgressed tribal code, he or she was not openly rebuked, but some elder would "go hunting" for that person by drawing on the vast reservoir of topographical memory and start telling a story about a place, a named location, at which certain events had happened, the place bearing equal weight in the story to the happenings. The story would contain some metaphorical element that related to the circumstances concerning the transgressor; it would contain an implied admonishment. The story, the arrow, belonging to the place would "shoot" the transgressor, and that place and that person would thereafter share a special and lasting bond: the place would constantly remind the transgressor and keep him and her in the right way of behavior. In effect, the place would take on the role of a stern elder, watching, prompting, reminding. "Even if we go far away from here to some big city," an elder told Basso, "places here keep stalking us. . . . The land looks after us. The land keeps badness away." Nevertheless, Basso was also told: "Our children are losing the land. It doesn't go to work on them anymore." Such is the manner in which the archaic whisper fades away.

Similarly, anthropologist Julie Cruikshank learned from Yukon native elders that their lives were "lived like a story." Her informants were women of Athapaskan and Tlingit ancestry. Their stories differed from men's stories and from those of nonnative women. "The recurring theme is one of connection—to other people and to nature," Cruikshank notes. "Connections with people are explored through ties of kinship; connections with the land emphasize sense of place. But kinship and landscape provide more than just a setting for an account, for they actually frame and shape the story."[43]

It is or was the same everywhere with primary, indigenous peoples. We have already seen that the Australian Aborigines followed mythic routes through the Outback, tracing and revivifying narratives in the land. Each place had its myth, its story, its song. The Aborigines sang the country, *and it sang them*. The mythic narrative provided tribal boundaries, defining landscape and mindscape simultaneously. The landscape became a "lifeworld of constituted meanings," as F. Myer has put it.[44] Setha Low remarks that for the Pintupi of Western Australia no place can be spoken of without a consideration of its mythological associations. "The landscape is interpreted by the stories of The Dreaming; the myth is used as a guide to what had been seen, whose ancestry is involved, and based on that interpretation, rights to the use of the land are determined," Low notes. "Thus the narrative, the telling of The Dreaming, actively brings together two constructs, that of the camp, country or land with family, relative or kin."[45]

The ancient Celts likewise drenched their native land with meaning; it spoke to them of their and its history, gave intimations of the otherworld, and told cautionary tales. As always, the language was mythic—there was the Gaelic *Dindsenchas*, for example. R. F. Foster tells us that, to the traditional Celt,

> . . . the literal representation of the country was less important than its poetic dimension. . . . The terrain was studied, discussed and referenced. Every place had its own identity and legend. *Dindsenchas*, the celebration of place-names, was a feature of this poetic topography, what endured was the mythic landscape.[46]

Such mythologized landscapes have been called "territories of the voice."[47] There seems to be a special relationship between the land and language—or the processes that underpin language. We have already noted a deep-rooted link between place and memory; and here we perhaps need to distinguish between written language and oral tradition. The spoken word requires a different action of memory from the written page. In spoken tales of places it is the place, the topography, that is the mnemonic, not the word: oral and written forms of language are the very reverse of one another. In the traditional *telling* of myth it is the land that is being told, that is the referent, rather than words being memorized. The land itself was a form of external memory, as Emily Lyle points out.[48] Emerson noted in similar vein the "immediate dependence of language upon nature."[49] What is happening within this relationship may be more complex than our culture would like to accept. It is one thing to acknowledge that we can invest the land with meanings we project onto it, but how about thinking of this transaction in a more interactive way? Could the land, the forms of nature, actually stimulate specialized effects with the brain-mind? Isn't this what we are really saying when we speak of the power and grandeur of nature forming a source of poetic or artistic inspiration? Are there receptive states or conditions within the brain-mind that have developed to interact with the ages-old data streaming in from nature? Is there, as I suggested earlier in this book, an interaction going on with the world that we rarely glimpse in our current "awake" monophasic conscious state?

During an interview with James Cowan, an Australian poet and writer who has studied Australian Aboriginal spirituality in considerable depth and spent many years in the Outback with tribal peoples, I questioned whether or not the myths that guide the Aborigines on their dream-journey routes were simply the constructs of tribal projections or, more heretically, whether their inherent form was somehow dormant in the landscape. In other words, are we dealing with *invention* or *recognition*—or, more probably, a combination of the two?

"To take a hypothetical case," I put it to Cowan, "let's say the Aborigines disappeared altogether in a particular area, and another tribal people eventually came and lived in that landscape. Do you believe that a similar mythic relationship would build up between them and the land?"

"Yes, I do," Cowen replied.

"In the sense of it [the mythic relationship] being seeds dormant in the earth?" I pressed.

"Yes. Provided that the people were amenable to that land as a non-material concept. I mean, if you were going to ask me were we going to send out a group of Wall Street stockbrokers to live in New South Wales, and whether they would camp out there and anything happen, I don't think it would. . . . But I do believe that if what you are trying to say, that the landscape has its own, let us say, metaphysical data imprinted in it which is unchangeable, my answer is yes. And, moreover, that that information could be invoked now or twenty thousand years from hence."[50]

The question I am toying with here is whether the information streaming from whatever the outer environment actually is contains data that are incorporated and used in the world model constructed by human beings in some cultures and not in others (specifically, not in ours). Of course, each society has its own names for its deities and spirits, its own social, religious, and ceremonial structures, and uses the interaction with the land for its own social needs and integrity. There is also no doubt that the landscape as a reservoir of mythic concepts, which can have social and other applications, only "comes alive" *as far as human beings are concerned* when human beings inhabit the landscape. It is also undeniable that when a people disappear the mental constructs formed from their experience of the land dies with them. But that isn't the point. Is there a *raw process* underlying all of this in which the natural configuration of a given topography can provoke basic images or ideas that are then embellished in the collective mind of a human group living within it? Is the first impulse of the process from land to mind—rather than the reverse, as we would now think to be the only possibility? Is there an interaction between external natural forms and the inner (also natural) neural architecture? If so, what are the brain-mind mechanisms that deal with this raw process?

Language may be such an integral part of the interactive experience with the land because it "turns out to be the key to solving the increasingly urgent problem of internal communication which the brain set up for itself," as cognitive psychologist Guy Claxton has written.[51] We referred in the introductory chapter to that inner dialogue running through our minds, the stories we tell ourselves, the perpetual inner chatter. So constant is this inner narrative that we often do not recognize how pervasive it is until our attention is drawn to it. Indeed, the stilling of this inner dialogue is the goal of meditational practice. Language is a tool the mind uses—a word can evoke a whole firing pattern of neurons, lighting up networks of memory and associations. But so, too, can forms, moods, lighting effects, vistas, places, and spaces in the landscape. We can also think of O'Keefe and Nadel's suggestion, encountered in the preceding chapter, that the hippocampus is a mapping device creating the matrix of space that is an organizing principle of mentation. We saw that memory could be encoded more readily in imagery than in abstract form—the "method of *loci*," for example. But images are not stored like neuron-sized videotapes; rather, a *pattern* is encoded in the neural architecture, a *deep-structure analogue*, which can reestablish the image and thus the memory as required. Moreover, O'Keefe and Nadel point out, language and imagery do not seem to operate on different systems—both rely on a common deep structure. So this proposed deep pattern of neuro-mental activity is not pictorial or linguistic in itself, but underpins such manifestations in the mind.

Perhaps the landscape can stimulate this deep structure or pattern, evoking imagery and narrative, which are then projected back onto the land. In the end, an indivisible resonance is established between the land and those who dwell close to it for generations. The mythic narrative is the means whereby that resonance is maintained from one generation to the next. So we can see how tragic it is for traditional peoples when a place is changed or destroyed, when it is taken out of the loop of resonance which oriented their society. When *humans* are taken out of the loop, on the other hand, the potential of evocation falls back into the land, to be restored or not, as time and circumstance dictate. As observed in the introductory chapter, if we in our culture had a closer relationship with the Earth and held a different view of it, we would notice how much of it is now falling silent. But we cannot hear that silence falling around us above the clamor we make. The archaic whisper becomes increasingly muted. It can only speak to us again if we pause to listen.

## THE SOUL OF THE WORLD

In terms of the brain, we may not yet know what are the precise mechanisms that handle this data input from the landscape, from nature, but in terms of the mind we can be sure that the basic nature of those data is mythic. *Mythic consciousness is the doorway between land and mind,* and it is the language of the soul. Poet and scholar Kathleen Raine says as much: "But the language of poets is a language of images upon which meanings are built, in metaphors and symbols which never lose their link with light and darkness, tree and flower, animals and rivers and mountains and stars and winds and the elements of earth, air, fire and water. The language of poetry is the language of nature. . . ."[52] She complains that the kind of education moderns receive is "a language without a memory." We learn from paper, from books, rather than from the living world. Memory is no longer inside us or a part of our natural environment; it is stored in external memory devices of our own making—libraries, audio and video tapes, computer databases, and so on. As Emily Lyle remarks, citing Merlin Donald, we are more engaged today with "memory management skills" involving how to find externally stored information.[53] As a culture, we are becoming more amnesiac, and our attention spans grow shorter.

Mythic consciousness (*not* specific myths or bodies of mythology) can be thought of as the mode in which the mind handles the extra-conscious data that stream in from the world of nature. It bears close resemblance to dreaming, as Joseph Campbell implied. We can take this literally as well as metaphorically, for throughout the ages people have resorted to certain places to dream for a cure or other special information. The Celtic seer, for instance, would wrap up in an animal skin, probably an ox hide, alongside a waterfall or pool of water, in order to have a prophetic dream. The vision quester, similarly, sleeps out in the wilderness in order to have a visionary dream, seen as being vouchsafed by nature. In the classical world, temple dreaming, or *psychomanteia*, was a highly organized activity. Over four hundred such temples existed in Greece alone, usually dedicated to the healing god Asklepios and always located at sources of water. People would attend a temple like this in order to seek healing. They were required to abstain from eating meat and fish or having sex, and undergo a series of purifications, which included drinking copious amounts of the temple water. Finally, the person went to sleep in a special cell, an *abaton*, in order to have the healing dream. These people were assisted by temple helpers or *therapeutes*—this was true therapy—who helped the patients to interpret their dreams, in which it was hoped Asklepios or some symbol relating to him would appear, revealing the way of curing the illness. Even the very act of sleeping at the temple was seen as being beneficial in some cases. Similar practices were conducted in European churches in the Middle Ages, and are still carried out in some Indian temples, and doubtless elsewhere.

A modern version of "temple sleep" is currently under way at the time of this writing. It is an Anglo-American effort, under the banner of the Dragon Project, a loose consortium of investigators founded in Britain in 1977 to study ancient sites from many different research angles, but especially with regard to ambient energies such as natural radiation, magnetism, ionization, and other environmental factors that might affect the body-brain-mind complex of users of those places. In the dreamwork program, four ancient sites in the United Kingdom were selected—a sacred mountain with a strong magnetic anomaly in Wales, and, in Cornwall, a Neolithic dolmen (stone chamber), an Iron Age underground passage, and a Celtic Christian holy well. The idea has been to have many people dreaming at these four places to see if any *site-specific* content recurs in their dreams. The person goes to sleep all night at the site, looked after by a helper, a modern-day *therapeute*. When the sleeper exhibits rapid eye movements (REMs), denoting dreaming sleep, they are awoken and their dreams recorded onto audiotape before they can be forgotten. These recorded dreams are transcribed onto a computer database, and in this way an extensive set of dreams is being accumulated for each site. These transcribed accounts are then sent to Dr. Stanley Krippner at the Saybrook Institute in San Francisco for analysis, along with normal home dreams recorded by the participants to act as individual controls. The site dreams are not being studied for personal analysis but are, rather, being cross-checked to see if any symbols, images, themes, patterns, or other characteristics can be identified in the dreams of different people that relate to a specific site. So, for example, if ten people dreamed of a little gnome at the dolmen, but only at the dolmen, we might reasonably suppose that something about that place promoted such dream imagery. (In reality, of course, any site-specific dream characteristics are likely to be more subtle, less clear-cut, and of greater complexity than this invented, simplistic example!) The work began in 1990; two of the sites now have a sufficient body of dream material for analysis to begin, and the other two places are continuing to have dreamwork conducted at them. The full analysis of all the dream material, totaling hundreds of dreams, will take a few years. At the least, it will be a unique body of dream data; at best, if site-specific dream content is identified, important questions will be raised. Is there a geography of consciousness? Is there such a thing as place memory, accessible in the dream state? Does memory exist as an information field outside of the brain, as biologist Rupert Sheldrake has proposed in his theory of morphic resonance? Is the dreaming state a particularly useful one for contacting such information fields? The implications will be considerable.[54]

Dreaming is, as I have suggested, one facet of mythic conscious-ness. Thoreau observed that mythology came closer to the language of the Wild than anything else.[55] Steven Foster and Meredith Little, in their book on vision questing, remind us that "Grandmother Na-ture . . . does not communicate in the English language."[56] Merlin Donald has proposed that primary human adaptation was not lan-guage in itself but, rather, "integrative, initially mythical thought," which created the need for improving the conceptual apparatus.[57]

A Dragon Project dreamwork session taking place at the Celtic Christian holy and heal-ing well at Madron, Cornwall, England.

But even here, Donald is thinking only in terms of the development of the human brain-mind; though not arguing one way or the other about this, I am suggesting here that mythic consciousness is an ac-tual faculty that can be used to gain access to greater information about the world than currently creeps into our cultural awareness. Mythic consciousness is the medium that can carry the language of both nature and the soul; it is the interface in which subtle aspects of a living Earth are translated into various forms of language that can be tapped into by human consciousness if it so chooses. A cul-

ture like ours, with a mainstream use of language that is not informed by mythic consciousness, has its attitude towards the phenomenon that is the Earth compromised.

But what is this inward dimension of the world, a dimension that
our culture dismisses to the sidelines if it accepts it at all? A belief in
"a non-physical or spiritual dimension of the material was ancient
in germ," Conrad Bonifazi informs us in his impressive historical
summary of the subject, *The Soul of the World*.[58] The ancient view of
the world was animistic—the Earth was alive. Bonifazi points out
that to the early Greeks "nature" did not mean the plethora of living organisms that we infer from the term today but, rather, an internal principle in things, a principle that related to the sensory
world in the way we conceptually associate the term "soul" with
body. "The thought of the natural world as a living being is one of
the oldest and most pervasive of human attempts to interpret the
universe," writes Bonifazi. It went back to times beyond documentation, and is a view still held by some indigenous non-Western
peoples to this day. It crept into earlier Western thinking via the ancient Greeks. They saw the regular motions of nature as expressing
an intelligence within things. The early-sixth-century-B.C. philosopher Thales, for instance, considered the world as being *ensouled*.
He felt that the planet was a great living organism. The Pythagore-
ans saw the essence of the world as an immaterial and impersonal
force which was intelligible through the principles of number and,
though not directly perceptible, was nevertheless real—a view also
held by Plato. To him, there was a transcendent sphere of pure
forms, of which the material world was but an inferior and transi-
tory reflection. But Plato still saw the tangible world of nature as
alive, transfused with and enveloped by its own soul, and he saw
"soul" as being an intermediary state between the sphere of pure
forms and the sensible, physical world. Aristotle saw existence as an
ascending scale, according to which base matter was not ensouled
but life, manifested in organisms from the level of plants upwards,
was. He saw the movements of the soul as being imagination,
memory, dreaming, and the passions, and suspected the mind and
the thinking faculty to be a "distinct kind of soul" which was immortal. The philosopher Zeno felt that a divine essence was dif-

fused through everything, but to variable degrees of purity. Zeno was the founder of the Stoics, a school of philosophy that maintained that each human soul was part of the world soul. Plotinus gave the idea of a world soul systematic philosophical form in the third century A.D. According to this, the great soul was the intermediary between intellect and the senses, between intelligence and matter, and permeated everything. It was both universal and local, every part containing the whole. "If the soul in me is a unity why need that in the universe be otherwise . . . ?" Plotinus argued.[59]

The doctrine of a world soul, the *anima mundi*, was a powerful current of thought in Europe through the Middle Ages and into the Renaissance. Among many thinkers who saw the world of appearances as being animated by its own soul was William of Conches, who Christianized it, identifying it with the Holy Spirit. Nicholas of Cusa explained that the *anima mundi* coexisted with matter, and did not exist as a separate mind within the material world. Cornelius Agrippa felt that the world, the heavens, and the elements have soul, and the soul of the world was rational, intelligent, and nothing less than a deity, filling all things and binding them together, "that it might make one frame of the world." The alchemist Paracelsus called the world soul "Archeus"—a volatile spirit that was invisible but acted visibly. It ordered, informed and *was* nature. Jan Baptista van Helmont claimed that the "whole efficient cause of Nature . . . is inward and essential." Bernardino Telesio held the interesting view that spirit "was a kind of psychological substance which received sense-impressions from external things, and was able to renew them in memory."[60]

Gradually, however, the view of an animated world became obscured, claiming ever-fewer adherents. By the seventeenth century, as the age of rationalism dawned, the universe began to be seen like a machine ticking in time to the laws laid down by a distant God, though even Sir Isaac Newton, the greatest single influence bringing about this change of worldview, could call on a version of an all-pervading world soul, *spiritus subtilissimus*, in some contexts. Though a straggle of champions for the *anima mundi* persisted, the doctrine had been relegated to "an intellectual twilight"[61] by the beginning of the eighteenth century. But it didn't quite die, and was reborn in changed and modified forms into evolutionary doctrines of varying kinds.

The concept of the *anima mundi* rarely rises in anything like its old form nowadays. An extreme teleological—evolutionary, goal-directed—version was propounded by the priest-paleontologist, Pierre Teilhard de Chardin. He felt that human beings were integral to the planet's evolution, that human consciousness was the spearhead of that evolutionary movement towards an ultimate "Omega Point" when godlike transcendence would be gained—a "Christogenesis." The brain was the most complex thing known of in the universe, and was achieving the "planetization" of consciousness. According to Chardin, we humans are the conscious outgrowth of the Earth, its means of becoming an entity in its own right.

Though this is an exciting idea, and others have presented similar versions of it, it is nevertheless a very anthropocentric view of things and brings in speculative assumptions about evolutionary goals. It is conceptual cargo we do not need. The message that is being pressed in this book is that we operate an informational model of the world that is kept in place by cultural gravity and the activity of the mechanisms of the brain-mind, which control what is included and edited out. Bonifazi comments that, because we are immersed in the culture it underpins, we tend not to see the limitations of the scientific view. Science is able to follow its worldview only "by abstracting from the whole of reality precisely those aspects which were amenable to its method. . . . What we are recognizing today is that the knowledge afforded by science does not exhaust reality, and that truths relating to the world in its totality, may be worth preserving."[62] If the information going into the makeup of our world model is expanded, then we can achieve a view of the world with some important differences. It really isn't a question of a war between a scientific outlook and something antiscientific, but simply bringing into our direct awareness a *further* strand of cognition—namely, the information that comes through the use of mythic consciousness. It will tell us an additional story about the world and about ourselves; it will deepen, enrich the worldview we already have, and inevitably modify it in ways that are quite urgently required. Myths in themselves may belong to ancient and specific strata of human history, but the *mythic process* is perennial, and is overly curtailed in our culture today or hived off into the pre-programmed mythic arena of film, television, and computer cyber-space. The repression of the active use and experience of organic mythic consciousness leads to all kinds of social pathologies—from rumors of satanic child abuse and UFO abductions, to drug abuse or submission to the control of mesmerizing millennial cults. In the larger sense, a culture without a healthy mythic consciousness exhibits damaging environmental behavior without clear aware-ness. We need to experience a direct link with nature, using the por-tals of mythic consciousness. We desperately need to see the Earth again with an open, dreaming eye.

A return to the use of mythic consciousness is being called for by various contemporary psychologists in differing ways, though usu-ally in the context of personal development and transformation. It is of course with individuals that any incorporation of the experi-ence of the mythic worldview must begin, but it also needs to be seen as a fundamental foundation for any emerging ecopsychology. To indicate how this generalizing process might practically develop, it is useful to start with an ecopsychologically critical myth—that of the fall of humanity from paradise, the myth of the lost Eden. Cer-tainly our culture acts as if it is cast out from the Garden, but the truth is we are still in the Garden, though stumbling around with our eyes closed. Blind in Eden. By opening the dreaming eye, we might begin to see where we are.

## THE EARTH OF VISIONS, OR PARADISE LOST? (RETURNING TO THE CENTER)

The myth of a once-and-future paradise is universal to humanity. It belongs to no particular culture or age—the idea of paradise is the birthright of human consciousness. Even in shamanic tribal tradi-tion there was a time when mankind and the gods coinhabited the Earth, a time also when animals and humans could talk with one another. The Judeo-Christian concept of the Garden of Eden was possibly adapted by Hebrew scholars from earlier Mesopotamian beliefs. The Greeks spoke of a Golden Age "in the time of Cronus," when people were happy, perfect, and living at ease. The ancient Celts had their Tir-na-nog, the "Land of Youth" and the Blessed Land of the West—and we saw earlier how the Irish Hy Brasil hung on even into the age of modern maps. The Chinese, the Native Americans, and the Africans all had their lost paradises. The Tibetans had Shambhala, the Polynesians Pulotu, and so forth. Heaven and Earth were once much closer to one another than now, and communication was easy between the two realms. But now we are banished, and contact is difficult if not impossible. Perhaps after death, or in another great cycle of time, Eliade's "eternal return,"[63] we will enter a new golden age, a celestial Jerusalem, or the Elysian Fields.

Descriptions of how paradise looked are fairly universal, too. Time there was mythic—Great Time. Vegetation, buildings, rocks, mountains, people all glowed with an inner light; everything seemed bejeweled. The *Ramayana*'s description of Uttarakuru, the Hindu paradise, is typical: "The land is watered by lakes with golden lotuses. There are rivers by the thousands, full of leaves the colour of sapphire and lapis lazuli. . . . The country all around is covered by jewels and precious stones, with gay beds of blue lotus, golden petalled. Instead of sand, pearls, gems and gold form the banks of rivers. . . ." The various paradises of humanity have also shared common geographic characteristics. There is a central tree or group of trees in some versions. In Eden, it was the Tree of Knowledge. The very word "paradise" comes from ancient Iran—*pairidaeza*, a walled garden. In mythic terms, this was the Var, the paradisal enclosure of Yima, a god figure of at least early–Indo-European antiquity. The Iranian paradise-garden symbolizes the Earth in all its levels, from material to the celestial Earth, and in its purest form involves a central arrangement of trees around a body of water. (There was also a symbolism of flowers in Mazdean Iran, in which certain flowers corresponded to certain angelic entities.) In other versions of paradise, there was a central mountain, or set of sacred peaks, centrally placed. There are usually four sacred rivers emerging from a fountain or a spring in a rock, and these flow in the cardinal directions. The Scandinavian *Edda* describes four rivulets emerging from the spring of Hvergelmir amidst the roots of Yggdrasil, the World Tree. The Chinese paradise mountain of Kwenlun is the source of the "four great rivers of the world." In Navajo myth, the paradisal Earth on which the First Man and First Woman lived had a spring from which rivers flowed to the Four Directions.

We can perhaps recognize that we have returned by a circuitous route to the Sacred Center, where we began our psychological journey through the world in chapter one. "Paradise, where Adam was created from clay, is, of course, situated at the center of the cosmos," religious historian Mircea Eliade pointed out. "Paradise was the navel of the Earth and, according to Syrian tradition, was established on a mountain higher than all others. . . . The center . . . is pre-eminently the zone of the sacred, the zone of absolute reality. . . ."[64] But we saw in chapter one that, the more we went into the center, the more we passed through the dissolving mists of the self—the crossroads of the Four Directions is haunted by its specter. This is of course the ultimate clue to the universal nature of paradise—it is located in the human mind, or, to put a different spin on that, it is not a physical place but a realm accessible only through the portals of human consciousness. This was eloquently grasped by Aldous Huxley when he experimented with the mind-altering drug mescaline in the 1950s. As he gazed around his garden, with his "doors of perception cleansed," flowers shimmered with supernaturally glowing colors on the brink of the otherworld. Trees seemed to "belong to some sacred grove . . . Eden alternated with Dodona, Yggdrasil with the mystic Rose."[65] He noted, too, the descriptions of inner landscapes seen by early experimenters with hallucinogens. He cited Weir Mitchel, who saw visions of a Gothic tower encrusted with gems and green and purple waves breaking on some otherworld beach creating myriad pinpoints of green and purple lights. These visionary paradises existed in the "antipodes" of the mind, according to Huxley's mapping of consciousness, and he was struck by the similarity of such visions of the altered mind to the traditional descriptions of paradise. The New Jerusalem, the Celestial City, in St. John's apocalypse had walls of jasper, and was made of glasslike gold and garnished with "all manner of precious stones." Huxley noted that preternatural light and preternatural colors were the hallmark of the self-luminous visionary worlds of paradise.

Paradise can be seen through the lens of the mind, and through the open dreaming eye. Paradise is a vision of the Spiritual Earth, the Earth before our fall. The scholar of Islamic spiritual traditions Henry Corbin gave us an outline of an exemplary form of this visionary Earth in the spiritual traditions of ancient Iran, which emerged from Zoroastrian Mazdaism of Persia. And Zoroastrianism originally derived elements from shamanism.[66] Within these traditions, to simplify what are actually more complex concepts, it is thought that the physical body inhabits the physical Earth, but the soul inhabits a visionary, celestial, or spiritual Earth, termed the *Imago Terrae* by Corbin. To put it another way, each level of the human being, from gross material to refined spiritual, projects, as it were, its own Earth, rather than passively experiencing an environment. So the Shi'ite adept, for instance, has "the Earth of his Paradise" as the projection of his spiritual body. If Adam's body was made from the clay of the material Earth, then his soul was fashioned from the "Earth of Visions." Various angels or powers represent—or project—the various levels of Earth. The Archangel of Earth, in this philosophy, is Spenta Armaiti, translated by Plutarch as Sophia, Wisdom. Corbin informed that there was a Mazdean sacrament of the Earth which "in its essence . . . can be described as a *geosophy*, that is to say as being the *Sophianic* mystery of the Earth."[67] This doctrine necessitated the existence of a *visionary geography*, Corbin maintained, because only a visionary geography can accommodate visionary events, the interaction of the outer, sensible Earth with the inner, symbolic or supramundane Earth. This visionary geography occupies the sacral space in the World Center. In the midst of it is Eran-Vej, mythologized as the Var of Yima, which issues light. The glowing inhabitants of this region will populate the Earth when it is transfigured from the mundane to the visionary at the end of time (which also means in personal postmortem terms). The mountain of Hukairya also stands in Eran-Vej and reaches to the stars. On it are the springs of the waters of life and the all-white Haoma, which grants immortality to those who partake of it (this is thought by some researchers to refer to an ancient hallucinogenic plant). Close to this is another mountain, made of ruby, the Mountain of the Dawns, the first peak to be lit by the sun's rays and the receptacle and provider of intelligence (there is a word play in Persian between "intelligence" and "dawn"). A third mountain in this visionary landscape is the Peak of Judgment, from which leads the perilous Bridge of Chinvat, reaching to the Beyond—a profoundly shamanic image. Elements of this visionary geography were projected onto the material, mundane geography of Iran, with physical mountains symbolizing their spiritual counterparts. Because this visionary geography was the scene of psycho-physical events, the details of which we need not discuss here, Corbin also called it a "psychogeography."

The twelfth-century mystic Suhrawardi carried over Mazdean philosophy into Islam, where it was further modified. The visionary land of the center became Hurqalya, "the Earth of the Emerald Cities," in which there was the cosmic mountain Qaf, which had an emerald slab, the *smaragdina*, on its summit. This stood at the junction of the visible and invisible worlds.[68]

This visionary land at the World Center is a notional zone "mediating between the sensory and the intelligible," as Corbin put it. It is *barzakh*, the interworld, where it is always the high noon of eternity, and thus where a person does not throw a shadow—a euphemism for saying that it could not be entered physically. For this is mythic space, the projection of mythic consciousness. Of course, we, being children of our culture, want to know what the *actual* nature of such a visionary world, such a paradisal realm, might be. Our scientists will say it is "all in the mind," hallucination. But could it be a glimpse into another dimension of reality, another world, with an actual, independent existence? Huxley remained ambivalent on the matter. Here, however, we can return to the idea of an informational model of the world. In such a model, it is meaningless to ask whether or not a visionary Earth is *real*, for the physical Earth whose reality we feel so sure of is in fact "only" a pattern of information sustained in our brain-minds and phase-locked by our culture. When Huxley looked around at a transfigured world during his mescaline experiments, he was as convinced as William Blake that his eyes had been cleansed, that he was receiving *more* information from "Mind-at-Large," as he put it. He felt the drug was inhibiting his normal mental filtering processes. The rationalist will disagree, arguing that it was simply that the drug caused his brain to embroider sensory data with hallucinatory material, and that this is even more patently the case when inner landscapes are seen. But the picture we build of the world in our brain-minds is in a sense a hallucination in any case, as has been noted several times. If we engage the "energy soup" that is our true environment with the steady gaze of the open dreaming eye of mythic consciousness, we can draw out of that matrix information that is filtered out of the data streams used by other mental functions. The informational model we then build does show the Earth in a transfigured, paradisal state—the Earth in its "archetype-Image," to use Corbin's phrase. In nonpsychological language, *this is the Earth viewed at the level of the soul rather than at the level of the physical body*. Corbin also used the term "imaginal" to describe this condition of cognition, this interworld in which sensory data are transmuted, where "spirits are embodied, and bodies spiritualized," as it was described by the seventeenth-century Islamic mystic Muhsin Fayz Kashani. The imaginal state was so named by Corbin to distinguish it from mere, pallid imagination; like Huxley, he was in no doubt that this mode of consciousness "*unveils* the hidden reality." If the mainstream thinking in our culture had access to the open dreaming eye of mythic consciousness, would we not invest our attitude towards the world with greater reverence? Would we not tell ourselves a different story about the Earth? Would our worldview not change dramatically?

The imaginal interworld state was lamented by Corbin as being a "vanished consciousness" in our times. He reported that the mystic adepts of Islam practiced a form of alchemical meditation to enter this intermediary world. Would not the development of some comparative cognitive tool that was accessible to our culture and provided such experience, a return to paradise, be the crowning achievement of an ecopsychology? Its *raison d'être*, even?

If all this sounds simply like theoretical, idealistic pie in the sky, let us consider practicalities. We have already noted that, whether a person changes consciousness through the use of psychoactive drugs, through deep meditative practice, or through shamanic trance-induction techniques, the experience of light, time, and space shifts; the world becomes transfigured. But there is no widely available training for navigating altered states of consciousness in the traditions of our culture. The use of drugs in such a cultural context can therefore be dangerous, and the spiritual training required to achieve altered mind-states by deep meditational methods is possible only for a relatively small number of people. But developments in recent years hold out the promise of an altered state of consciousness that may well prove to be profoundly useful and effective in exploring the imaginal interworld state of mind we have been discussing. The state of consciousness in question is usually referred to as "lucid-dreaming."

The term, coined by Frederick Van Eeden in 1913,[69] is somewhat unfortunate, because it gives the impression to those who have never experienced the state that all that is involved is particularly vivid dreams. This is not the case. The lucid-dream state is a discrete state of imaginal consciousness, usually achieved through normal dreaming sleep, in which the sensible world is modeled with extraordinary "reality": all senses can be operative, including touch; space is fully three-dimensional; and the scenery and objects within it seem "objective" and detailed—perspective changes convincingly as one moves, and the sense of motion can be completely convincing. There can be differences from normal waking reality, however: the lucid dreamer can fly or leap along the ground with great, graceful bounds; words or numbers seen on a page or surface seem unstable, changing each time they are looked at; and the lighting in a room can behave erratically. In the lucid-dream state, a person is physiologically in dreaming sleep, but "awakes" to full consciousness *within* the dream. Whereupon the dream, however vivid it may have been before, suddenly takes on a totally sensory presence, just as if the dreamer had awoken to the world of waking consciousness. Lucid-dream scenery can be "otherworldly" at one extreme, or, at the other, can reproduce the dreamer's bedroom and sleeping body. Because of this, aspects of some lucid dreams are highly reminiscent of so-called out-of-body experiences (if we assume that "we" are "in" our bodies to begin with), and some researchers consider the two conditions to be, in fact, one and the same.

So remarkable is this state of consciousness that, although vari-

ous people have reported and written about it for decades, not until 1975 did science reluctantly start accepting its existence. In that
year, British dream researcher Keith Hearne was able to demonstrate the condition instrumentally. During dreaming sleep, much
of the body is paralyzed—only the eye muscles and respiratory system are unaffected. Hearne hit on the idea of using REMs as a
means whereby a lucid dreamer in a sleep laboratory could communicate with the "outside world."[70]

Hearne's subject in this experiment was Alan Worsley, a man who
had regular lucid dreams. Hearne suggested that Worsley use a pre-
arranged set of eyeball movements when he was experiencing lucid
dreaming. Eventually the set of signals were received from Worsley
while physiological monitoring confirmed that he was asleep. A
year or two later, dream researcher Stephen LaBerge at Stanford
University, California, not knowing of Hearne's success, independently came up with the same idea and result.[71] Serious research
into the lucid-dream state had begun.

It remains, however, a new frontier of consciousness research,
and something of a Cinderella research area, still largely ignored or
downplayed by mainstream sleep-and-dream researchers. But its
potential is enormous; as transpersonal psychologist Roger Walsh
has declared, lucid dreaming is a powerful new psychological tool
in our quest for understanding the nature of consciousness.[72] It will
better enable us to understand how we model the world of the
senses in our minds. Lucid dreaming can also act as a springboard
for further altered states of consciousness: people have reported
episodes of "cosmic consciousness" experienced from within the
lucid dreaming state.[73,74] The accomplished lucid dreamer is also in
a better position to benefit from the study of Tibetan dream yoga,
in which the ultimate aim is to stay conscious in all states, and to
wake up from consensus waking reality as one wakes up from a normal dream.

Clearly, this state of consciousness has great potential for both
personal and collective discovery. Though there are a thousand and
one ways of achieving altered mind-states, lucid dreaming may well
prove to be the wisest, most applicable way of doing it within our
culture, for we all sleep and we all dream (whether or not we re-

member our dreams)—a yoga for the West, perhaps. Regarding our specific concerns in this book, it offers a direct experiential way of opening the eye of mythic consciousness, so we can all learn how to see the ensouled Earth, the "White Earth" of alchemical tradition, what Buddhists call "the Shining."[75] The mind is as much a part of nature as is a rain forest, and in the imaginal state of lucid dreaming it is thus possible for nature to contemplate nature, rediscovering its own interiority, because ego boundaries are softened back to the early dreamtime state of humanity, a state that is perennially present if we can learn to tap into it. In this state the informational model of the world is extended and can yield profound experiences and insights. Only when we again find out how to pass through the portal of the Sacred Center to paradise will we be able to add the required soul to our material ecological concerns.

The overarching mission of this book has been to offer historical contexts, intellectual arguments, and experiential techniques to promote the idea of the existence of a mental mode—which can best be termed "mythic" or "imaginal"—that is effectively missing from the modern worldview, from modern consciousness, and which could be used to heal our relationship with the Earth. Incorporation of this mythic mode into our consciousness requires a "softening" of our tenacious hold on the consensus, "waking" worldview that our hard-edged ego and the culture of the West consider not only normal but the *only* way of apprehending nature, the world. It seems to me that such a softening is what an ecopsychology must be able to provide. In these pages we have been looking back at much older and longer-lived ways of seeing the world, and I have been suggesting that we give ourselves permission to think strange thoughts, to test the edges of our perceptions, to allow ourselves to be animistic on one track of our being to balance the rationalistic tracks that otherwise govern us. "Rationalism" is just the name of one type of dream, one that we are culturally locked into. It is within the framework of that dream that the flood of material on brain and mind now issuing from cognitive science is placed. It

tends towards a form of neuro-reductionism, as though the phenomenon of the mind (and consequently the phenomenon of
Earth) can be reduced to neural circuitry. But we do not yet know
where consciousness enters the system—the brain itself could be an
act of consciousness, for all we know. To return to the metaphor
used in the introductory chapter, the cognitive scientists could be
making the error of the TV engineer in equating the TV receiver with
the broadcasting studio. Or, to use a similar analogy, they may be
dissecting the computer, and even finding evidence for its software,
while ignoring the programmer. We must continually remind ourselves that we are yet as children in the study of mind, to which the
neural architecture of the brain is but the human doorway. The
findings of cognitive science can be accepted and welcomed, but it
would be presumptuous to assume that our studies of the brain will
tell us all there is to know about the mind. Brain-mind need not be
a neat, balanced equation; it is not necessarily the case that
brain = mind. Cognitive science has jumped too quickly and ea-
gerly to that assumption, and nature is rarely so simple.

In mythic consciousness, we can rove outside the bandwidth of
the rational dream. We have already noted that Emerson claimed
the world was "a divine dream." An old Bushman once told Laurens
van der Post: "There is a dream dreaming us."[76] Pushing at our rational limits, perhaps we should think, at least occasionally, that
the Earth is *dreaming us*. (It is healthy to reverse normal assumptions occasionally.) Waking in that dream, becoming "lucid" within
it, means entering the imaginal state. We have mapped the material
Earth, the Earth of our physical bodies; it is time now for us to become as equally acquainted with the ensouled Earth—to learn to
map *chora* again. We carry the pattern of paradise embedded in the
deepest levels of our mind; the choice is ours as to whether we remain blind in Eden. We can, if we wish, create the opportunity for
the land to re-mind us. We can learn once again to treat the Earth as
if it was, on one level, sentient. We cannot do that with rational
consciousness, but we *can* do it in mythic mode. In that state, we
can engage in a dialogue with the Earth, and find ways of translat-
ing gleanings from that interaction into rational consciousness. If
we do so, then our relationship with Earth will inevitably—if grad-

ually—heal, as surely and as naturally as day follows night. Redis-covering the *anima mundi*, perhaps in a way and on a scale that has never happened before, might lead us back to the estranged human soul.

## EXPERIENTIAL

In our symbolic journey through the world in the preceding chap-ters, exploring the bases of various psychological frameworks for re-assessing our relationship with the Earth, the suggested experiential activities have, to some extent, followed a course. You have been en-couraged to pick and choose amongst these activities (see the in-troductory chapter), but the practice of some of them will be important for preparing for the work to be accomplished here, in this final "Experiential" section, where procedures are outlined that will help you to experience actually, directly, the Earth of Visions.

### Temple Sleep

In chapter two we discussed "monumenteering." To extend the range of suggested mnemonic activities at the selected ancient site, why not take a nap there, if that is practicable? As has already been suggested, ancient sacred places are themselves analogous to dreams recalled upon awakening. Live the analogy! Immediately on waking up, jot down any dreams you can recall, and add that note to the memorabilia you assemble relating to the site. I well re-call that I had an afternoon nap at the ancient Celtic holy well at Madron, one of the sites selected for the Dragon Project dreamwork program discussed earlier in this chapter, in Cornwall. It was a warm, drowsy summer afternoon, and I fell deeply asleep on a ledge on the north wall of the little ruined medieval chapel, with the springwater rushing and gurgling in the stone reservoir in the southwest corner as background sound. I awoke suddenly about ten minutes later and sat bolt upright. I had seen two feminine hands dipping into water; they came up dripping and massaged the muscles around my eyes in a specific way. I immediately went over to the water, about which there were numerous healing legends, and acted out the procedure the hands had demonstrated in the dream, using my fingertips to massage the edges of my eye sockets with the ice-cold water. (This so strongly re-minded me that, even a few years afterwards, I was able to re-enact this dream experience at the Madron chapel for the TV cameras of the *Sightings* team when they visited Britain.) Your dream at your selected site may not be so obviously related to the place as this unusual dream was, but, however obscure it is, make a note of it.

If sleeping at your selected monument is not possible for whatever reason, then select a place in nature that is convenient and safe for you. Develop a dreaming relationship with it. Make it your sleeping partner! Keep a dream journal for just that place. After a time, compare this with the dream journal you keep by your bedside (see the "Living the Dreamtime" exercise below).

Finally, it is just possible that the Dragon Project dreamwork program mentioned above may still be operative at one or two of the selected sites when you read this; if you would like to take part in the program, the contact address is given in the appendix on further resources at the end of this book. You will be sent appropriate details.

## Calling the Spirits

Indulge in a little animistic play. Select some liminal spot in nature. A good choice would be a wood or forest, either at dusk or on a dull day or at a place where dense foliage makes the lighting dim and eerie. Alternatively, it could be a lone tree, bush, or group of rocks at dusk. The chosen spot needs to be free of human noise, and, indeed, as quiet as possible. Tread as respectfully and as quietly as you would if entering an ancient cathedral. Find a comfortable position and sit still and silent. Breathe calmly and evenly. Let the gloaming creep into your vision. In Japan, places haunted by *kami* or spirits are called *shiki*, and are just such places as described above. (In Ireland, lone thorn trees are a typical haunt of those nature spirits called fairies.) *Shiki* are often marked by white paper ornaments, hung with ropes, or cleared and laid with gravel.[77] The traditional method of summoning the *kami* is to clap your hands twice. Do this, then sit perfectly silent and still and wait. During this period, suspend your disbelief in such things, try not to argue with your rationalistic track, and reassure yourself that no one from your culture is watching you. Sit and *expect*. For just a little while, you have chosen to be a good old-fashioned animist.

Swiss writer Blanche Merz describes a remarkable encounter with place spirits or elementals which was also witnessed by a companion. They sat in sight of what had been identified as a spirit place close to the water's edge along the upper reaches of Lake Leman. They remained immobile for more than two hours, identifying with the trees and the high grass.[78] They made no sound. Eventually there was a sudden swirl of warm air, and they could just discern a "pale glow, opaque and phosphorescent," between some trees about thirty feet away. The birds seemed to increase their chirping, then fell silent. Merz and her companion didn't take their eyes off the light, and watched it gain in intensity and form the shape of "a giant dull green egg." Eventually delicate little elflike beings with formless faces began to appear in the light. They skittered nervously and all disappeared when Merz was stung by an insect and reacted with a sudden movement.

In Ireland, my wife and I both saw something that we have never been able to explain, but which may also have been an elemental. Emerging as if from camouflage from the grass alongside a country road, we both glimpsed (a better word than "saw") a "something" a little under two feet in height. It was as if the background suddenly took on a localized, discrete three-dimensionality. Circumstances made us lose sight of it very rapidly, but not before we saw this three-dimensional lump of greenish background begin to move. . . .

You may not be blessed at first attempt with such appearances, but be on the watch for any hint—an unexplained rustle in the leaves or grass around you; a tiny swirl of wind; or even a change in mood or feeling. Merz reckons the technique requires "blending what you know with what you feel." I recall on one occasion being on the tree-covered long barrow called East Kennet, a mile or two from Avebury, a powerfully atmospheric and remote spot. While I was engaged there in photography, the leaves and twigs on the ground suddenly snapped and crackled like firecrackers in a rapid sequence in a semicircle around me. The hairs bristled on my neck, and I got out of there fast—I wasn't ready to go into mythic mode, and my sense of the mood of the place had changed dramatically!

After your hour or so of sitting quietly, get up and leave the spot, whatever may or may not have happened in your opinion, openly or inwardly thanking all the life-forms visible and invisible that may be present. When you move away, switch out of "mythic mode" and resume your normal consensus consciousness. If you feel a bit embarrassed or foolish about undertaking this exercise, just smile—it is only your hard rational ego becoming irritated and perhaps a bit threatened by your getting out of line. Remind your ego that it is not the total sum of your consciousness, but just one mode. In another culture, another time, your actions would have been perfectly sane, honorable—and even expected of you!

## Nature the Dream-Maker

Quite often Mother Nature presents ways to lull you into reverie, into those liminal mind-states leading to mythic mode (if you don't nod off to sleep first). Use such reveries, Earth dreams, whenever you can. Keep your mythic eye open for opportunities. For instance, a fire. We mentioned earlier that every home should ideally have a hearth, an open fire. A fire is a tool for the mind as well as a source of warmth for the body. Gaze into the flickering flames or, late in the evening, the glowing embers. I have done this from childhood, and have seen a thousand faces, golden cities, shimmering lands. On one particular late-winter eve, I well remember, I was already in an altered state of consciousness before staring into the embers in a wood-burning stove. I became rapt in the complexities of one glowing log, as its burning light pulsed in varied intensities over the gnarled surface. Suddenly I was looking into another world. What had at one moment simply looked like suggestive shapes and forms became a true scene, like a tiny movie. I saw a wayside cottage, and a man come out of its door and walk up to the garden gate. I looked on past this, down the lane, to the distant fields, trees, and hills of the landscape beyond. I started to look into this, and saw minute detail everywhere opening up in waves before my gaze. So intense was the experience that I had to call a halt to the exercise. One really has to be in serious mythic mode to see like this, but any fire will prompt reverie. Use the fire to get used to that state. Learn to recognize it and operate within it.

Another, similar type of nature reverie is afforded by sunlight sparkling on a body of water or a dancing stream. Relax, lie back, and let your eyes go out of focus, so you just see a soft, dazzling, dancing sparkle filling your visual field. The shimmer and movement of the light on the water, like that of the fire, seems to massage, perhaps entrain, the rhythms of the brain into deep states of reverie—we can be sure that nature connects all things.

Then there are clouds. Nature produces clouds to invoke the mythic mind as well as to yield rain. You knew this as a child, but you have forgotten. Well, re-mind yourself—be a big kid again. Sprawl out somewhere comfortable—nobody will know what you are up to, so ignore the admonishments of your rationalist ego, which will be getting quite concerned about you by now. Choose a day when big fluffy white clouds are sailing across the blue yonder. Try to cut anything on the ground out of your field of view; fall visually into the great bowl of the sky. See how the clouds move majestically, their edges constantly changing, folding, dissolving. See and enjoy the soft play of light and shadow. What can you see? Faces? Old Zeus himself? A huge poodle? A dragon? The towers of a dreaming city? Let it all pass; let the clouds drive a parade of imagery and associations through the vault of your mind.

And do it whenever you get the chance—build up your mythic muscles.

## Bark with a Bite

A wonderful visual portal for mythic vision is gnarled tree trunks and even quite small areas of complex tree bark. Inspect trees in your vicinity and see what you can mythically see. Take a photo of the gnarled section of trunk or bark that most conjures images in your mind, or, if it is a loose piece of bark, take it home with you.

Whether you take a photo or a sample, use it for several minutes a few times every week to conjure the image(s) that you first saw, and always look to see what fresh images can come forth. It is said that the great Renaissance artist and inventor Leonardo da Vinci used to get his apprentices to stare at stains on the studio walls for a few hours every week so they could learn to see imaginally faces, battles, and so on.

Use bark, stains, and whatever else helps keep your mythic eye in training.

### Rock On

Let us now consider a more structured example of this imaginal seeing. In Plate O, you are shown a view of a particular named rock on one of the Scilly Isles—the string of islands and islets that stretch into the Atlantic from Cornwall's Land's End at England's most southwesterly point. The name of the rock and its exact location are given in note 79 for this chapter, at the back of this book, but it would be better not to look the information up until you've carried out this activity: it might affect your mythologizing.[79] These islands are said to be all that is left of the legendary sunken land of Lyonnesse. Not too far away across the mouth of the English Channel is Brittany in France, where there are also legends of a lost land, called Ynys. There is in fact clear evidence that parts of the coastlines of Cornwall and Brittany were inundated. Like mainland Cornwall, the Scilly Isles have many ancient monuments scattered over them, dating from remote prehistory, through the Roman period, and to Romano-Celtic times and later. Also like Cornwall, their geology is granitic, and the mighty Atlantic and the prevailing southwesterly winds have worn away at their coastal rocks, carving many fantastic shapes, since granite doesn't crumble away like most rocks. A number of the more spectacular forms were given names by the islanders generations ago. The rock in the picture is one of these, though a small example, being only about ten feet high. Look at it. What image does it conjure in your mind? What does your imaginal eye see when you are looking at it? When an image emerges from the rock, use associations that come with it to try to incorporate it into a legend, a myth, that accounts for how it became fossilized, locked into the rock. Mythologize the rock. Write your myth down, then tape-record it. Play this tape and look at the photograph immediately before going to sleep that night. Try to *dream your myth*. See if the legend can develop its own life in that mythic arena we call dreaming. Try this one or two nights every week for a month or two, and make sure you at least glance at the photograph every day. Play the tape of your legend when you get a chance—in your car, perhaps.

A view of the weathered, named rock on St. Agnes, Scilly Isles, U.K.

Rather than working from the photo in this book, or in addition to doing so, you might like to find your own rock with imaginal shapes in it. Take its photograph and use that in the same way described above. If the rock shown in this book tells you a wild pre-Celtic story, your rock might speak to your mythic mind of a Native American foundation legend, or some lost hero or goddess.

Another way to use the photograph of the rock in this book, or your own pictures, is instead of reading a bedtime story to a child. I recall an uncle visiting my sickbed one time in the 1950s, when I was very young. He brought along a book called, I think, *Nature Through the Seasons*. It was a big picture book—quite rare at that time. One double-page photograph showed a snowy scene, with scattered trees and bushes. There was a dark, soft patch of snow beneath one of the bushes that looked, my uncle and I decided, like a little boy in a pointed hat lying on the ground, partly obscured by the bush. My uncle convinced me that was what it was and that, moreover, the little boy was dead. A tale unraveled about how he had become separated from his parents one dark winter night, and had wandered lost through the wilderness. Various adventures befell him, until, at last, he fell dying from cold and exhaustion. It was all very sad, and I shed some tears over that patch of melting snow! Make your rock photographs a subject to be explored with a child no older than ten years of age. Let a story develop from the images seen in the rock, and try to get the child to lead in this process, with you just adding bits and pieces to help things along. Don't try to stop the process for the child's sake if the story becomes sad or scary—children are past masters at this sort of thing! *Listen to the child*—let the mythic narrative emerge through your collaboration with this young mind.

## Listening to Mother

Now you be the child. This time we'll use the auditory sense, which can provide the same access to reverie as the visual stimuli we described earlier. For example, the sound of rain falling on the canopy of a forest—or sometimes even on the roof of a building—can make the relaxed mind drift away. Likewise the muted roar of wind blowing through many leaves. The psychologist Julian Jaynes has suggested that the wind trembling the leaves of a huge sacred oak tree at the oracle center of Dodona in ancient Greece may have provided the matrix of sound out of which the priestess heard the voice of Zeus give the answers to questions. Jaynes also proposed that a similar function was provided by murmuring springs and water gushing through a narrow ravine at the oracle of Lebadea, where the voice of Trophonius could be heard by those who listened in the right way. Jaynes found a cell-like pit in the rock there that led into an "ovenlike" shrine over an undergound flume.[80]

The psychologist, parapsychologist, and dream researcher Stanley Krippner tells of a tradition among the ancient Slavic tribes. It involved digging a hole in the ground with bare hands and placing an ear to it, so that they could hear what *Mati-Syra-Zemlya*, Moist Mother Earth, was telling them.[81] Try it yourself, in soft soil or in stretch of flat, wet sand at the beach. What is Mother saying to you?

## The Vasudeva Crossing

We can undertake a more structured form of this kind of listening, based on the famous, moving climax to Hermann Hesse's novel *Siddhartha*.[82] Siddhartha, after a lifetime of seeking spiritual truth, stays with an old ferryman sage called Vasudeva when his quest seems at its most hopeless. One day, while the two men are crossing the river, as they had done so many times before, Vasudeva entreats Siddhartha to listen to the rushing water. And Siddhartha hears the "many-voiced song" of the river. It laughs and cries. Its voice becomes full of longing, full of yearning, full of woe. Good and evil voices, voices of pleasure and sorrow, the sounds of laughing and lamenting, voices of men, women, and children. Suddenly these thousands of voices merge into one interwoven tapestry of sound— the river is in reality singing just one great song of life. Siddhartha's sense of self similarly melts into one flow, his desperate clinging to things ceases, and he gains enlightenment. Although he had crossed the river many times with Vasudeva, only this time did he truly make the crossing.

Our intent here is somewhat more modest, but uses part of this process. First of all, you need a river. Actually, much better, find a waterfall or a gushing mountain stream, for both these kinds of water produce that rushing, roaring noise that is such a rich matrix of sound. Take along a good-quality tape recorder and make a long audiotape (twenty minutes at least) of the sound of the water. While this is happening, sit calmly or lie down, close your eyes, and listen. At first, the movement of the water will sound like radio static, for it is technically a similar sound. After about five minutes, though, you may begin to hear various beats within the sound that result from the specific location, the way the rock walls are reverberating the sound, and so on. This is the signature of the place; the waters are telling you their story. Continue listening. Soon you will seem to catch the sound of voices in the water. A name is called. Perhaps your name, perhaps the name of a relative or friend; quite often, and curiously, it is the name of someone you knew who has died. The waterfall or mountain stream will now start telling you your story, the story of other people, or possibly the story of the spirits that haunt the place *or that you brought with you.* Don't edit or resist what you hear. Just let the waters speak. A voicelike sound may spark off a string of associations in your mind. Let it. The Earth is speaking to you.

Use the tape made at the waterfall or stream frequently at home. Listen in your city room, or wherever, to that voice of the Earth. New voices will emerge from the sound as you listen with your eyes closed shortly before going to sleep. Conjure a memory of the place; see it in your mind's eye. Turn off the tape (or let it click off automatically), and go to sleep. Dream well. Dream the Earth's dream.

## Living the Dreamtime

If you practice some or all of the above activities, you will be suitably prepared for this final one, in which we shall work our passage to the Imaginal Earth.

First we need to ensure that the mythic arena which is our dreamlife is fully prepared. You have already cleared the ground with some of the experiential activities above and earlier in this book. Now get serious about your dreams. If you don't already, start keeping a dream journal. Keep a booklet and pen handy to your bedside. Every morning when you awake, spend a moment lying quietly with your eyes closed, trying to remember as many dreams as you can. If you open your eyes and move about, the delicate fabric of dream memory falls asunder more rapidly. Jot down what you can recall. If you can't remember anything, there is always another night; as you persist in this habit, it will come easier to you, and you will find you are remembering more and more of your dreams. Read through your journal regularly, especially before falling asleep.

When you recall your dreams, pay specific attention to the background, the scenery. All too often it is the events and people in a dream that hold our attention. If you have artistic skills, you might want to make sketches in your dream journal of some dream scenes you recall. Eventually, you might find yourself beginning to notice the scenery deliberately while in your dreams, or even having dreams that show only scenery (this is often the case with the fleeting visions of the hypnagogic state—see "Finding your Warp Factor" in chapter two). If so, this is an important development towards the next stage.

And that is—learning to have lucid dreams. There are many ways you can train yourself in this, and various authors have offered their own methods. Stephen LaBerge and Howard Rheingold's *Exploring the World of Lucid Dreaming* gives numerous techniques, for instance.[83] But most techniques boil down essentially to forming mental habits in waking consciousness that eventually begin to appear in the dreaming state. The requirement is somehow to trigger awareness while in a dream: waking up in the dream without waking up from sleep. It is a delicate operation, but if it has been done once it is much easier to repeat. One habit is to ask yourself several times each day, as you go about your business, "Am I dreaming?" If it is appropriate, you could even set your wristwatch to beep you every hour or so as a reminder. Get thoroughly in the habit of questioning whether you are asleep or awake. That mental habit will only have to appear once during a dream to start you on the road to lucidity. Work at it. Another technique is a special form of the "method of *loci*." Make a pact with a friend or partner to meet him or her in your dreams at some specific place known to you both. We have already noted how place and memory are tightly linked, so make the dreamtime rendezvous a place that you see every day in waking consciousness, perhaps the front of a building you pass every day on your way to work, or, even your own kitchen! In this way, the place will "stalk" you and keep reminding you of the pact every time you pass it or enter it. Keep the intention in your mind as you go to sleep. Similarly, and always, keep the intention to become lucid in the forefront of your mind every time you go to sleep. Writing down your intention, speaking (or singing!) it out loud, or making some similar active display before retiring for the night strengthens it even further. This is called "incubating" a dream, and eventually (though sometimes quite quickly) the intent works its way into the dream state.

Periods of dreaming (REM) sleep occur roughly every hour or two during a normal night's sleep, the longest being the couple of hours before waking. It is in this last period that the lucid dream is most likely to occur. LaBerge and colleagues have suggested waking up two hours earlier than usual, carrying out some activity, then going back to bed and catching up with those lost two hours of sleep at the time you normally awake.[84] So, for example, if you normally awake at 7 A.M., set your alarm at 5 A.M., get up, read, or get on with some task, then come back to bed at 7 A.M. and sleep until 9 A.M. Your chances of having a lucid dream are greatly enhanced during this period. Another trick is to take an hour's nap during the day, incubating in the usual manner. A nap can often be more productive of lucidity than deeper nighttime sleeping.

But unless you are a natural lucid dreamer, as only relatively few people are, you will need to work at all this. If after a couple of months' consistent effort you still haven't had a lucid dream, then think about obtaining some artificial assistance. There are two fairly effective ways of doing this.

The first—more expensive but for many people more acceptable than the second—is to use an electronic lucid-dream machine. La Berge's Lucidity Institute already supplies a programmable electronic eye-mask that is quite comfortable to use, and Hearne is said to be about to come out with a dream machine at the time of this writing. These machines are designed to pick up your physiological signs of dreaming sleep—a change in breathing rhythms, or REMs. They then use various types of prompts to awaken you within your dream. Further details on the Lucidity Institute's machine can be found in the appendix. These machines sell for a few hundred dollars. They are not, however, instant answers to the problem, and even they have to be worked with over a period of time.

The other option requires a raid on the spice shelf in the kitchen. This was how I personally started lucid dreaming (although I had had earlier in life what I took to be out-of-body experiences). I took two level (five-millimeter) teaspoonfuls of ground nutmeg just before retiring for the night. My skin became dry and hot, a little like having a fever—I must admit I was a bit concerned that my experimental zeal might be making me ill. But I managed to drop off to sleep. During my long REM period, around 6 A.M., I had a startlingly powerful and fully lucid dream. I have written about this in detail elsewhere,[85] and so will not bother to recount it in full here. Suffice it to say I awoke in a dream in which I was stumbling around in the crypt of some ancient temple and then experienced two versions of the traditional "tunnel" entoptic—one a dark subterranean passage and the second a long row of huge marble trilithons—and flew out over a magnificent landscape with blue distant hills and sunlit rolling fields and woodlands. I looked down on a scatter of houses and saw people who looked perfectly normal except that they were wearing curious sage-green tunics. Everything was totally "real"; I could even tug at tree branches as I glided by, and could feel the waxy texture of the leaves. Above all, it was the stunning scenery that made me gasp, along with the extraordinary physical sensation of flight. I knew I was looking out over the paradisal, Imaginal Earth. In the months after that experience, I had a series of spontaneous lucid dreams, without needing nutmeg or even incubation. That is why the first lucid dream is so important: once you have had one, others become easier, as if the brain-mind has somehow "primed" itself.

*If you choose this nutmeg method, however, be careful and responsible.* Don't take nutmeg in excess, because that would risk damaging your body. Don't take nutmeg at all unless you are in good health and are satisfied that for you it is safe (as is the case with all the suggested experiential activities in this book). Nutmeg can be a bit "rough." It has been known to be smoked by people who couldn't get hold of cannabis. Used like this, it can apparently give unpleasant headaches afterwards, like extreme hangover effects. Don't use it this way; *use it only as an adjunct to the sleeping process.* Start modestly with small amounts, perhaps by incorporating it in dishes you cook yourself. If you take it directly, start with no more than a half-teaspoonful sprinkled on ice cream, or, if you have a savory tooth, on a peanut-butter sandwich, about a half hour before going to bed for a full night's sleep. If that has no effect—and factors such as body weight and how much you have eaten before taking the nutmeg (try to eat lightly that day) all have a bearing—then a week later try one level teaspoonful. (I am talking here of a five-millimeter teaspoon, a third of a tablespoon in U.S. measure.) Never go beyond two level teaspoons. Don't make a habit of it (unlikely as that might be, for nutmeg isn't very pleasant to the taste in these larger doses)—you only need it for your first lucid dream. Your nutmeg experiments may not trigger lucidity, but they will almost certainly make your dreams more numerous, or at least more powerful, visionary, and robust, and so more easily remembered and usable as entrances into lucidity.

When you start having lucid dreams by whatever method, then you are effectively out on your own (though more support and information are becoming available all the time). You will be able to remember your lucid dreams as easily as you remember events in waking life. The sheer novelty of lucidity will excite you to begin with, but the time will come when you will want to gain more control; then you can start using the mind-state to explore the Imaginal Earth. The lucid-dream state provides you with the raw material of mythic consciousness. One experiment to try would be to perceive in a lucid-dream landscape the sort of imagery mentioned at the beginning of this chapter, concerning simulacra of gods, goddesses, and heroes in hills, mountains, and rocks. *Animate* the landscape around you, and see what develops. *Live the dreamtime.* Another experiment would be to call forth nature spirits during a lucid dream. The fabulous complexity and mystery of the human mind will never cease to amaze and instruct you.

# NOTES

INTRODUCTION

1. James Lovelock, "Gaia—Science or Myth?," *Resurgence*, May–June 1993.

2. James Lovelock, *The Ages of Gaia*, Oxford University Press, 1988.

3. James Lovelock, "Planetary Medicine," *Resurgence*, September–October 1991.

4. Theodore Roszak, quoted in Daniel Goleman, "Psychology's New Interest in the World Beyond the Self," *New York Times*, August 29, 1993.

5. Theodore Roszak, *The Voice of the Earth*, Touchstone, Simon & Schuster, 1992.

6. Ibid.

7. Robert Greenway, quoted in Goleman, "Psychology's New Interest."

8. Quoted in Goleman, "Psychology's New Interest."

9. Reported in ibid.

10. Theodore Roszak, "The Voice of the Earth," *Resurgence*, January–February 1992.

11. Theodore Roszak, *The Voice of the Earth,*" Touchstone, Simon & Schuster, *1992.*

12. *Deep Ecology and Transpersonal Psychology: An Enlightening Confrontation?*, Open Eye Publications, n.d.

13. Cited in ibid. (emphasis added).

14. Ralph Waldo Emerson, *Nature* (1836), Beacon Press ed., 1991.

15. G. W. Russell ("Æ"), *Song and Its Fountains* (1932), in Raghavan Iyer and Nadini Iyer, eds., *The Descent of the Gods*, Colin Smythe, 1988.

16. G. W. Russell ("Æ") *The Candle of Vision* (1918), in Iyer and Iyer, *Descent of the Gods.*

17. Ibid.

18. John Perkins, *The World Is As You Dream It*, Destiny Books, 1994.

19. Emerson, *Nature.*

20. David Turnbull, "Local Knowledge and Comparative Scientific Traditions," *Knowledge and Policy*, vol. 6, nos. 3–4 (Fall–Winter 1993–94).

21. Ibid.

22. D. Haraway, *Symians, Cyborgs and Women: The Reinvention of Nature*, 1991; and T. Nagel, *The View from Nowhere*, 1986; both cited in Turnbull, "Local Knowledge."

23. S. L. Star, "The Structure of Ill-Structured Solutions: Boundary Objects and Heterogenous Distributed Problem Solving," in L. Gasser and N. Huhns, eds., *Distributed Artificial Intelligence*, 1989, cited in Turnbull, "Local Knowledge."

24. Christian Rätsch in conversation with Paul Devereux, in *The Ley Hunter*, vol. 112 (1990).

25. Julian Jaynes, *The Origin of Consciousness in the Breakdown of the Bicameral Mind*, Houghton Mifflin, 1976.

26. Charles D. Laughlin, John McManus and Eugene G. d'Aquili, *Brain, Symbol and Experience*, Columbia University Press, 1990–1992.

27. Ibid.

28. Cited in Jaynes, *Origin of Consciousness.*

29. Guy Claxton, *Noises from the Darkroom*, Aquarian Press, 1994.

30. Ibid.

31. Owen Flanagan, *Consciousness Reconsidered*, MIT Press, 1992.

32. Charles D. Laughlin, *Glossary of Technical Terms Used in Biogenetic Structuralism*, privately published, 1994.

33. Claxton, *Noises from the Darkroom.*

34. Rupert Sheldrake, *A New Science of Life*, Blond & Briggs, 1981.

35. For example, Stuart Hameroff thinks that cytoskeletal microtubules within neurons could possibly be a site for quantum effects. See, for instance, his "Quantum Coherence in Microtubules: A

Neural Basis for Emergent Consciousness?," *Journal of Consciousness Studies*, vol. 1, no. 1 (Summer 1994).

## CHAPTER 1: CENTERING

1. Robert Temple, *The Sirius Mystery*, BCA ed., 1976.
2. Jean Richer, *Sacred Geography of the Ancient Greeks*, SUNY Press, 1994.
3. Marie Delcourt, *L'Oracle de Delphes*, cited in ibid.
4. Leonard Cottrell, *The Penguin Book of Lost Worlds*, Penguin, 1966.
5. Mircea Eliade, *Shamanism—Archaic Techniques of Ecstasy* (1951), Bollingen ed., 1964.
6. Hilda Ellis Davidson, *The Lost Beliefs of Northern Europe*, Routledge, 1993.
7. Michael Dames, *Mythic Ireland*, Thames & Hudson, 1992.
8. John Michell, *At the Centre of the World*, Thames & Hudson, 1994.
9. Cited in William Stirling, *The Canon* (1897), Garnstone Press ed., 1974.
10. Eliade, *Shamanism*.
11. Mircea Eliade, *Occultism, Witchcraft and Cultural Fashions*, University of Chicago Press, 1976.
12. John G. Neihardt, *Black Elk Speaks* (1932), Pocket Books ed., 1972.
13. Cited in Joan Halifax, *Shaman—the Wounded Healer*, Crossroads, 1982.
14. Paul Devereux, *Secrets of Ancient and Sacred Places*, Blandford Press, 1992.
15. Ray A. Williamson, *Living the Sky*, University of Oklahoma Press, 1984.
16. Richard F. Townsend, *The Aztecs*, Thames & Hudson, 1992.
17. Halifax, *Shaman*.
18. Raymond Bloch, *The Etruscans*, Thames & Hudson, 1958.
19. J. McKim Malville and John M. Fritz, "Mapping the Sacred Geometry of Vijayanagara," in Gavin D. Flood, ed., *Mapping Invisible Worlds*, Edinburgh University Press, 1993.

20. Ibid.

21. J. McKim Malville, "Astronomy at Vijayanagara: Sacred Geography Confronts the Cosmos," Rana P. B. Singh, ed., *The Spirit and Power of Place*, National Geographic Society of India, Benares Hindu University, 1993.

22. Gary Urton, *At the Crossroads of the Earth and the Sky*, University of Texas Press, 1981.

23. Eliade, *Occultism*.

24. Ibid.

25. O. V. Ovsyannikov and N. M. Terebikhin, "Sacred Space in the Culture of the Arctic Regions," in Carmichael, David, et al., eds., *Sacred Sites, Sacred Places*, Routledge, 1994.

26. Trudy Griffin-Pierce, "The Hooghan and the Stars," in Ray A. Williamson and Claire R. Farrer, eds., *Earth and Sky*, University of New Mexico Press, 1992.

27. A. Carmichael, *Carmina Gadelica*, cited in Dames, *Mythic Ireland*.

28. Dames, *Mythic Ireland*.

29. Keith Critchlow, *Time Stands Still*, Gordon Frazer, 1979.

30. Rana P. B. Singh, "Kashi as a Cosmogram: The Sacred Geometry," in Singh, ed., *Spirit and Power of Place*.

31. Ibid.

32. Dorothy Lee, in *Explorations*, vol. 2, no. 4 (1954–55).

33. Jean Piaget and Bärbel Inhelder, *The Child's Conception of Space*, Routledge & Kegan Paul, 1967.

34. O. Francis G. Sitwell, "Sacred Space Reconsidered," in Singh, ed., *Spirit and Power of Place*.

35. C. G. Jung, "The Spirit of Psychology," in Joseph Campbell, ed., *Spirit and Nature*, Bollingen ed., 1954.

36. Eliade, *Occultism*.

37. Jim DeKorne, *Psychedelic Shamanism*, Loonpanics Unlimited, 1994.

38. See, for example, Nigel Pennick, *Practical Magic in the Northern Tradition*, Aquarian Press, 1989.

39. Chantal Radimilahy, "Sacred Sites in Madagascar," in Carmichael et al., eds., *Sacred Sites, Sacred Places*.

40. J. Donald Hughes, "Spirit of Place in the Western World," in James A. Swan, ed., *The Power of Place* (1991), Gateway Books ed., 1993.


CHAPTER 2: PLACING

1. Sigmund Freud, *Standard Edition of the Complete Psychological Works of Sigmund Freud*, vol. 12, Hogarth Press, 1978.
2. Eugene Victor Walter, *Placeways*, University of North Carolina Press, 1988.
3. Edmunds V. Bunkśe, "Post-Industrial Landscape and Sense of Place," in Rana P. B. Singh, ed., *The Spirit and Power of Place*, National Geographic Society of India, Benares Hindu University, 1993.
4. Ibid.
5. Kathleen Raine, "Outer World as Inner World," in John Button, ed., *The Green Fuse*, Quartet, 1990.
6. As translated by Desmond Lee, Penguin, 1965.
7. Ibid.
8. Gaston Bachelard, *The Poetics of Space*, 1969, cited in Walter, *Placeways*.
9. Charles Mountford, *Winbaraku and the Myth of Jarapiri*, Rigby, 1968.
10. Chantal Radimilahy, "Sacred Sites in Madagascar," in Carmichael et al., eds., *Sacred Sites, Sacred Places*, Routledge, 1994.
11. Jane Hubert, "Sacred Beliefs and Beliefs of Sacredness," in Charmichael et al., *Sacred Sites, Sacred Places*.
12. David C. Carmichael, "Mescalero Apache Sacred Sites and Sensitive Areas," in Charmichael, ed., *Sacred Sites, Sacred Places*.
13. Rudolf Otto, *The Idea of the Holy*, Oxford University Press, 1924.
14. I am grateful to William H. Rosar of California for pointing out to me this history of the term.
15. Eric Partridge, *Origins*, Macmillan, 1958.
16. I am grateful to John Steele of California for originally drawing my attention to this instructive etymological fact nearly two decades ago.

17. See Peter Duerr, *Dreamtime—Concerning the Boundary Between Wilderness and Civilization* (1978), Blackwell ed., 1985, for a particularly effective discussion of these issues.

18. Walter, *Placeways*.

19. Ibid.

20. Julian Jaynes, *The Origin of Consciousness in the Breakdown of the Bicameral Mind*, Houghton Mifflin, 1976.

21. J. A. Symonds, *The Revival of Learning*, John Murray, 1923, cited in Walter, *Placeways*.

22. Walter, *Placeways*.

23. As experimental psychologist William H. Rosar has put it to me in a personal communication (1995): "What we commonly call the physical world . . . is really the perceptual world. . . . So sacred space is really a division *within the perceptual world*, not the physical world."

24. O. V. Ovsyannikov and N. M. Terebikhin, "Sacred Space in the Culture of the Arctic Region," in Carmichael et al., eds., *Sacred Sites, Sacred Places*.

25. Victor Turner, *The Ritual Process* (1969), Cornell University Press ed., 1977.

26. Maria Reiche, quoted in Tony Morrison, *The Nasca Lines*, Nonesuch Expeditions, 1987.

27. Patricia Lysaght, "Bealtaine: Irish Maytime Customs and the Reaffirmation of Boundaries," in Hilda Ellis Davidson, ed., *Boundaries & Thresholds*, Katharine Briggs Club, 1993.

28. Ruth Richardson, "Death's Door: Thresholds and Boundaries in British Funeral Customs," in Davidson, ed., *Boundaries & Thresholds*.

29. J. Bagford, 1774, cited in Karin Kvideland, "Boundaries and the Sin-Eater," in Davidson, ed., *Boundaries & Thresholds*.

30. Richardson, "Death's Door."

31. John Palmer, "The Deathroads of Holland," *The Ley Hunter*, vol. 109 (1989).

32. For further information on this material, see Paul Devereux, *Shamanism and the Mystery Lines* (1992); Llewellyn, 1993.

33. Lage Wahlström, "Places and Regional Identity," in Singh, ed., *Spirit and Power of Place*.

34. Thomas Bender, "Making Places Sacred," in James A. Swan, ed., *The Power of Place* (1991), Gateway Books ed., 1993.

35. Charles D. Laughlin, John McManus, and Eugene G. d'Aquili, *Brain, Symbol and Experience*, Columbia Univeristy Press, 1990–92.


CHAPTER 3: JOURNEYING

1. G. T. Fechner, *Über die Seelenfrage*, C. F. Amerlang, 1861, cited in Conrad Bonifazi, *The Soul of the World*, University Press of America, 1978.

2. Jay Appleton, *The Experience of Landscape*, John Wiley, 1975

3. Philip O'Connor, *Vagrancy*, Penguin, 1963.

4. Ibid.

5. Theodore Roszak, *The Voice of the Earth*, Touchstone, Simon & Schuster, 1992.

6. James Lovelock, "Gaia—Science or Myth?" *Resurgence*, May–June 1993.

7. Kim Taplin, *The English Path* (1979), Boydell Press ed., 1984.

8. Bobi Jones, "Small Paths," in *Selected Poems*, trans. Joseph P. Clancy, Christopher Davies, 1987.

9. Satish Kumar, *No Destination*, Resurgence Books, 1992.

10. Gary Urton, "Andean Social Organization and the Maintenance of the Nazca Lines," in Anthony F. Aveni, ed., *The Lines of Nazca*, American Philosophical Society, 1990.

11. Rana P. B. Singh, "Panchakroshi Yatra, Varanasi: Sacred Journey, Ecology of Place and Faithscape," *The National Geographic Journal of India*, vol. 1, no. 2 (1991), cited in Kaj Noschis, "Powerful Places and an Inner Dialogue," in Rana P. B. Singh, ed., *The Spirit and Power of Place*, National Geographic Society of India, Benares Hindu University, 1993.

12. Simon Coleman and John Elsner, "The Pilgrim's Progress: Art, Architecture and Ritual Movement at Sinai," *World Archaeology*, vol. 26, no. 1 (June 1994).

13. Eugene Victor Walter, *Placeways*, University of North Carolina Press, 1988.

14. Ibid.

15.  Walter L. Brenneman, Jr., "Sacred and Loric Space in Irish Pilgrimage," in Singh, ed., *Spirit and Power of Place.*

16.  Michael Haren and Yolande de Pontfarcy, *The Medieval Pilgrimage to St Patrick's Purgatory,* Clogher Historical Society, 1988.

17.  Ibid.

18.  Ibid.

19.  Peter Harbison, "Early Irish Pilgrim Archaeology in the Dingle Peninsula," *World Archaeology,* vol. 26, no. 1 (June 1994).

20.  Ibid.

21.  John Blofeld, *The Wheel of Life* (1959), Rider ed., 1972.

22.  Paul Devereux, *Earth Lights Revelation,* Blandford Press, 1989.

23.  J. M. Kitagawa, "Three Types of Pilgrimage in Japan," in Sumner B. Twiss and Walter H. Conser Jr., eds., *Experience of the Sacred,* Brown University Press, 1992.

24.  Amita Sinha, "Pilgrimage-Journey to the Sacred Landscape of Braj," in Singh, ed., *Spirit and Power of Place.*

25.  Rana P. B. Singh, "Sacred Geometry of India's Holy City, Varanasi: Kashi as Cosmogram," in Singh, ed., *Spirit and Power of Place.*

26.  Rana P. B. Singh, "Sun Images, Shrines and Alignments at Varanasi," in *The Ley Hunter,* vol. 123, (1995).

27.  Sinha, "Pilgrimage-Journey."

28.  Wendy Pullan, "Mapping Time and Salvation," in Gavin D. Flood, ed., *Mapping Invisible Worlds,* Edinburgh University Press, 1993.

29.  Coleman and Elsner, "Pilgrim's Progress."

30.  Tom Zuidema, cited in A. F. Aveni, "Order in the Nazca Lines," in Aveni, ed., *Lines of Nazca.*

31.  Barbara G. Myerhoff, "Peyote and the Mystic Vision," in Kathleen Berrin, ed., *Art of the Huichol Indians,* Fine Arts Museums of San Francisco/Harry N. Abrams, 1978.

32.  Weston La Barre, "Anthropological Perspectives on Hallucinations and Hallucinogens," in R. K. Siegel and L. J. West, eds., *Hallucinations,* John Wiley, 1975.

33.  Joseph Epes Brown, quoted in Jay Hansford C. Vest, "Sacred Geography of the Blackfeet," in James A. Swan, ed., *The Power of Place,* (1991), Gateway Books ed., 1993.

34. Brian Reeves, "Ninaistákis—the Nitsitapii's Sacred Mountain: Traditional Native Religious Activities and Land Use/Tourism Conflicts," in Carmichael et al., eds., *Sacred Sites, Sacred Places*, Routledge, 1994.

35. Steven Foster with Meredith Little, *The Book of the Vision Quest*, 1989. Fireside, Simon & Schuster ed., 1992.

36. Cited, alongside a reproduction of the picture, in *The Picture History of Photography*, Harry N. Abrams, 1977.

37. Ernst Pfeiffer, ed., *Sigmund Freud and Lou Andreas-Salomé Letters*, cited in Walter, *Placeways*.

38. John Perkins, *The World Is As You Dream It*, Destiny Books, 1994.

## CHAPTER 4: MAPPING

1. Jan DeBlieu, "Mapping the Sacred Places," *Orion*, vol. 13, no. 2 (Spring 1994).

2. Kevin Lynch, *The Image of the City*, 1960, cited in ibid.

3. Gavin D. Flood, "Introduction," in Gavin D. Flood, *Mapping Invisible Worlds*, Edinburgh University Press, 1993.

4. Stephen S. Hall, "I, Mercator," *Orion*, vol. 13, no. 2 (Spring 1994).

5. Eugene Victor Walter, *Placeways*, University of North Carolina Press, 1988.

6. Juliette Wood, "Another Island Close at Hand," in Hilda Ellis Davidson, ed., *Boundaries & Thresholds*, Katherine Briggs Club, 1993.

7. T. J. Westrop, "Brâzil and the Legendary Islands of the North Atlantic," *Proceedings of the Royal Irish Academy*, vol. 30c (1912-14), cited in Michael Dames, *Mythic Ireland*, Thames & Hudson, 1992.

8. David Turnbull, *Maps Are Territories* (1989), University of Chicago Press ed., 1993.

9. Ibid.

10. D. P. Dubey and Rana P. B. Singh, "Chitrakut: The Frame and Network of the Faithscape and Sacred Geometry of a Hindu Tirtha," in Rana P. B. Singh, ed., *The Spirit and Power of Place*, National Geographic Society of India, Benares Hindu University, 1993.

11. P. C. Poudel and Rana P. B. Singh, "Pilgrimage and Tourism at Muktinath, Nepal: A Study of Sacrality and Spatial Structure," in Singh, ed., *Spirit and Power of Place*.

12. Dorothea J. Theodoratus and Frank LaPena, "Wintu Sacred Geography of Northern California," in Carmichael et al., eds., *Sacred Sites, Sacred Places*, Routledge, 1994.

13. Emily Lyle, "Internal-External Memory," in Flood, ed., *Mapping Invisible Worlds*.

14. Per Hage, "Speculations on Pulawatese Mnemonic Structure," *Oceania*, vol. 49 (1978), cited in ibid.

15. Richard Bradley, Felipe Criado Boado, and Raḿon Fabregas Valcarce, "Rock Art Research as Landscape Archaeology: A Pilot Study in Galicia, North-West Spain," *World Archaeology*, vol. 25, no. 3 (February, 1994).

16. Richard Bradley, "Symbols and Signposts—Understanding the Prehistoric Petroglyphs of the British Isles," in Colin Renfrew, ed., *The Ancient Mind*, Cambridge University Press, 1994.

17. Ibid.

18. Robin Baker, ed., *The Mystery of Migration*, Macdonald, 1980.

19. Helen Watson, "Aboriginal Australian Maps," in Turnbull, *Maps Are Territories*.

20. Robert Tonkinson, *The Mardu Aborigines*, Holt, Rinehart & Winston, 1978 and 1991.

21. James Cowan, *The Mysteries of the Dream-Time*, Prism Press, 1989.

22. Charles Mountford, *Winbaraku and the Myth of Jarapiri*, Rigby, 1968.

23. Watson, "Aboriginal Maps."

24. T. G. H. Strehlow, *Aranda Traditions*, Melbourne University Press, 1947, cited in Joseph Campbell, *The Way of the Animal Powers*, vol.1, pt. 2, Harper & Row, 1988.

25. Probably W. Thomas, in T. F. Bride, ed., *Letters from the Victorian Pioneers*, quoted in Lucien Lévy-Bruhl, *Primitive Mythology* (1935), trans. Brian Elliot, University of Queensland Press ed., 1983.

26. David Lewis, "Observations on Route Finding and Spatial Orientation Among the Aboriginal Peoples of the Western Desert Re-

gion of Central Australia," *Oceania*, vol. 46 (1976); David Lewis, "The Way of the Nomad," in *From Earlier Fleets: Hemisphere—An Aboriginal Anthology*, 1978; both cited in Turnbull, *Maps Are Territories*.

27. Kingsley Palmer, cited in Turnbull, *Maps Are Territories*.

28. This is discussed in three Latin works: the *Ad Herennium* of c. 84 B.C., Cicero's *De Oratore* of 55 B.C., and Quintilian's *Institutio oratoria* of the first century A.D.

29. Referred to by Helen Watson in Turnbull, *Maps Are Territories*.

30. John O'Keefe and Lynn Nadel, *The Hippocampus as a Cognitive Map*, Oxford University Press, 1978.

31. Ibid.

32. Joan Halifax, *Shaman—the Wounded Healer*, Crossroads,1982.

33. Campbell, *Way of Animal Powers*, vol. 1, pt. 2, fig. 276.

34. Ibid., figs. 278, 279.

35. Mircea Eliade, *Yoga* (1958), Arkana ed., 1989.

36. Halifax, *Shaman*.

37. Alan Ereira, *From the Heart of the World*, BBC-TV, December 4, 1990 (transcript). See also his book *The Heart of the World*, Jonathan Cope, 1990.

38. Hall, "I, Mercator."

39. I give an extended history of dowsing in chapter 7 of my *Earth Memory* (1991), Llewellyn ed., 1992.

40. Christopher Bird's *The Divining Hand* (1979) is a thoroughgoing study of dowsing in all its aspects, including a useful review of work testing dowsers for electric and magnetic sensitivity. My copy, published in the U.K. by Macdonald & Jane in 1980, is under the title of *Divining*.

41. Käthe Bachler's *Earth Radiation* (1976) is probably the best study of typically German energy-dowsing currently available in English translation. My copy was published in the U.K. by Wordmasters in 1989. Nevertheless, although this is fairly sane, some of the energy claims should be viewed with caution.

42. *Dowsing and Church Archaeology*, by Richard N. Bailey, Eric Cambridge, and H. Denis Briggs, published in the U.K. by Intercept in 1988, is a splendid account of truly objective dowsing for ancient church foundations, verified by archeological excavations.

CHAPTER 5: DREAMING

1. Ralph Waldo Emerson, *Nature* (1836), Beacon Press ed., 1991.

2. V. A. Donohue, "The Goddess of the Theban Mountain," *Antiquity*, vol. 66, no. 253 (December 1992).

3. Ibid.

4. Personal communication; ibid.

5. Erich Neumann, *The Great Mother* (1955), Bollingen ed., 1963.

6. *The Time Team Reports*, Channel Four Television, 1995.

7. Anne Ross, "Landscape and Ritual in the Pagan Celtic World," paper presented at The Ley Hunter Moot, Dinas Mawddwy, Wales, 1991.

8. Vincent Scully, *The Earth, The Temple and the Gods*, Yale University Press, 1962.

9. Ibid.

10. Rachel Fletcher, "Ancient Theatres as Sacred Spaces," in James A. Swan, ed., *The Power of Place* (1991), Gateway Books ed., 1993.

11. Scully, *Earth, Temple, Gods*.

12. Paul Devereux, *Symbolic Landscapes*, Gothic Image, 1992.

13. James Mooney, *Myths of the Cherokee*, report 19, pt. I, Smithsonian Institution, 1900, cited in Lucien Lévy-Bruhl, *Primitive Mythology* (1935), trans. Brian Elliot, University of Queensland Press ed., 1983.

14. A. P. Elkin, "The Secret Life of the Australian Aborigines," *Oceania*, vol. III (1932–33), cited in Lévy-Bruhl, *Primitive Mythology*.

15. Lévy-Bruhl, *Primitive Mythology* (emphasis added).

16. Olive Pink, "Spirit Ancestors in a Northern Aranda Horde Country," *Oceania*, vol. IV (1933–34), cited in Lévy-Bruhl, *Primitive Mythology*.

17. James Hillman, "And Huge Is Ugly," in John Button, ed., *The Green Fuse*, Quartet, 1990.

18. Paul Wirz, *Die Marind-anim von Holländisch-Sud-Neu-Guinea*, 1922, cited in Lévy-Bruhl, *Primitive Mythology*.

19. Jack M. Broughton and Floyd Buckskin, "Racing Simloki's Shadow: The Ajumawi Interconnection of Power, Shadow, Equinox, and Solstice," in Ray A. Williamson and Claire R. Farrer, eds., *Earth and Sky*, University of New Mexico Press, 1992.

20. Paul Devereux, "Shamanism and the Mystery Lines," *The Ley Hunter*, vol. 116 (1992).

21. Paul Devereux, *Shamanism and the Mystery Lines* (1992), Llewellyn, 1993.

22. Paul Devereux, "Acculturated Topographical Effects of Shamanic Trance Consciousness in Archaic and Medieval Sacred Landscapes," *Journal of Scientific Exploration*, vol. 7, no. 1 (1993).

23. Charles D. Trombold, "Causeways in the Context of Strategic Planning in the La Quemada Region, Zacatecas, Mexico," in C. D. Trombold, ed., *Ancient Road Networks and Settlement Hierarchies in the New World*, Cambridge University Press, 1991.

24. Payson Sheets and Thomas L. Sever, "Prehistoric Footpaths in Costa Rica: Transportation and Communication in a Tropical Rainforest," in Trombold, ed., *Ancient Road Networks*.

25. David Browne, Royal Commission on Ancient and Historical Monuments in Wales, personal communication.

26. Weston La Barre, "Anthropological Perspectives on Hallucination and Hallucinogens," in R. K. Siegel and L. J. West, eds., *Hallucinations*, John Wiley, 1975.

27. Richard Evans Schultes and Robert F. Raffauf, *Vine of the Soul*, Synergetic Press, 1992.

28. Marlene Dobkin de Rios, "Plant Hallucinogens, Out-of-Body Experiences and New World Monumental Earthworks," in Brian M. Du Toit, ed., *Drugs, Rituals and Altered States of Consciousness*, A. A. Balkema, 1977.

29. J. D. Lewis-Williams and Thomas A. Dowson, "The Signs of All Times," *Current Anthropology*, vol. 29, no. 2 (April 1988).

30. David Lewis-Williams and Thomas Dowson, *Images of Power*, Southern Book Publishers, 1989.

31. Thomas A. Dowson, *Rock Engravings of Southern Africa*, Witwatersrand University Press, 1992.

32. See Siegel and West, eds., *Hallucinations*, for instance.

33. David S. Whitley, in Lewis-Williams and Dowson, *Images of Power*.

34. David S. Whitley, "By the Hunter, for the Gatherer: Art, Social Relations and Subsistence Change in the Prehistoric Great Basin," *World Archaeology*, vol. 25, no. 3 (February 1994).

35. G. Reichel-Dolmatoff, "Drug-Induced Optical Sensations and Their Relationship to Applied Art Among Some Colombian Indians," in Michael Greenhalgh and Vincent Medaw, eds., *Art in Society*, Duckworth, 1978.

36. Arthur Grimble, *A Pattern of Islands*, John Murray, 1952.

37. Cheryl Straffon, in *Meyn Mamvro*, vol. 25 (Autumn 1994).

38. Barry Lopez, *The Rediscovery of North America*, Vintage Books, 1990.

39. Paul Devereux, "Three-Dimensional Aspects of Apparent Relationships Between Selected Natural and Artificial Features Within the Topography of the Avebury Complex," *Antiquity*, vol. 65, no. 249 (December 1991).

40. Paul Devereux, *Symbolic Landscapes*, Gothic Image, 1992.

41. Keith H. Basso, "'Stalking with Stories': Names, Places, and Moral Narratives Among the Western Apaches," in Daniel Halpern, ed., *On Nature*, North Point Press, 1987.

42. Ibid.

43. Julie Cruikshank in collaboration with Angela Sidney, Kitty Smith, and Annie Ned, *Life Lived like a Story*, University of Nebraska Press, 1990.

44. F. Myers, *Pintupi Country, Pintupi Self*, Smithsonian Institution, 1986, cited in Setha M. Low, "Place Attachment in Cultural Anthropology," in Rana P. B. Singh, ed., *The Spirit and Power of Place*, National Geographic Society of India, Benares Hindu University, 1993.

45. Setha M. Low, referring to Myers' work, in Low, "Place Attachment."

46. R. F. Foster, *Modern Ireland:1600–1972*, Allen Lane, 1988, cited in Gabriel Cooney, "Sacred and Secular Neolithic Landscapes in Ireland," in Carmichael et al., eds., *Sacred Sites, Sacred Places*, Routledge, 1994.

47. See L. A. De Salvo, K. W. D'Arcy, and C. Hogan, eds., *Territories of the Voice: Contemporary Stories by Irish Women Writers*, Virago Press, 1990.

48. Emily Lyle, "Internal-External Memory," in Gavin D. Flood, *Mapping Invisible Worlds*, Edinburgh University Press, 1993.

49. Ralph Waldo Emerson, *Nature* (1836), Beacon Press ed., 1991.

50. "Mysteries of the Dreamtime," James Cowan in conversation with Paul Devereux, in *The Ley Hunter*, vol. 118 (1993).

51. Guy Claxton, *Noises from the Darkroom*, Aquarian Press, 1994.

52. Kathleen Raine, "Outer World as Inner World," in John Button, ed., *The Green Fuse*, Quartet, 1990.

53. Lyle, "Internal-External Memory."

54. I have written at some length about energetic aspects of ancient sacred sites in *Places of Power*, Blandford Press, 1990 (distributed in the U.S.A. by New Leaf Distributors), but little has been written about the dreamwork research program, since it is still in progress. An outline, with photographs of some of the sites involved, is given in my *Secrets of Ancient and Sacred Places*, Blandford Press, 1993 (distributed in the U.S.A. by Sterling Publishing Co.). There have also been filmed sequences on Paramount TV's *Sightings* in the U.S.A., and also on the Learning Channel. Occasional progress reports are given in *The Ley Hunter* (Box 92, Penzance, Cornwall TR18 2XL, U.K.). The whole operation is run strictly as an experiment, and if there are significant results, probably not available until nearly the end of the 1990s, there will be academic papers and, doubtless, a special book on the whole effort. Finally, I should remark that the program arose out of a powerful dream I had while in New York in 1988. Interestingly, it was the tradition in classical times that people not try to sleep at a temple unless they had already experienced a dream instructing them to do so.

55. Henry David Thoreau, "Walking," 1862.

56. Steven Foster with Meredith Little, *Vision Quest*, Fireside, Simon & Schuster, ed., 1992.

57. Merlin Donald, *Origins of the Modern Mind: Three Stages in the Evolution of Culture and Cognition*, Harvard University Press, 1991, cited in Lyle, "Internal-External Memory."

58. Conrad Bonifazi, *The Soul of the World*, University Press of America, 1978.

59. Plotinus, *The Enneads*, trans. Stephen MacKenna, Faber & Faber, 1962, quoted in ibid.

60. All quotes this paragraph from Bonifazi, *Soul of the World*.

61. Ibid.

62. Ibid.

63. Mircea Eliade, *The Myth of the Eternal Return* (1949), Bollingen ed., 1954.

64. Ibid.

65. Aldous Huxley, "The Doors of Perception" (1954), in *The Doors of Perception and Heaven and Hell*, Penguin, 1959.

66. Mircea Eliade, Shamanism—Archaic Techniques of Ecstasy (1951), Bollingen ed., 1964.

67. Henry Corbin, *Spiritual Body and Celestial Earth* (1976), I. B. Tauris ed., 1990.

68. Ibid.

69. Frederick Van Eeden, "A Study of Dreams" (1913), in Charles Tart, ed., *Altered States of Consciousness*, John Wiley, 1969.

70. Keith Hearne, *The Dream Machine*, Aquarian Press, 1990.

71. Stephen La Berge, *Lucid Dreaming* (1985), Ballantine ed., 1986.

72. Roger Walsh, unpublished paper presented at "Toward Earth Community: Ecology, Native Wisdom and Spirituality," the 13th International Transpersonal Association Conference, Killarney, Ireland, May 1994.

73. LaBerge, *Lucid Dreaming*.

74. Susan Blackmore, *Beyond the Body*, Granada, 1983.

75. I am grateful to archetypal psychologist and author Alan Bleakley for these latter two traditional examples of the transfigured Earth.

76. Laurens van der Post, *The Heart of the Hunter* (1961), Harvest/HBJ ed., 1980.

77. Kazuo Matsubayashi, "Spirit of Place: The Modern Relevance of an Ancient Concept," in James A. Swan, ed., *The Power of Place* (1991), Gateway Books ed., 1993.

78. Blanche Merz, *Points of Cosmic Energy* (1983), C. W. Daniel ed., 1987.

79. Don't read this unless you have already done the exercise! The rock is known as The Nag's Head, and is situated on St. Agnes, one of the most westerly isles of Scilly, above Porth Warna.

80. Julian Jaynes, *The Origin of Consciousness in the Breakdown of the Bicameral Mind*, Houghton Mifflin, 1976.

81. Stanley Krippner, "The Living Earth and Shamanic Traditions," in Swan, ed., *Power of Place*.

82. Hermann Hesse, *Siddhartha* (1922), Picador ed., 1991.

83. Stephen LaBerge and Howard Rheingold, *Exploring the World of Lucid Dreaming*, Ballantine Books, 1990.

84. Stephen LaBerge, Leslie Phillips, and Lynne Levitan, "An Hour of Wakefulness Before Morning Naps Makes Lucidity More Likely," in *NightLight* (Lucidity Institute), vol.6, no. 3, (Summer 1994).

85. The main account is in Paul Devereux, "An Apparently Nutmeg-Induced Experience of Magical Flight," in Christian Rätsch, ed., *Yearbook for Ethnomedicine and the Study of Consciousness*, Verlag für Wissenschaft und Bildung, 1992.

# SELECTED BIBLIOGRAPHY

Appleton, Jay. *The Experience of Landscape*. John Wiley, 1975.

Aveni, Anthony F., ed. *The Lines of Nazca*. American Philosophical Society, 1990.

Berrin, Kathleen, ed. *Art of the Huichol Indians*. Fine Arts Museums of San Francisco/Harry N. Abrams,1978.

Blackmore, Susan. *Beyond the Body*. Granada, 1983.

Blofeld, John. *The Wheel of Life* (1959). Rider ed., 1972.

Bonifazi, Conrad. *The Soul of the World*. University Press of America, 1978.

Button, John, ed. *The Green Fuse*. Quartet, 1990.

Campbell, Joseph. *The Way of the Animal Powers*. Vol.1, Pt. 2. Harper & Row, 1988.

Campbell, Joseph, ed. *Spirit and Nature*. Bollingen, 1954.

Carmichael, David, Jane Hubert, Brian Reeves, and Audhild Schanche, eds. *Sacred Sites, Sacred Places*. Routledge, 1994.

Claxton, Guy. *Noises from the Darkroom*. Aquarian Press, 1994.

Corbin, Henry. *Spiritual Body and Celestial Earth* (1976). I. B. Tauris ed.,1990.

Cottrell, Leonard. *The Penguin Book of Lost Worlds*. Penguin, 1966.

Cowan, James. *The Mysteries of the Dream-Time*. Prism Press, 1989.

Critchlow, Keith. *Time Stands Still*. Gordon Frazer, 1979.

Cruikshank, Julie, in collaboration with Angela Sidney, Kitty Smith, and Annie Ned. *Life Lived like a Story*. University of Nebraska Press, 1990.

Dames, Michael. *Mythic Ireland*. Thames & Hudson, 1992.

Davidson, Hilda Ellis. *The Lost Beliefs of Northern Europe*. Routledge, 1993.

Davidson, Hilda Ellis, ed. *Boundaries & Thresholds*. Katharine Briggs Club, 1993.

DeKorne, Jim. *Psychedelic Shamanism*. Loonpanics Unlimited, 1994.

Devereux, Paul. *Symbolic Landscapes*. Gothic Image, 1992.

Devereux, Paul. *Shamanism and the Mystery Lines* (1992). Llewellyn ed., 1993.

Dowson, Thomas A. *Rock Engravings of Southern Africa*. Witwatersrand University Press, 1992.

Duerr, Peter. *Dreamtime—Concerning the Boundary Between Wilderness and Civilization* (1978). Blackwell ed., 1985.

Du Toit, Brian M., ed. *Drugs, Rituals and Altered States of Consciousness*. A. A. Balkema, 1977.

Eliade, Mircea. *The Myth of the Eternal Return* (1949). Bollingen ed., 1954.

Eliade, Mircea. *Shamanism—Archaic Techniques of Ecstasy* (1951). Bollingen ed., 1964.

Eliade, Mircea. *Occultism, Witchcraft and Cultural Fashions*. University of Chicago Press, 1976.

Eliade, Mircea. *Yoga* (1958). Arkana ed., 1989.

Ereira, Alan. *The Heart of the World*. Jonathan Cape, 1990.

Flanagan, Owen. *Consciousness Reconsidered*. MIT Press, 1992.

Flood, Gavid D., ed. *Mapping Invisible Worlds*. Edinburgh Unversity Press, 1993.

Foster, Steven, with Meredith Little. *Vision Quest*. Simon & Schuster ed.,1992.

Greenhalgh, Michael, and Vincent Medaw, eds. *Art in Society*. Duckworth, 1978.

Grimble, Arthur. *A Pattern of Islands*. John Murray, 1952.

Halifax, Joan. *Shaman—the Wounded Healer*. Crossroads, 1982.

Halpern, Daniel, ed. *On Nature*. North Point Press, 1987.

Haren, Michael, and Yolande de Pontfarcy. *The Medieval Pilgrimage to St Patrick's Purgatory*. Clogher Historical Society, 1988.

Hearne, Keith. *The Dream Machine*. Aquarian Press, 1990.

Hesse, Hermann. *Siddhartha* (1922). Picador ed., 1991.

Huxley, Aldous. *The Doors of Perception and Heaven and Hell*. Penguin, 1959.

Iyer, Raghavan, and Nadini Iyer. *The Descent of the Gods*. Colin Smythe, 1988.

Jaynes, Julian. *The Origin of Consciousness in the Breakdown of the Bicameral Mind.* Houghton Mifflin, 1976.

Kumar, Satish. *No Destination.* Resurgence Books, 1992.

LaBerge, Stephen. *Lucid Dreaming* (1985). Ballantine Books ed., 1986.

LaBerge, Stephen, and Howard Rheingold. *Exploring the World of Lucid Dreaming.* Ballantine Books, 1990.

Laughlin, Charles D., John McManus and Eugene d'Aquili. *Brain, Symbol and Experience.* Columbia University Press, 1990–92.

Lévy-Bruhl, Lucien. *Primitive Mythology* (1935). Trans. Brian Elliot. University of Queensland Press ed., 1983.

Lewis-Williams, David, and Thomas Dowson. *Images of Power.* Southern Book Publishers, 1989.

Lopez, Barry. *The Rediscovery of North America.* Vintage Books, 1990.

Lovelock, James. *The Ages of Gaia.* Oxford University Press, 1988.

Merz, Blanche. *Points of Cosmic Energy* (1983). C. W. Daniel ed., 1987.

Michell, John. *At the Centre of the World.* Thames & Hudson, 1994.

Morrison, Tony. *The Nasca Lines.* Nonesuch Expeditions, 1987.

Mountford, Charles. *Winbaraku and the Myth of Jarapiri.* Rigby, 1968.

Neihardt, John G. *Black Elk Speaks* (1932). Pocket Books ed., 1972.

Neumann, Erich. *The Great Mother* (1955). Bollingen ed., 1963.

O'Connor, Philip. *Vagrancy.* Penguin, 1963.

O'Keefe, John, and Lynn Nadel. *The Hippocampus as a Cognitive Map.* Oxford University Press, 1978.

Otto, Rudolf. *The Idea of the Holy.* Oxford University Press, 1924.

Pennick, Nigel. *Practical Magic in the Northern Tradition.* Aquarian Press, 1989.

Perkins, John. *The World Is As You Dream It.* Destiny Books, 1994.

Piaget, Jean, and Bärbel Inhelder. *The Child's Conception of Space.* Routledge & Kegan Paul, 1967.

Rätsch, Christian. *Yearbook for Ethnomedicine and the Study of Consciousness.* Verlag für Wissenschaft und Bildung, 1992.

Renfrew, Colin, ed. *The Ancient Mind.* Cambridge University Press, 1994.

Richer, Jean. *Sacred Geography of the Ancient Greeks.* SUNY Press, 1994.

Roszak, Theodore. *The Voice of the Earth.* Touchstone, Simon & Schuster, 1992.

Schultes, Richard Evans, and Robert F. Raffauf. *Vine of the Soul.* Synergetic Press, 1992.

Scully, Vincent. *The Earth, The Temple and the Gods.* Yale University Press, 1962.

Sheldrake, Rupert. *A New Science of Life.* Blond & Briggs, 1981.

Siegel, R. K., and L. J. West, eds. *Hallucinations.* John Wiley, 1975.

Singh, Rana P. B., ed. *The Spirit and Power of Place.* National Geographical Society of India, Benares Hindu University, 1993.

Swan, James A., ed. *The Power of Place* (1991). Gateway Books ed., 1993.

Taplin, Kim. *The English Path* (1979). Boydell Press ed., 1984.

Tart, Charles. *Altered States of Consciousness.* John Wiley, 1969.

Tonkinson, Robert. *The Mardu Aborigines.* Holt, Rinehart & Winston, 1978 and 1991.

Trombold, C.D., ed. *Ancient Road Networks and Settlement Hierarchies in the New World.* Cambridge University Press, 1991.

Turnbull, David. *Maps Are Territories* (1989). University of Chicago Press ed., 1993.

Turner, Victor. *The Ritual Process* (1969). Cornell University Press ed., 1977.

Twiss, Sumner B., and Walter H. Conser, eds. *Experience of the Sacred.* Brown University Press, 1992.

Urton, Gary. *At the Crossroads of the Earth and the Sky.* University of Texas Press, 1981.

Vander Post, Laurens. *The Heart of the Hunter* (1961). Harvest/HBJ ed., 1980.

Walter, Eugene Victor. *Placeways.* University of North Carolina Press, 1988.

Williamson, Ray A., and Claire R. Farrer, eds. *Earth and Sky.* University of New Mexico Press, 1992.

When writing to any of the following organizations, please remember always to include a stamped self-addressed envelope for reply, or, if sending overseas, one or two international postal-reply coupons—obtainable from your post office—paper-clipped to a self-addressed envelope.

## WILDERNESS EXPERIENCE

Should you wish to attempt a vision quest, or obtain greater experiential knowledge of wilderness psychology, you ought to seek skilled and experienced professional advice and assistance. It is not something to undertake lightly. I am sure there are several groups that can help with this, but my own recommendation would be that you initially contact Robert G. Greenway of the Northstar Wilderness Group, Box 1407, Port Townsend, Washington 98368.

## LUCID DREAMING

If you have decided that you require an electronic aid to help you attain lucidity in the dream state, then the most accessible instrument at the time of this writing is the "Nova Dreamer," produced by the Lucidity Institute, 2555 Park Boulevard, Suite 2, Palo Alto, California 94306, Fax: (415) 321-9967. It consists of a lightweight eyemask that can be worn quite comfortably while you sleep. The clever miniature electronics built into it provide detectors that pick up your rapid eye movements when you are dreaming, and then flash red LEDs into your eyes to alert you within dreaming sleep without awakening you. The sensitivity to REMs, the intensity of the LEDs, and the sequences in which they can flash are all programmable for individual requirements. There is also a program that allows for a review of the number of times the LEDs signaled you in the night. Send to the institute for details on the Nova Dreamer and the other lucid-dream aids they offer.

The Lucidity Institute also publishes a quarterly newsletter called *NightLight*, which gives tips, lucid-dreaming techniques, the results of experiments, an exchange of personal experiences, and news of workshops, lectures and so forth.

In the U.K., the Lucidity Institute is represented by LifeTools, Sunrise House, Hulley Road, Macclesfield, Cheshire SK10 2LP.

## ORGANIC LUCID-DREAMING AIDS (ESSENTIAL OILS)

If you feel more drawn to organic lucid dream aids but don't like the idea of taking ground nutmeg on its own, as described in chapter five, then I suggest you use a generous pinch in cooking your evening meal, followed by a sprinkle of nutmeg essential oil on your bedclothes just before going to bed. I have found that combination to work very well. The oil does need to be powerful therapy-standard, pure essential oil, however, rather than the more cosmetic, diluted varieties often available. There are various sources for such quality oils, but one I can vouch for in the U.S. is Butterbur & Sage, Box 940, Beacon, New York 12508. In addition, I have prepared for this company a small "Dreaming Kit," which consists of a relaxant essential oil, a hypnotic essential oil prepared for massage application, and nutmeg essential oil, plus a leaflet describing how to use these in sequence and with safety to promote dreaming and, perchance, lucidity.

## ECOPSYCHOLOGY

Some of the core, founding group of psychologists and other professionals promoting the development of an ecopsychology now produce a publication, *The Ecopsychology Newsletter*. Write to: P. O. Box 7487, Berkeley, California 94707-0487.

## THE DRAGON PROJECT ANCIENT SITES DREAMING PROGRAM

As indicated in chapter five, work at two of the four selected sites in the U.K. is still ongoing into 1997. If you would like to volunteer as a dreamer (preferably bringing along a friend or partner), inquire in the first instance to see if the work is still ongoing, and state when you would be available. Write to: The Dragon Project Trust, 39 Alma Place, Penzance, Cornwall TR18 2BX, U.K.

## KEEPING UPDATED

If you are interested in keeping abreast of the ideas and developments in the range of topics covered in this book—consciousness research related to ecopsychological concerns, site dreaming, Dragon Project updates, and research and information relating to archaic mind-sets, sacred sites, landscapes, and traditions, together with modern developments in Earth relationships—then you will probably find the small magazine I am Consultant Editor of value. It is *The Ley Hunter*, Box 258, Cheltenham GL53 0HR, U.K. Information can also be obtained by mail from B&S USA, Dept. TLH, Box 940, Beacon, New York 12508. Published three times a year, it carries the latest research, news, reviews of literature, and so forth, and is pitched somewhere between an academic and a popular style. Its E-mail address is leyhunt@aol.com.

## THE ANTHROPOLOGY OF CONSCIOUSNESS

A more academic but still accessible and fascinating look at research into ancient and traditional mind-states, along with contemporary implications and developments, can be found in *The Anthropology of Consciousness*, published quarterly by the Society for the Anthropology of Consciousness, 2267 Clinton Avenue, apartment C, Almeda, California 94501-4910. Electronic: hwautisc@sl.csuhayward.edu

## SCIENTIFIC EXPLORATION

For those with a serious scientific bent, the quarterly *Journal of Scientific Exploration* provides a useful peer-reviewed forum for inquiry into phenomena at the edges of mainstream acceptability (the liminal area where change is most likely to occur!). It is published by the Society of Scientific Exploration, ERL 306, Stanford University, Stanford, California 94305-4055.

## CONTINUING EXPERIENTIAL

If the demand is sufficient for workshops, gatherings, conferences, and other group activities for the furthering of experiential work on mythic, or imaginal, consciousness in its various forms, then it might prove possible to arrange events along these lines. Let me know if you would be interested in this. I can be contacted through the addresses given above for *The Ley Hunter* ("Keeping Updated").

# INDEX